AF291923

A Life Under Sail

The first and prime rule of the Royal Cruising Club is 'to associate the owners of small yachts, boats and canoes used for cruising on sea, river or lake, and any other persons interested in aquatic amusements'. Here is a selection of my aquatic amusements from over the years.

By the same author

Military histories and biographies

Reasons in Writing: A Commando's View of the Falklands War
Amphibious Assault Falklands: The Battle for San Carlos
Blondie: A Life of Lieutenant Colonel H.G. Hasler, DSO, OBE, RM
The Next Moon: A Special Operations Executive Agent in France
HMS Fearless: The Mighty Lion
3 Commando Brigade, Helmand
Commando Assault, Helmand
Nothing Impossible: A Portrait of The Royal Marines 1664 – 2010 (Editor)
Exocet Falklands
Paid to Predict: Duplicity and Deceit Among 'Allies'
A Life in Letters
Amphibious Warfare Post World War II

Fiction

Skeletons for Sadness. A Story of Espionage, Love and War in the Falklands
Death's Sting: Duplicity and Deceit in the Balkans

Reference

Falkland Islands Shores
Jane's Amphibious Warfare Capabilities (Editor)
Jane's Special Forces Equipment Recognition Guide (Editor)
Jane's Amphibious and Special Forces (Editor: bi-annual)

A Life Under Sail

The Aquatic Adventures of a Royal Marine

Ewen Southby-Tailyour

Pen & Sword

MARITIME

First published in Great Britain in 2026 by
Pen & Sword Maritime
An imprint of
Pen & Sword Books Ltd
Yorkshire - Philadelphia

ISBN 978 1 03614 856 0

Typeset in INDIA by IMPEC eSolutions
Printed and bound in England by CPI Group (UK) Ltd, Croydon, CRO 4YY

The Publisher's authorised representative in the EU for product safety is Authorised Rep Compliance Ltd., Ground Floor, 71 Lower Baggot Street, Dublin D02 P593, Ireland.
www.arccompliance.com

For a complete list of Pen & Sword titles please contact

PEN & SWORD BOOKS LIMITED
47 Church Street, Barnsley, South Yorkshire, S70 2AS, England
E-mail: enquiries@pen-and-sword.co.uk
Website: www.pen-and-sword.co.uk

or

PEN AND SWORD BOOKS
1950 Lawrence Rd, Havertown, PA 19083, USA
E-mail: uspen-and-sword@casematepublishers.com
Website: www.penandswordbooks.com

Contents

Introduction

This is a collection of essays and stories written over the years to amuse, enlighten, instruct and perhaps, warn. Some come as a reminder to other seafarers of the pitfalls and joys that attend a life at sea under sail and motor, both privately and professionally. Some stories are light-hearted, others rather less so. Many offer advice and lessons learned, while also warning of unexpected consequences. A fair few have a moral undertone.

Many of these articles cover significant incidents in my life as a yachtsman which may be of interest to my family and those long-suffering friends who were often involved. Inevitably there is some overlap and repetition where I have discussed the same subject but from a different viewpoint.

In the Foreword to the book *A Life in Letters*, I suggested that it was more suitable as a Christmas stocking-filler followed by demotion to the downstairs loo, rather than any formal bookshelf - to be dipped into at random and in a haphazard order. The same may be said of *A Life Under Sail*.

Chapter 1

In the Beginning, 1942

On Christmas Day 1942, at Stobs Camp in the borders of Scotland, three miles to the south of Hawick, my heavily pregnant mother, unable to bend down to the oven and the large turkey roasting inside, gave up and took a sip of an equally large measure of 'Horses Neck'. The author and Royal Marines lieutenant, Evelyn Waugh, knew how to baste a bird. 'Let me help,' he offered.

Outside, the snow was drifting against the front door of the isolated and exposed Barns House, while inside, June Tailyour stood up straight, stretched her back and gladly accepted Waugh's offer. Down the hill, in neatly laid lines, were Nissen huts occupied by 5th Battalion, Royal Marines where, in the NAAFI, the marines were enjoying beer, whisky and a roast. The battalion was part of the 101 Infantry Brigade, Royal Marines and had been billeted at the camp since late October 1941.

I was born on Sunday, 18 January 1942, in Hawick's Haig Maternity Home and was early – thanks to my father, Norman, skidding the family car, a draughty and unreliable, convertible Vauxhall into a snow drift, thus frightening my mother into labour.

The christening was held in that same NAAFI hut on 1 March 1942, (Norman and June's first wedding anniversary) and was conducted by the battalion's RNVR padre using my father's yacht's bell filled with melted snow as the font. Thinking this too cold, the vicar actually daubed my head with precious champagne. Thus began a lifetime's involvement with ships and the sea.

Chapter 2

The Wake-up Call, 1949

A seven-year-old boy stands on the deck of a 35-ton, 56-feet, Bristol Channel Pilot Cutter lying to her moorings off St Mawes. He has climbed to the truck of the mast via the ratlines and pole-topmast many times but this day is different; he is in tears.

The yacht's owner, exasperated, demands for the third time, 'Are you going up the mast?'

'No, Uncle Patrick!'

'Right. Give this to your mother when you get to London.' The brief letter read: *Darling June, You sent your son to me to be taught seamanship. He has failed! Love Patrick.* A note for the various guards *en route* was tied to the lapel of the boy's overcoat.

The journey from Falmouth Docks station took many hours and a number of changes. On arrival at Waterloo the boy's mother glanced at the tear-stained paper, took him home to Richmond, washed and fed him and the next morning, after changing the label, bundled him onto the Falmouth-bound, steam train, like a parcel in the hands of the guards. Four, now-familiar, changes later, the yacht's owner - warned by a telegram - was handed the same, even grubbier letter and read on the reverse: *Darling Patrick, I sent my son to you to be taught seamanship. You appear to be failing! Love June.* I climbed the mast.

The year was 1949, the vessel was *Olga*, and her owner was the late Lieutenant Colonel Patrick William O'Hara Phibbs, the boy's godfather, guardian and honorary grandfather.

Chapter 3

Six Old Gaffers, 1946-2022

In the early 1920s, Pat Phibbs of the Royal Cruising Club (RCC) joined the Royal Marines and soon bought a 7-ton quarter-decked Polperro 'hooker' called *Elizabeth Mary*. *EM* as she became known, was built in Looe in 1908 by R. Pearce. Pat immediately fitted a cabin, hoisted a jackyard tops'l and, in light airs, set a jib tops'l from the truck to the bowsprit's cranse iron. The mains'l was loose-footed while a hideous engine, complete with massive flywheel, skulked in the fore-peak, offering (when it could be goaded into life) a nod towards the twentieth century.

In 1935, my father, Norman Tailyour, also of the RCC (and, later of the Royal Yacht Squadron, RYS), had built in Egypt a small gaff cutter he named *Sea Vixen*. Although just 21 feet long she was constructed to the same lines as the well-known Pilot Cutter *Dyarchy*. *Sea Vixen* was shipped home before the war then cruised almost non-stop and even attended the RCC's 1938, Beaulieu 'meet'.

In 1947, Pat retired from the Royal Marines and in the same year bought *Olga* which was to be his permanent home until he died in 1975. In 1993 I commissioned the third of four *Black Velvets*, this one being a 12-ton 35-feet gaff cutter, whose sail plan I had designed specifically for high-latitude exploring.

Between these seven gaff cutters (and many other yachts including junks, brigs, dhows, outriggers and the rest) lies a lifetime of nautical memories. Although I never sailed in *Sea Vixen* countless early childhood hours were spent scraping her wooden spars with broken glass while her hull, still in its wartime resting place, slowly dried out to the point of no return. Dozens of photographs remind me of what had been for father and what might have been for me. But then there was 'Uncle Pat'. In 1946 my family moved into bachelor Pat's married quarters in the Royal Marines Barracks at Stonehouse where he also kept *EM*. The days were few indeed when we were not trawling, under sail, in Cawsand and Whitsand Bays before wheeling the assorted catch to the barrack's main galley. I was only four but revelled in being part of the process.

In 1949 Pat retired from the Royal Marines and purchased *Olga*, a Bristol Channel pilot cutter designed and built by J. Bowden of Porthleven in 1909, that had worked out of Barry for the first years of her life. Pat moved on board and took up his deceased father's moorings (the family's gaff schooner had long since been sold) off the St Mawes house where his disliked stepmother still lived: on her death he re-deployed her bronze bust as one of the mooring's sinkers. It is still there. Throughout the winter months *EM* and *Olga* were often the only yachts moored in the Percuil river.

Slowly a routine developed. Easter meant the annual working cruise to St Peter Port where the spring tides suited *Olga*'s draught of 9 feet, for her annual application of noisome, red anti-fouling - always declared 'out-of-date' and thus free from Plymouth dockyard. These were no holidays for a young, 'un-paid, paid hand' nor were they for the fainthearted, as we sailed regardless of weather. Pat 'put back' just once when, after slipping her moorings off Moody's Yard in the Hamble - the Channel weather was so foul that even he was forced to run for Portland. It was touch-and-go yet there was no choice but to keep the canvas set. Thankfully the jib held long enough to get us through the harbour entrance, and then, as though glad to be free of its responsibility, it burst with an almighty crack leaving little but the three bolt ropes. It was the only occasion he lost a sail.

Thanks to my father's foreign postings, Pat's duties embraced those of guardian and tutor which were tasks he took so seriously, that while I was boarding at Stubbington House School (not far from the Hamble - then mercifully clear of pontoons and marinas) in the early 1950s, *Olga* was moored in midstream for the winters so that he could entertain my friends on Sundays. But I quickly discovered that it was really so that I could spend the laying-up and fitting-out seasons either up the mast, over the side or among the iron 'pigs' in the bilges. Providing we had completed the set tasks; we could then row off the effects of lunch and get up to all the innocent mischief that boys do when among unexplored muddy creeks. There was always a waiting list at school to join me but it was the roast beef and ice cream rather than the pots of varnish that influenced my popularity.

The rest of the year followed an established pattern. Sailing from St Peter Port now with a clean bottom *Olga* would head for the stepmother's bust at St Mawe's from where the summer cruises would begin. Eight was the normal complement, with the mains'l alone needing four men to hoist - two each on the throat and peak falls, and when they were belayed the two pairs would move to the port-side purchases until Pat was satisfied with the way the sail was set. We occasionally sailed with four, until towards the end of his life it was sometimes just Pat and me. This was heavy work as he would not, then, leave the cockpit but in their heydays these vessels had been sailed home from their deep-sea rendezvous by the off-duty pilot and the cabin boy. Any complaint from me received short shrift over the 30,000 nautical miles I must have sailed under his command.

Before sailing, the praam dinghy – in its secondary role as a water barge – would be filled at a convenient spring until its gunwales were nearly awash, then towed gingerly back by the larger dinghy to have its contents pumped into *Olga*'s capacious tanks, while the never-used bath would also be filled.

Invariably the first port of call for each cruise was Camaret, where we would anchor off the slipway and, once victualed with wine, cheese, fresh fish, (and having been measured the year before) new, red-canvas Breton smocks, it was away to the south. In no particular order we would visit Audierne, Benodet, Loch Tudy, Île Tudy, Belle Île, Île de Ré, Île d'Yeu, La Rochelle, d'Étel and so on, with all these anchorages unvisited by other yachts. In a good year we would get as far as the north Spanish coast.

Those were the days when tunny fisherman still sailed *en masse* out of Concarneau, and the sardine fishing fleets with their distinctive blue nets, out of Camaret and Douarnenez. Camaret's *filet bleu* festival was always a must. Dog-watch entertainment was rifle shooting at the green-glass fishing floats that, then, littered the ocean followed by 'mess dinners' in the saloon with port-fired contests of agility over the beam that ran beneath the skylight or races to the end of the 14-feet long bowsprit or over the crosstrees.

The saloon was a large, snug cabin dominated by a substantial teak, gimballed table along the starboard side while a coke stove lay against the forward bulkhead. Various sideboards, chests of drawers and bookshelves completed the furniture while the whole was lit by a ferocious Tilley Lamp the ritual igniting of which was an unpredictable, early evening evolution.

Forward of the saloon, a port-side passage led to the large fore-cabin, workshop and sail lockers – the large heads occupied the whole of the starboard side of this passage. This narrow space to port, ventilated by the fore-hatch, doubled as the galley, yet through here all sails had to be passed, usually at the critical stage of a meal's preparation. For some reason, serving meals and tops'l-setting had to be conducted at the same time so just as the cook called *au table*, the predictable response from the upper deck was 'wait a moment, we'll just set the tops'l'. Pat enjoyed good food, although when alone, he existed on a diet of pink gin, raw onions, bully beef or sausages and cigarettes. A staple diet was an unlimited supply of wartime, lifeboat biscuits - acquired free at the end of hostilities, and yes, we did tap out the occasional weevil!

Offshore, the routine depended little on the weather, for reefing or heaving-to were seldom considered until the wind strength was at least Force 7. I recall only once reefing the No. 2 grade, flax canvas mains'l with the huge reefing handles and worm and screw roller gear. In practice, the first 'reef' was the handing of the Indian cotton jib tops'l, then the flax main tops'l, followed by the stays'l then, once we were down to the mains'l and jib, we would sit it out until, we would sit it out until the blow had passed. Bristol Channel pilot cutters are about as sea-kindly and safe as it is possible to be.

Many on-board facilities had seen service elsewhere: the after cabin's washbasin was a folding type, from apparently, an RAF bomber, and the windlass was turned by a car's self-starter motor connected to a light aircraft's dynamo, powered by a concrete-mixer engine. The main engine lay at right angles to the centreline and was linked to a truck's rear axle that turned the drive through 90 degrees. The propeller was offset to port.

Stories from those days are legendary: a steamer's log line wrapped around the topm'st fore-stay after a foggy, channel crossing was a sobering discovery while on one occasion my friends and I (recently commissioned into the Royal Marines) were sitting in the cockpit congratulating ourselves on a successful, if complicated, dusk anchorage under sail off Audierne. With the first gin in our hands and talk of the run ashore on our lips, we were silenced by a reminder that the ship comes first. 'Who is going to clear the propeller?' Pat demanded and while we procrastinated, he stood, took out his glass eye and with a cry of 'Call yourselves bloody commandos!' leapt overboard with a knife. We did not launch the dinghy.

Cruises were conducted with impeccable seamanship and, despite Pat's gruff exterior and occasional shout, with great good humour. Nothing short of full self-reliance was required in all departments before Pat considered his crews to be true seamen - accolades that would not have been bestowed had they called for navigational, meteorological or medical advice over a (then non-existent) telephone. Unlike some modern sailing 'heroes' he did not need to know the breaking strains of his flax sails, nor the tensile strength of his manila and hemp cordage, for he judged instinctively, what they could stand. He never lost a spar, only once carried away a sail and never parted a halyard (the ratlines, though, were another matter!). He needed no shore-side, computer-literate technician to suggest a reef or alteration of course because of the impending weather.

Discipline was tough and sometimes even harsh, while all the time various maxims were drummed into me such as: 'Seamanship, boy, not showmanship'; 'Blades forrard in the dinghy, please, as the ladies sit in the stern sheets!'; 'If you fall overboard, you are dead'; 'One hand for the ship, the other for the King'; 'Yachts have destinations not times of arrival. No voyage should ever be constrained by a time limit for that can lead to bad decisions'; 'Never set out to sea unless you are prepared and equipped to stay there'; 'Always wear sea boots that are two sizes too big' and so on. This last, in particular, was to save my life - twice.

With my parents often abroad, living with Pat on board *Olga*, and with *EM* moored nearby, made for an 'interesting' childhood, often remembered by Pat's constant reminders to 'get it right'. Self-responsibility was the cry, not reliance on third parties, while his overriding mantra was always 'seamanship not showmanship'. Pat's was a hard, unforgiving school.

The late 1940s was the time when so few yachts were at sea that on sighting a sail we would alter course towards it, dip ensigns, shout sailing instructions for the last port each had visited then on parting, dash below to look up details and addresses in *Lloyds Register of Yachts,* so we could exchange photographs. Now we tend to turn away!

Other memories include 'shooting the trammel' at dusk from the pulling dinghy off Carricknath Point, helped by Mary Ford (later a sought-after London fashion model) who was living on board a nearby converted Brixham trawler. It was quite a row for two 8-year-olds. We would then return before dawn to 'hand' the net, before selling the contents on St Mawes's quay - the only source of pocket money for this unpaid paid hand! And if the unpaid paid hand wasn't burnishing the brightwork or scrubbing the bottoms of both *Olga*'s dinghies on the beach, Pat and I would sail *EM* (one aged between 8 and 12 - as the summers multiplied - and the other between 48 and 52) to trawl, under sail, off Porthbeor and Towan beaches.

My godfather's relationship with my mother was to me then, a puzzling one and one that required *Olga* (then painted light grey as a nod to the higher temperatures) to sail to Malta in 1956. And so it was from that island that much Mediterranean cruising was enjoyed along the Sicilian and southern Italian coasts.

When my father's tour of duty ended in 1957 and with *Olga*'s return home it was back to the old routine of St Peter Port at Easter and the Bay of Biscay for the summer, with the occasional trawling excursion in *EM*.

Neither of Pat's vessels had life jackets or safety harnesses, thus sharpening the senses and encouraging a greater awareness of hidden dangers. With no life raft, in an emergency the dinghy's gripes would be cut, the praam - which was inverted inside the large sailing dinghy - turned, and a prayer offered that both would float off upright. Flares were not carried and there was no means of communicating other than by Aldis Lamp (assuming the batteries were above any bilge water). Navigation was by one of two sextants (a bubble and a quadrant) and Consol, but more commonly by dead reckoning, instinct and local knowledge, with every new anchorage an adventure preceded by the dinghy and lead line. The few charts had been 'acquired' from the naval service with some still retaining the D-Day cross-channel plans while the sole Western Approaches chart was precious enough to live under a Perspex sheet so that courses and fixes could be drawn with wax pencils and then rubbed off. To save on fuel, the paraffin navigation lights were not lit unless others were sighted.

Pat Phibbs died in 1975. As my mother had pre-deceased him, he had torn up his will, although his wish remained that I should inherit. However, I knew that *Olga*'s safest bet was to be sold. This we arranged just before he died, but not before Bill Tilman's offer had been dismissed: 'I will not sell *Olga* to that murderer of pilot cutters!'

Elizabeth Mary had already been sold - well - to be raced successfully. When I saw her in 1999, she was undergoing the third rebuild of her life in a Salcombe boatyard. In 2008 she sailed past my then current *Black Velvet* while we were 'resting' on a buoy off Fowey. A great and nostalgic sight.

In 1975, Patrick was discovered after lying for thirty-six hours at the foot of the companion ladder with a Calor gas cylinder pinned across his chest. He died shortly afterwards in Plymouth's naval hospital from cancer (he could smoke one hundred cigarettes a day when at sea), and despite origionally having been left to my mother who predeceased him, *Olga* was sold - badly. Luckily she was then discovered just in time at Maldon by the Swansea Maritime Museum, who had her 'shipped' across the width of England on a lorry. She is still sailing now and in as good a condition as she probably ever was.

With the loss, first of *Sea Vixen* then *EM* and now *Olga*, it was my turn to take up gaff rig ownership but not without a brief and interesting foray into the simpler joys of Bermudian rig with the first *Black Velvet*. The second *Black Velvet* - tiny but purposefully convenient for equally small children (no guardrails taught them to hold on tight) - was a 24-feet, Cornish Crabber that lasted us well until I retired from the Royal Marines. Then I was able to commute a fair amount of my pension and spend it all - plus rather more - on the third *Black Velvet*. The money raised did not extend to (in descending order of desire) – wood, steel, aluminium or cement, so I sought a suitable hull shape onto which I could design a gaff-rigged cutter with a squares'l. The Tradewind 35's glass reinforced plastic (GRP) hull fitted the bill and so *BV3* was launched at Lymington in 1993 and immediately entered for the following year's two-handed Round Britain and Ireland Yacht Race (RB&I) with my son, Hamish (RCC) as co-skipper. We came last into Plymouth but a good number of others had retired while we had butted around the islands at our own comfortable pace. Another RB&I (out of six in all) ended, unplanned in Brest in time for Éric Tabarley's magnificent nautical funeral service.

Six summers taking ornithologists deep into the Western Approaches looking for the elusive (in these waters) Wilson's petrels (known to Devon Wildlife Trust as 'willy-watching patrols'), helped *Black Velvet* pay her way, as did three expeditions into the Arctic with mountaineers, the last of which ended as a rather sobering chapter in Peter Bruce's seminal *Heavy Weather Sailing*.

Patricia was not a yachtswoman but enjoyed living on board, so the solution was to unship the spars, remove all heavy equipment, buy a collection of the canal guides, apply for a licence and enter the French canal system via the Somme. A deep-draught yacht is not ideal, but for one glorious year, in bursts of a fortnight, we bumped and scrapped our way through the canals to the north-east of Paris while exploring further with bicycles. If *Black Velvet* had moved any distance, then an easy train ride to collect the car always worked – on time and cheap. This idyll came to an abrupt halt when, on her 365th day away, *Black Velvet* was visited by *les voleurs* while moored in the immigration town of Creil. This sad episode is covered in detail later.

By 2011 *Black Velvet* was not yet beginning to feel her age, but I was. So after two years trying not to make the decision – an electric windless helped stave off the inevitable – it was time she found an owner who could do her justice, while I looked for a vessel more suitable for a 70-year-old who still enjoyed single-handed pottering – under a gaff rig of course.

I did, and found a very smart, immaculately maintained, 30-feet Cornish Crabber 'pilot cutter' at a Mylor boatyard. I renamed her *Black Velvet of Tamar*. She was sold in my 80th year having been, by far, the most favourite of all my vessels.

Chapter 4

Esso Norway Salvage Attempt, 1964

Account written for the Royal Marines' journal the *Globe & Laurel.*

In August 1964, I was the officer commanding the Royal Marines detachment on board HMS *Anzio* based at Bahrain in the Persian Gulf. She was a wartime-built, tank landing ship (assault) (LST(A)) with the Seaborne Tank Force of sixteen Centurion tanks embarked for a voyage from Bahrain to Aden, when on 24 August 1964 we received an SOS from the British oil tanker *Esso Norway*. Once our part in the salvage attempt was over, I was invited to write an article about it. The following is the result.

We never believed that we would be involved, for when we finally arrived on the scene there were seven other merchant ships standing by. However, they seemed to be waiting and just watching, so we barged in to pick up the tanker's delightful master, Captain J. Petrie, a north–countryman. He and ten of his crew were in one of their ship's lifeboats and had just left the tanker for the second time. He wanted us to tow her, and not a Norwegian ship that was standing by and who had asked verbally to do so before we arrived. I was never sure why Captain Petrie preferred a British warship to a Norwegian merchant vessel. While *Anzio* was manoeuvred upwind of the tanker, which was still blazing aft in the engine room and crew's quarters, I lowered one of my eight assault landing craft (LCA) crewed by a corporal and two marines, and set off for the Norwegian ship to pick up each of the remaining survivors.

Despite a heavy sea running against the side of the ship we managed to get 30 of *Esso Norway*'s crew into the landing craft, including three badly injured men. On the way back to *Anzio* we passed the tanker, still blazing, so we returned to put a team of our chaps on board to prepare the tow and fight the fire. The initial objective was to pass a line of any size so that no one else could claim her. It was a tricky evolution in the heavy sea that was running but eventually we managed to pass a wire hawser. She displaced about 43,000 tons but had taken on about 70,000 tons so we reckoned she was almost 100,000 tons or the equivalent of two, light aircraft carriers. Not surprisingly, we could only make one-and-a-half knots and took three hours turning her around to the west. *Anzio* displaced a mere 4,000 tons.

During the first night and in an increasing swell, the tanker began to 'take charge' so HMS *Anzio* had to slip the tow to steam around her all night to prevent anyone else from pinching her. What apparently had happened was that a cooling water pipe had burst and began flooding the engine room. To counterbalance the extra water on board they had to jettison 1,000 gallons of crude oil, which immediately came back into the ship through the broken pipe. The gas from this oil then exploded at 0330.

During the morning of the second day I was called to lower a landing craft and take the two worst injured men to an Italian guided missile cruiser. This was quite a feat for the corporal cox'n as there was a very heavy sea running alongside a high hull, but the Italian equivalent of a Neil Robertson stretcher saved the day - and further injury. On our return to *Anzio* hoisting the landing craft was frankly, dangerous, made even more so, as I was continually being shouted at by my captain. I refused to hoist unless he gave us a lee from the swell but this he declined to do. One moment we were almost at deck level on a wave, then the next we were about 20 feet down. There was little the crew and I could safely do as it was too much work for one man trying to attach the one-hundred weight blocks into the davit's hooks, then take up the weight on the falls. Finally, with superhuman effort from the crew, the forrard and aft hooks were secured. This stopped the up and down movement, but we were now being swung out 10 or 12 feet and back again against the ship's side. By good fortune, and no thanks to our captain, we had no injuries despite having to be lowered and hoisted four more times that morning. The worst thing about the whole salvage operation was the complete lack of encouragement and support from the captain who never said anything to hearten my marines.

After breakfast that next day, I took across a fresh boarding party to pass another tow, this time, and thankfully, under the first lieutenant's calm, professional command. We were also tasked with collecting the ships officers' private gear. The crew's quarters aft were burnt out: a most unpleasant task as we didn't really know what to take or to leave behind. All the mid-ship cabins were water free, so it was difficult to believe that the tanker was a derelict, except for the angle of the deck and the complete silence, broken only by the crashing surf as it swept across and into the aft superstructure. At Captain Petrie's insistence, for as the Master he owned the contents, the tanker's chief officer and I used a fire axe to liberate the bonded stores locker where we found thousands of cigarettes, three crates of gin and three of brandy. These were shipped into the landing craft for the eventual and welcome benefit of *Anzio*'s crew.

During the second night *Esso Norway* settled a further six feet aft with the sea now breaking right over the stern superstructure. Throughout the second day we worked on board salvaging all the moveable items of value and navigation gear. While supervising this evolution *Esso Norway*'s shipwright asked me if I would help him go aft to see if we could find any trace of three men who, it was assumed, had been killed in the explosion. I did not relish the idea yet it was vital, so we made our way along the sea-washed catwalks which was when for the first time I thought she might go down at any second. The idea was to climb to the top of the aft superstructure to look down into the engine room through what had been the main skylights.

We found an enormous, jagged hole above the engine room with everything blown completely clear, allowing us to see into the flooded compartments. There were gruesome bits and pieces lying around, but thankfully, as none of these were recognisable, we decided to quietly return to the landing craft.

All that night *Anzio* towed *Esso Norway* at one-and-a-half knots, really just trying to keep her off the coast which by then was about three miles to starboard. As she now drew 60 feet we could not afford to get much closer in the heavy, monsoon-induced, on-shore sea that was running.

All the while I and my different crews were required to hoist and lower landing craft in the most appalling sea state as we changed the towing crews on board *Esso Norway* and sent continual reports on her rate of sinking. That evening we again took a party across to stay on board the tanker for the whole night in case the tow parted, which with the heavy sea still running, was more than likely. There was indeed, one hell of a swell running alongside the tanker, so once again, we were surprised and relieved that we suffered no injuries getting the men on board. This was thanks largely to the remarkable skills of the marine cox'ns. Just when we needed it least, a thick fog now descended as we prepared to spend the night off the tanker's stern watching for further signs of deterioration.

It was a terrible night in the open landing craft, with me and six marines. We couldn't see a thing through the fog and fine rain while we laboured in the heavy sea - way beyond any peacetime safety limits.

At one stage we had to pass a new tow which was done in excellent time but at about 0200 I reported to *Anzio* that the *Esso Norway* was settling further and now with a list to starboard. As there was a significant amount of crude oil flooding to the surface it was decided to take the boarding party back to *Anzio*, which we did before standing by for the rest of the long night, sending back regular reports.

In the morning I changed the landing craft crew and had breakfast sent into the boat, after which we were tasked to collect the captain of a Danish tug that had appeared. At the subsequent conference it was decided that we should hand over responsibility so that the tanker could be beached, under control, in shallow water until the end of the monsoon. The plan was then to pump out the engine room and tow the *Esso Norway* to Aden where the remainder of the crude oil could be saved. With relief we left her in charge of the tug and steamed on to Aden to unload the Seaborne Tank Force, refuel and get some rest.

As an aside, having refuelled and while on our way back to Bahrain there was a high chance that my assault squadron would be put ashore in Oman to 'look after a few people' but unfortunately it didn't come off.

The *Esso Norway* saga was the subject of considerable discussion across the maritime world and can still be followed on Google. About two years later I received £150 as my share of the salvage money.

Chapter 5

Two-handed Watchkeeping, 1970

In 1970 and with the enthusiastic permission of my commanding officer I entered Philip Tuckett's beautiful, 49-feet, wooden yawl *Speedwell of Cremyl* in the second of Colonel 'Blondie' Hasler's two-handed Round Britain and Ireland (RB&I) races. I had tried to enter for the first, four years earlier, but a posting to the Sultan of Oman's Armed Forces was considered more important for my career.

Having taken command of *Speedwell*, three hurdles needed to be addressed. First the crew, second, the self-steering gear and third a watchkeeping system that ensured maximum efficiency and minimum exhaustion. The crew problem was solved with the arrival of Roger Dillon whom I had not met previously but who was to become a lifelong and much-valued friend. My original crew, Johnny Ackroyd-Hunt, had almost at the last moment, been denied leave as he was a helicopter pilot required elsewhere. The self-steering gear was solved by Blondie who jumped at the challenge to design and build, at no cost to us, the largest servo-pendulum gear he had made so far, and one with the added complication of having to fit it to a wheel rather than a tiller.

The watchkeeping conundrum was less easy to solve. There was the standard four-on, four-off routine adopted by most two-handed crews, but this meant that socialising, cooking, eating together, and even sail changing had to be at the expense of someone's rest. Some yachts adopted an even more tiring two-on, two-off watch system. Others had no system but just woke the off-duty crew when they were tired. Who then did the cooking, sail changing and general chores and when? I was determined to find a better way of managing our time while ensuring the maximum of undisturbed rest - apart of course from emergencies.

Following hours of doodling I came up with the following suggestion which we put into action:

0700 – 0800	Breakfast	Both on watch.
0800 – 1300		Crew A on watch for five daylight hours.
1300 – 1400	Lunch	Both on watch for one hour of social time and chores.

1400 – 1900		Crew B on watch for five daylight hours.
1900 – 2200	Dinner	Both on watch for three hours. Evening sail changes if necessary. Drink, chat and chores.
2200 – 0100		Crew A on watch for three night-hours having had five hours off watch during the afternoon.
0100 – 0400		Crew B on watch for three night hours but who will then have five hours rest during the morning.
0400 – 0700		Crew A on watch for three dawn hours.
0700 – 0800	Breakfast	Both on watch for one hour of social time and chores.
0800 – 1300		Crew B on watch having had a total of six hours off watch during the night.

Once we had slipped into this unique routine, both Roger and I agreed that it suited a two-handed crew perfectly. After the race we managed to persuade others to adopt it, including the Amateur Yacht Research Society who publicised it widely. The extraordinary seaman Mike McMullen, sadly lost during the 1976 Observer Single-handed Transatlantic Race (OSTAR) used it most successfully with Martin Read, when they were two-handed. I regarded this as firm endorsement and have used it ever since.

To summarise the advantages:

1. There are three periods in every twenty-four hours when the crew are together without losing any rest. This to my mind is vital.
2. The crew with the two-night watches will have had five hours rest during the afternoon between 1400 and 1900, and then five hours rest the following morning between 0800 and 1300. Conversely the crew with just one night watch will have had the two longest day watches.
3. The system is flexible enough to allow for a crew to be shaken while off watch, without too much loss of rest. If necessary, he/she can sleep in during the next joint/social watch.
4. The routine changes every day.
5. We found we had more sleeping/resting time than was necessary!

Finally to my mind it is essential when sailing short or two-handed, that a good, firm watch-keeping system is in place and adhered to, to make things tick smoothly. This ensures less risk of argument or complaint that a rest period had been eaten into by chores. My system can of course be adopted for any number of crew assuming that a two-watch system is in place.

To some it may seem dogmatic but during the many occasions I have used it, we fared far better and were certainly less tired than those who had no system or used one of those mentioned at the beginning.

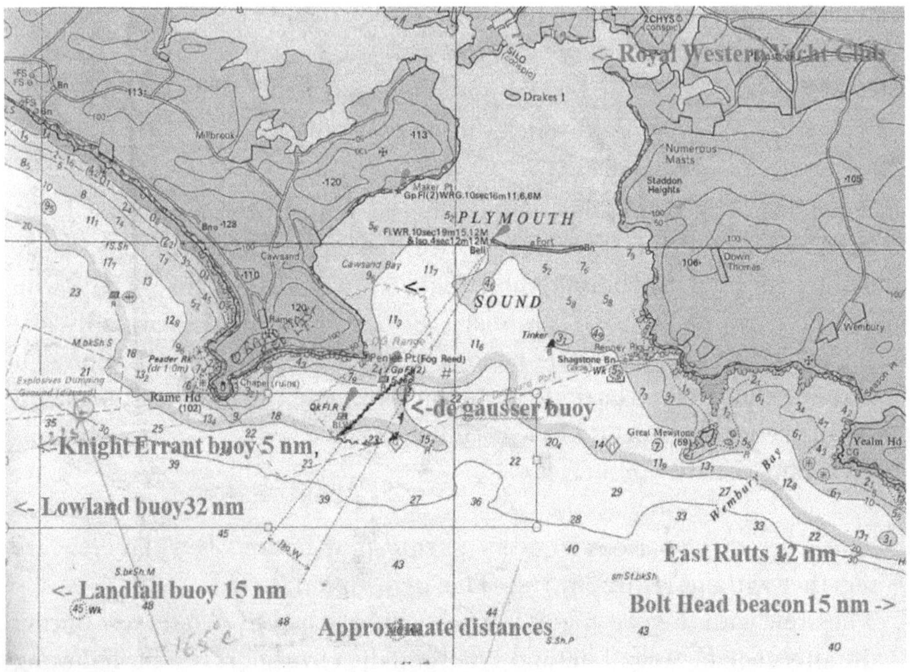

The relevant buoys for the Silver Jubilee Race 1977 (Royal Naval Hydrographic Department).

Chapter 6

Royal Thames Yacht Club
Silver Jubilee Race, 1977

**The then secretary of the Royal Navy Sailing
Association asked me to write about the race
for the club's journal. This is the result.**

The Silver Jubilee Challenge Cup was first presented to the Royal Thames
Yacht Club by His Royal Highness the Prince of Wales in 1935. In 1977, the
same yacht club decided to mark the Silver Jubilee of Her Majesty the Queen
by organising a race in conjunction with ten other yacht clubs around the
country, in order that as many people from across the nation could compete.
The balance of entry fees after expenses had been paid would be donated to
the Queen's Silver Jubilee Appeal, thus yachtsmen and women from every
corner of the British Isles were given the opportunity to celebrate the Jubilee
by sailing a highly imaginative race, at the same time knowing that they were
contributing to a worthy cause.

The object of the race was to 'endeavour to sail the greatest number of
nautical miles around a set number of listed marks within a 24-hour period'.
Each yacht club was responsible for publishing the listed marks for their area,
in concert with the official rhum line distance between them. After the start
yachts were free to choose their own course and order of rounding each mark,
while it was not obligatory to round all marks listed. The crux of the race
was that only the rhum line distance between each mark would count. That
forced skippers and navigators to do their sums very carefully to ensure their
yacht was, where possible, always with a fair tide and wind, and that each mark
rounded would leave them with a choice of at least two others in different
directions. This to allow for wind shifts, changing tides and expected boat
speed. It was apparent that the courses chosen by the largest yachts would
differ considerably from those taken by the smallest, as for instance, a small
yacht might take a whole tide to reach a distant mark.

If a foul tide was unavoidable then a mark had to be chosen which would allow a passage in the least tidal stream, with preferably, a reaching or running wind. Planning ahead for at least two legs, depending on the expected boat speed for the expected conditions, was essential in order to avoid being down both wind and tide for the next leg.

In 1977 I owned the first of my four *Black Velvets*. This one had been built for me especially for the two-handed Round Britain and Ireland Yacht race in 1974. She was a standard Hurley 24 with a 17-feet 6 inch waterline. Rigging was a size larger than specification, and her hull was strengthened at all the obvious stress points. She carried ten sails, was fitted with a useless QME self-steering gear, and by then, an equally useless Vire 6hp petrol engine. Up to that year her greatest 24-hour recorded mileage was 102 nautical miles in a southerly gale 60 miles north-west of Ireland on our way to Barra in 1974. This may not sound much but was achieved under either bare poles or just the storm jib in very heavy seas.

Excited by the idea of something different, I managed to persuade two sailing friends that this was not an event to be missed. Thus two well-known and hugely experienced West Country yachtsmen, Peter Seldon and Graham Adam, agreed to join me, once I had explained that it was not, in my view, a race, but a fascinating navigational challenge which made it far more interesting – and fun.

The listed marks chosen from Plymouth meant that we could really only sail to the west or the east. Consequently, the turning points were split between reasonably close marks (presumably for the smaller yachts to be able to round at the turn of a tide if lucky) and two distant marks at opposite ends of the area, which a larger yacht might be able to cover in one tide. From west to east they were:

Lowland buoy off the Manacles rocks, to the north-east of the Lizard.
Landfall buoy approximately 15 miles west-south-west of the Eddystone lighthouse.
Knight Errant buoy, east of Looe.
The southern most of the two Admiralty degaussing buoys, east of Rame head.
East Rutts buoy, west of Bolt Tail.
Skerries buoy, off the Skerries bank, east of Start Point.

The start was across the Royal Western Yacht Club's line off its West Hoe clubhouse, around the South-West Winter buoy within Plymouth Sound, but from then onwards in whichever direction the various skippers decided. The rest would be up to us as dictated by wind direction and strength, the tide times and our speed over the ground.

At 1100 on 6 June, *Black Velvet* started in company with sixteen others, divided about equally into two classes, one for larger 'rated' yachts and one for smaller yachts with a 'Portsmouth yardstick' for handicapping. That was us and our newly acquired number was 129, not that I had the slightest idea what that meant. We were the smallest yacht in the fleet with a planning speed for the wind at that moment of about 4 knots. The wind in the Sound was from the west at Force 3.

Before we set off through the western entrance of the breakwater there was no doubt in any of our minds that to gain the advantage of wind and tide, we should first head downwind for the East Rutts buoy. However, now that we were actually underway, thoughts of heading up-wind first, to the Knight Errant buoy off Looe began to make more sense. Even before we had passed the breakwater, we held the first of many quick cockpit conferences for the wind was already increasing and expected to veer, as a depression passed to the north. In the end we cut our losses and made for East Rutts which, with help from the tide, we reached in two hours. We then enjoyed a cracking, close reach to the distant Lowland buoy. Only two of the smaller yachts followed us to the west.

Once we had rounded the mark and had settled onto the windward leg *Black Velvet* was decidedly over canvassed in the now rising wind, so we changed from the heavy genoa to the number one jib. With one full reef now in the mains'l we began to haul away from the next astern.

At 1526 we rounded the southern degausser buoy with the wind now constant from the southwest, increasing to Force 6 and gusting above, while kicking up a most nasty, short, steep sea.

At 1735 we rounded the East Rutts for the second time. Visibility was now bad but with no real change in wind strength or direction. It dawned on us that if the visibility deteriorated further we might be looking for this unlit buoy again, but next time in the dark. Yet luck was on our side for through the murk could now be seen what must have been the first of many Jubilee beacons being lit along the coast. Its position was quickly marked on the chart for future reference as a navigating mark.

We were now punching into a worsening sea fine on the port bow which *Black Velvet* was finding more and more difficult. She, as did I, longed for the longer, more manageable swell of an Atlantic gale!

During this leg the wind increased markedly accompanied by violent rain squalls to Force 7, each lasting for about 40 minutes. The conversation in the cockpit took on a different tone as the forecast was for a veer to the north-west and an increase to Force 8. While under the lee of Penlee Point we hove-to, pulled down a second reef, changed to the smallest jib above the storm jib, heated a ready-made casserole and poured three large whiskies.

Fortified and more comfortable we headed back into the Channel. The wind was definitely increasing but still from the same direction so it was off to East Rutts yet again. The tide had turned in our favour and the broad reach in the gloom of dusk and the rainstorms was boisterous - and exciting. We became almost euphoric and poured another six whiskers. To the north along the skyline, when the squalls permitted, five enormous bonfires could be seen stretching from above Millbrook to our plotted one near to Boat Tail, we could even see my village beacon on Dartmoor.

It was a beautiful sight from a small yacht bouncing around the Channel on a wild night and made us even more determined not to give in, but to continue with our unique way of celebrating the Jubilee. As luck would again have it, we were in the middle of a squall when he had run our distance, but just for a moment, we could make out the glare of the Bolt Tail beacon. A position line was followed by a running fix. We were on the right course and almost immediately the East Rutts buoy appeared dead ahead. We had now covered just under 50 miles in less than twelve hours and, although not likely to win the race, we were on track to beat *Black Velvet*'s previous best 24-hour run. This fact hardened our resolve to continue despite the appalling conditions.

We headed back towards the degausser once more. As the forecast wind shift had not occurred it seemed a pity not to make use of the winning combination of wind direction and tide.

Halfway towards the Mewstone, an even larger than usual wave thundered out of the dark, breaking either side of us for as far as we could see in the gloom.

I shouted, 'Hold on!' before all hell was let loose together with a great deal of water above the cabin sole with Peter displacing much of it. I had never heard of a yacht pitch-poling stern first, but we must have come dangerously close. Everything that was movable, plus a number of objects that were not supposed to be, ended up as far aft as was possible.

There was no damage except to the log line which had been torn from its shackles. We were going to miss that as it was a vital key to navigation in the bad visibility. Then, while we were sorting ourselves out, the wind veered sharply to the north-west. We needed no lengthy discussion for the only course now open to us was to head directly for the distant landfall buoy away to the south-west.

Navigationally, I had achieved a reasonable departure from our position off the Mewstone, but that was as far as it went, despite a chart that was so sodden that it was impossible to use a pencil. Luckily, every so often we could take a back bearing of Bolt Tail's distant beacon, and in those conditions, we were well aware that when we crossed the Hands Deep, the echo sounder would confirm our position - roughly. As the visibility was so poor, to ease our collective consciences we decided to sail an estimated five miles further than the buoy's known position before turning for home. By chance this was suddenly not necessary, as dead ahead, was the more than welcome sight of a red light flashing every ten seconds. Not often have I been so glad to see a buoy, and although we were soaked through, very cold, extremely tired, hungry and not a little thirsty, seldom have government-issue oatmeal blocks and cold sardines tasted so good, as we settled down for an exhilarating close-reach towards the north-east and the finish line. Even so, we were puzzled that apart from when rounding the first mark, we had not seen one other yacht. Yes, the visibility had been bad, but not for the whole twenty-four hours.

The rest of the race became academic as far as we were concerned. We knew nothing of the others but we were happy to have sailed 105 rhum line, nautical miles, so as we approached the finishing line, we hoisted the signal flags to indicate the distance sailed. In actual miles covered it was, of course, rather more.

As we crossed the line, what we hadn't realised was that the Royal Western Yacht Club was hosting its Queen's Silver Jubilee cocktail party and so were surprised to see so many people apparently welcoming us back. While we sculled *Black Velvet* into the Royal Marines' small-boat camber and drove round to the clubhouse to hand in our log, in our absence the significance of our flag-hoist was being debated, and especially so by the crews of the larger yachts who were already accusing us of showing off - or even cheating.

We didn't understand. We must have come last.

'Quiet everyone, please,' the commodore shouted, 'Now that the last yacht has finished, we have the results. Third, the yacht *Blue Eyes* - 83 miles. Second, the yacht *West Wind* - 84 miles, and first *Black Velvet* - 105 miles. She is also the smallest yacht to have taken part, and the only one to have completed the whole course in the channel.' We were astounded as the three of us received a handsomely engraved ship's decanter.

Where is She? The Search for the
Bonhomme Richard, 1979

A North Sea navigation puzzle

A version of this essay was first published in *Yachting Monthly*.

It appears to me to be the province of our infant Navy to surprise and spread alarm with fast sailing ships. When we grow stronger we can meet their fleets and dispute with them the sovereignty of the ocean. This strategy against the Royal Navy was the brainchild of the 'Honourable Captain John P. Jones, Commander-in-Chief of the American Squadron now in Europe', and that was how he described himself.

At 1100 on 25 September 1779, America's most famous warship foundered in the North Sea. Watching her from a captured British man-of-war was her captain, John Paul Jones. For over two hundred years the exact position of the *Bonhomme Richard* has been studied by historians, navigators and nautical archaeologists, but never solved.

To Americans, Jones is their greatest naval hero but to the British of that time he was little more than a rapacious pirate. John Paul was born a Scot in 1747, and having quickly risen to command his own merchant ship, he deserted the *Betsy* after a sword fight in which he killed his opponent while at anchor off Tobago in 1773. Apart from a quick temper, he was undoubtedly skilled as a leader, ship handler and naval tactician.

Changing his name to John Paul Jones he was commissioned into the embryo United States Navy and soon instructed to 'distress' the British population. No match for the Royal Navy, he resorted to hit-and-run tactics with the sloop *Ranger*. In 1778, as part of that strategy, he attempted to abduct the Earl of Selkirk from his house on St Mary's Isle in Kirkcudbright Bay. The Earl was to have been used as a hostage for the release of prisoners but he was absent. The raid is fascinating, not for its lack of success, but for the manner in which it failed, and the subsequent and charming letters of apology to the Countess – who had been alone at the time…!

At 1530 on 23 September 1779, and now captain of the *Bonhomme Richard*, the chance for which Jones had been waiting presented itself – a forty-four-ship convoy, under the command of Captain Richard Pearson in HMS *Serapis*, was sighted off Flamborough head, making its landfall from the Baltic with a cargo of wood.

The battle that followed was the first night engagement of the era, and while the American won the fight, he lost his ship and gained immortality. Pearson saved the convoy before he surrendered and was eventually knighted. From the American point of view, the only nation that came out of the affair badly was France. Three of Jones' ships were commanded by Frenchmen, all of whom, at dusk and in the crucial moment of the first engagement, hauled their wind and stood off. Jones knew that without their support he had to take the Englishman by boarding, for now he was outgunned.

By brilliant manoeuvring – one of his specialities – Jones laid his ship alongside the *Serapis* and was able to write later:

> *The battle thus begun was continued with unremitting fury. Having ensured the safety of his charges, Pearson was obliged to strike his colours but not before he shouted to me if I had, myself struck, only to the receive my reply, I have not yet begun to fight!*

He, Pearson, had done his duty, and in keeping with the custom of the day, was invited on board the victor's ship, where Jones handed back the proffered sword, with his compliments on a gallant defence of the convoy – plus a glass of wine. The two flagships, still grappled and on fire, swung to the *Serapis'* anchor, while a survey confirmed that the *Bonhomme Richard* was now not only greatly decayed with age but also… 'mangled beyond description': a condition that forced a reluctant Jones to transfer his command to the newly captured *Serapis*.

The *Bonhomme Richard* was cut adrift at 2230 that night and although in a slowly sinking state, her first lieutenant remained on board in an endeavour, it is believed, to sail her to the safety of Texel. His attempts, though valiant and strenuous, were in vain, for at 1100 on 25 September and after a fight with the elements nearly as fierce as that with the *Serapis*, Jones watched with 'inexpressible grief, the last glimpse of my flagship as she slid, bows first, beneath the North Sea'.

Shortly before the two hundredth anniversary of the Battle of Flamborough Head, the American author Clive Cussler recruited a team to carry out academic studies, prior to a practical search to find, but not to recover, the *Bonhomme*

Richard. I was appointed navigational advisor and the British motor-yacht *Arvor III* was chosen as the research vessel. She would sail under the highly unofficial Texan flag, rather than her more usual White Ensign of the Royal Yacht Squadron.

My task was two-fold: first, to work out where the warship was cut loose in 1779 and then plot her likely drift pattern up to the point of foundering. Later, I would use the *Arvor* to conduct a 1979 drift-study then with both tracks to hand and allowing for variables, suggest the most likely area for our search.

The battle has always been known as the Battle of Flamborough Head and certainly that is where the opposing captains first engaged each other. It is also the headland mentioned throughout in a Midshipman Fanning's journal, written on board the *Serapis*. But midshipmen's journals are notorious for their inaccuracies, even in the eighteenth century. Mine, produced in 1960, is a remarkable document of creative writing to satisfy my captain.

The first encounter was certainly off Flamborough Head, but with light southerly winds and the north-setting tide, I concluded that the *Serapis* was finally anchored about four miles due east of Filey Brig. The midshipman refers only to Flamborough in his journal but, I believe, the headland he was watching was, in the varying visibility and falling darkness, the next one to the north - Filey Brig. It is an easy mistake to make, especially in the heat of battle. Fanning also states that when they anchored it was in 16 fathoms which would not have been possible off Flamborough.

Contemporary reports from ashore also suggest Filey Brig as no one from Bridlington saw the events. There was only talk of the 'sound of the battle' to seaward. However, plenty of onlookers at Scarborough spoke of flashes of gunfire in the moonlight at five or six leagues to the east-south-east - roughly thirteen and fifteen and a half nautical miles respectively. Wreckage was washed up on the north shore of Flamborough and survivors scrambled to safety from a ship's boat across the beach beneath Buckton.

Other factors helped. My estimated track taken by the *Bonhomme Richard* ran down a line of magnetic anomalies discovered earlier and thought to be jettisoned cannon. The track I plotted also passed through the area where a rudder pintle had been brought to the surface, along with a French musket dated 1778, with a ball half-way up the barrel. I therefore felt sure that I had chosen the correct anchorage position.

For our own drift we needed the same weather and tidal conditions as those 200 years before. I had worked out the tides for 1779, while the weather was gleaned from contemporary documents. The *Bonhomme Richard* had been cut adrift towards the last of the north-west-setting tide two days before springs when the current has a maximum set of 3 knots.

An important variable, for which I had to make an allowance, was this unanswered question: did the *Bonhomme Richard* drift with the tide and rising wind or was there a definite policy to sail her to safety? Details are vague but I was able to make a number of deductions based on the state of the vessel at the battle's end and what I knew of her construction. Eventually, I would subtract our own wind-induced drift and apply that which might have affected a ship of the *Bonhomme Richard's* construction, either under jury rig or as a near-bare hulk.

I needed to estimate her rate of sinking, and to do that I had to know her draught when cut adrift and compare that to her draught shortly before foundering. From this I could deduce the lessening effect of windage and the increasing effect of the tidal stream.

To help the scientific team interpret the side-scan sonar and the magnetometer readings, and to aid the divers in their positive identification, it was important to know the positions of the cannon, relative to one another - what cannon were still on board when she foundered, the type and quantity of her ballast, and the type and stowage area of her spare anchors.

To add to these identification problems, the White Fish Authority's 'Fastening Chart' of the likely search area, revealed over 2,000 fastenings, many of which are piles of stones containing ferrous metals. A pile of stones containing ferrous metals was what we would be looking for.

Precise details of the ship were hard to find. She began life as a French East Indiaman, built for the Oriental trade, and when she came to Jones' notice in early 1779, had completed four voyages to China. However, she had not been his first choice to replace the *Ranger*, for he wished to have no connection with any ship that 'does not sail fast as I intend to go in harm's way'. Yet when Louis XVI thought it proper to 'place at your disposal the ship *Le Duc de Barras* of forty guns now at Lorient' and gave Jones permission to sail under the American flag and to recruit Frenchmen, he accepted. There followed a six-month refit, during which he was able to gather the other ships for hit and run raids.

Although we know that this was a frustrating time for the American captain, there were compensations, for he had declared earlier that he enjoyed nothing more than 'fitting out and making love'. This latter occupation was to bring him much anguish in later life and was partly the cause of his lack of recognition until after his death in France in 1792 as a pauper, despite having been an admiral in the Russian navy. When he was asked by a lady, why in all his battles, he had never been hurt, his reply summed up his private affairs: 'I have only been wounded with arrows that no enemy discharged.'

The *Bonhomme Richard*, as Jones renamed his new command, was reported to have had a 'burthen' of 900 tons, giving an estimated wartime displacement of 1,400 tons, but it is more likely that her actual displacement was 900 tons with a burthen (the number of tuns of wine a ship could carry) being rather less. This would make more sense, as her dimensions were in the order of 140 feet by 35 feet.

It was important to ascertain her ballast as this was all we really expected to find. French ships were ballasted with washed river stone, supplemented with shingle and rejected shot to add weight and fill in the gaps. Jones was known to favour the British system, so it is possible that 300 pigs of iron were added to her bilges, each marked with the French *livres* notation and with large holes for ease of handling.

We think that she carried four anchors when she left Lorient and assume that each was engraved with the customary Fleur de Lys. The bower and sheet anchors weighed 3,000 livres each, with the stream anchor weighing 1,500 and the kedge 1,000, roughly 3,237, 1,618 and 1,749 pounds respectively. It is likely that she carried extra stream and kedge anchors in her holds and that these were not jettisoned in the fight to save her from sinking.

When the two captains met over their glasses of wine, the *Bonhomme Richard* had an estimated draught of 19 feet 6 inches, with 5 feet of water in her bilges. She had many shot-holes below the waterline caused by the frigate *Alliance* (commanded by a fellow American), which had circled the two flagships, firing indiscriminately. Her draught increased to 20 feet just before foundering, as the sea 'rushed in and out of the lower gun ports'. We presumed that at some stage she jettisoned her 18-pounder cannon and her three main anchors, and if so, this would have decreased her displacement by 11 tons.

Finally, the one point that our research had yet to clarify, was the question of drifting or sailing. We do know that she had her mizzen set on the stump of that mast, and we think to begin with, she may have set her fore course on the lower foremast. She had no main mast. Her rudder was hanging by just one pintle out of the five, helping us to deduce that sails were set for steering and steadiness, rather than perhaps for speed. The wind and sea were increasing and the first lieutenant would not have wanted to put more strain on the battered hull than was necessary. The quarterdeck was in danger of falling into the gunroom, for it was largely unsupported by the transom as a result of faulty 18-pounder cannon exploding.

Fire remained the constant worry until brought under control at 1100 on the morning after the battle. By 1900 on 24 September, Jones agreed that his salvage crew was losing the struggle and so at 1930 he removed his flag, but not the ensign. At 2200 he was obliged to pass the final order to abandon ship, an evolution that took all night. Cutters and gigs transferred the wounded and stores, until at 0400 on 25 September, his exhausted men were forced to halt their labours as the sea reached the lower gun ports. The last man left at 1000 and she foundered within the hour.

All this detail was acquired over months of trans-Atlantic telephone calls and nationwide visits, enlisting the help of experts on windage and eighteenth-century rigging, until I was left with a simple plotting exercise.

Armed with my assumed drift chart it was time to compare it with reality. So in May 1979 we arrived in Newcastle where ten of us were allocated five of *Arvor*'s double cabins – and it was here that we met our first obstacle. No American was prepared to let another share a cabin with the only girl, the dark-haired and attractive expedition cook. After much seriously heated and time-consuming argument (which, initially, I kept out of) I was forced to suggest, very quietly, that peace would only be guaranteed if the sole Englishman had the privilege. After a stunned silence, the internecine fight was ended by the expedition leader exclaiming loudly, 'Gentlemen, if anyone is going to sleep with the cook it had better be the limey!'

This decision was made despite the innocent cook not being asked her preference throughout the 45-minute long debate. Nevertheless, honour was now satisfied and kept by all parties. A small point, but one which, at the time, so very nearly scuppered the whole trip.

Our drift started close to the assumed position of the *Serapis*' anchorage – and at the same state of tide – and went according to plan, with sights taken every 15 minutes for 36 hours, using all the aids available to us – horizontal and vertical sextant angles, lines of soundings, RDF, sun and star sights, and compass bearings. Once all the variables such as drift and windage had been applied, I had a track remarkably similar to that which had taken me several months to plot on paper. We started the engines and turned for Bridlington and British food. Every time I had been faced with a Texan 'delicacy' I was obliged to retaliate with sardines flambéed in gin and whisky on my morning porridge. Alongside and in the pubs, I evaluated our findings until able to produce the long-awaited 'area of highest probability', ready for the arrival of Clive Cussler, with his side-scan sonar and magnetometer teams – courtesy of the Massachusetts Institute of Technology.

The 10-square mile search area was fed into a computer which in turn fed one and a half million coordinates into two transponders that were set up ashore. From then onwards, *Arvor*'s track up and down preselected lanes was machine guided. All the helmsman had to do was steer the computed course and react to a signal which sounded each time he was three yards off track.

For three months (without me on board) *Arvor* ploughed a tiny section of the North Sea towing a 300-yard-wide sonar and magnetometer footprint, one cable apart, but with a generous overlap. Despite the hiring (in desperation) of a spiritual medium who flew over the area in a light aircraft with her eyes shut and while also vastly increasing the number of fastenings on the White Fish Authority's charts, we found nothing that resembled what we sought. There were many piles of stones, yet none that could have been identified as ballast. There were previously untabulated wrecks, but not one that could have been an eighteenth-century man-of-war.

Finally, we were certain of only one thing: she was not in the search area and we would have to return to our academic studies to solve the 'sail or drift' enigma. Despite our failure, it had been an absorbing navigational adventure, far removed from my normal work, and one which, as a sideline, had given us all a sobering insight into life at sea 200 years before.

Chapter 8

Impact Hydrography Around
the Falklands, 1979

'*These notes and charts are the amateur jottings of an itinerant yachtsman and are of no interest to this department*'. Chief Hydrographer of the Royal Navy quoted in a letter relayed to me circa 1980.

The commanding officer of the Amphibious Training Unit at Poole in Dorset looked at me, a youngish Royal Marines captain, across his desk.

'I want you to give a lecture to the next Naval Party 8901 when they arrive here for their Falkland Islands pre-deployment training in two weeks' time,' he said.

'But I don't know a thing about them, colonel.' I replied

'You soon will!'

Neither the colonel nor I could have guessed how prophetic his last comment would be, and as I wandered off in search of the education officer and his *Times Atlas of the World*, I cursed myself for having been in the wrong place at the wrong time.

The year was 1976 and the Naval Party with the funny number was the Royal Marines detachment stationed outside Stanley as the Foreign Office-sponsored tripwire against an aggressor. The role of tripwire in the military sense – in any sense – is not an enviable one for tripwires are, by and large, expendable.

I studied and lectured then became so fascinated by the place, the work involved and the sparsest of published nautical detail, that I volunteered to go there myself, then promptly forgot this aberration.

One year later, the chickens – or should I say kelp geese – came home to roost, when I was – without warning and now serving in 42 Commando stationed near Plymouth – told that I had been 'specially selected' to command Naval Party 8901.

I was to return to Poole in November 1977 to form up, and train for three and a half months, the new detachment of forty-four Royal Marines - and to listen to my own lecture on life 'down south' delivered by someone who, like me, had never been there!

I hadn't so much been in the wrong place, for as I have admitted, I had earlier been a volunteer for this most out-of-the-way British military postings, but now with two very young children, it was very definitely the wrong time. Nevertheless, orders are orders for, after all, I had volunteered - and the Royal Marines' head office has a long memory.

My interest in beaches goes back to the 1940s and 1950s, when significant chunks of my holidays from boarding schools would be spent on board the family's Bristol Channel Pilot Cutter *Olga* (still in commission and regularly raced and cruised by Tectona Sailing, supervised by Swansea Council) under the sole tutelage of *Olga*'s owner, my godfather, a retired Royal Marines, bachelor colonel. Earliest recollections include being sent ashore by myself, aged seven, in the dinghy clutching a lead line and sounding pole (a boathook with notches). My duty was to find a beach with the correct weight-bearing surface and gradient, so that when *Olga* was driven ashore mid-season, to be scrubbed and re-antifouled, her water line was horizontal. Thus my soundings had to take account of the keel not being horizontal. I would bring back various soundings for Uncle Pat to draw to scale on the backs of old charts, after which I was often required to sally forth again.

Within eight months of becoming a Royal Marine, in 1960 I found myself a 'Young Officer under training' on board one of the three Dartmouth Training Squadron frigates, HMS *Wizard*, in the West Indies. The ship's enlightened first lieutenant (later an admiral), puzzled how to occupy his four embarked Royal Marines young officers, until deciding that it was easier to put us ashore to fend for ourselves, while the ship, with its far larger complement of midshipmen under training went to sea to practice nautical manoeuvres. The *quid pro quo* of this superb arrangement was that we were to survey Bequia's then little-known Friendship Bay - and for a few glorious days that is what we did, living on the beach and existing off what we could catch or snare - nothing. Wisely we had brought ashore the staples and a fair supply of rum (for bartering purposes for vegetables of course).

Having qualified as a landing craft officer my Royal Marines career prior to 1978 (and subsequently) had involved me in the practicalities of amphibious warfare in general and the use of landing craft in particular. Both disciplines required a serious working knowledge of beaches, their approaches, gradients, exits, 'trafficability', defence from land and seawards, plus their susceptibility to surf, as well as their general weather and hydrographic conditions.

Such work then became part and parcel of my life as a Royal Marine. As a lifelong yachtsman, when the opportunity came to continue this military duty and private hobby among the barely surveyed (since the 1800s) Falkland waters, it was not difficult to summon up the enthusiasm for the appointment. There was, conveniently, an even more serious background to this desire: to compile a simple yachtsman's guide to this seldom visited, cruising paradise.

Until 1978, the role of Naval Party 8901 had been, on hint of invasion, to rush into the hills and play at guerrilla warfare – harrying the invaders for three weeks or until the United Kingdom 'did something'. This was a remit that could only have been invented by someone who had never been to the Islands – despite years of protestations by successive commanding officers.

Nobody though, in the Ministry of Defence, knew what that 'something' should be, for no contingency plans existed. Meanwhile, the Foreign and Commonwealth Office (FCO) slowly and remorselessly allowed the Argentines to believe that the place was theirs, almost for the asking. Certainly, three years later the imminent loss of the Ice Patrol Ship HMS *Endurance* was a good sign from the Junta's point of view, while wider hints at Britain's lack of commitment came with the proposed sale of all of the Royal Navy's amphibious ships and most of the aircraft carriers that supported such operations.

So, how does all this lead back to what I have for years called, with good and sometimes embarrassing reasons, the amusing art of impact hydrography?

In 1977, something actually stirred in Whitehall, when, in concert with the MOD, the FCO decided that their tripwire was, in the future, to buy 'three weeks bargaining time' in the United Nations. To my mind, as the junior officer now in command of the embryo Naval Party under training at Poole and thus about to be responsible for implementing this new policy once we relieved our predecessors 'in theatre', that could only mean one thing: forcing an enemy into a stand-off position while negotiations in New York took place.

My 1978-1979 tour was to become what I termed the 'buffer' detachment while I wrote, and my marines (against the then Governor's wishes for he was being briefed by a totally different section of the FCO) practiced the new routine – one that required us to stay and fight while, falling back under control to Government House. The idea being, that if we forced the invaders to fight in Stanley itself, they may well back-off for fear of killing civilians. After all, the Argentines thought they were coming to relieve an oppressed people who could hardly wait to drag from beneath their beds illegally held Argentine national flags.

From our military point of view, this was good on paper and gave my marines something to concentrate on, but in practice was almost as farcical, as had been the original planned reaction to an invasion: 'take to the hills'. My cynicism has no place here, other to explain that I was to carry out this newly aggressive stance against the expected full-scale amphibious assault by a close-to-modern navy, with the just forty-four marines, no defence stores, no heavy weapons and no communications (other than for eight hours a day) with which I could tell the outside world including - rather tellingly - the MOD, what was happening.

What does have a place here is that part of my plan - eventually approved at Cabinet level once it had been properly 'staffed' by the experts in Fleet Headquarters - involved choosing a suitable beach to which a covert stay-behind party would, purposefully not be involved in any fighting, make its way. Here we were to cache arms, survival stores and communications. This secure and secured beach, far from any settlement would be, so the plan went, the beach into which any reconnaissance force from the Royal Marines' Special Boat Service would be guided in advance of a re-invasion. Assuming, still against any official - and indeed, unofficial - announcements that that would happen.

My job, among all the others implicated in this three week bargaining time, was to choose that beach. Those were, though, the days of great suspicion for the talk across the camp settlements and in Stanley's bars, sitting rooms and even Government House's drawing and dining rooms, was never 'if the invasion occurs', but always, 'the when, how and where'. As I have hinted, I had the perfect cover because, long before our arrival on 5 April 1978, I had made it known that, in addition to my military duties, I was keen to compile, in my spare time, a 'yachtsman's guide to the Falkland coastlines' - all 15,000 miles of them.

Within the Naval Party's order of battle was a 150-ton, civilian-manned, bright-red-hulled coaster, the MV *Forrest*. My immediate predecessor as NP 8901's commanding officer had been a helicopter pilot, and so when the 'local' pilots were on leave, or to give them a welcome break, he had flown the Beaver float 'plane' around the settlements. A previous commanding officer had been a motorcycle enthusiast and another was an accomplished horseman and so on. I was a landing craft officer and yacht owner.

The one thing I could not do was to make a beeline in *Forrest* for - as it was to be the chosen one - Campa Menta Bay on the north coast of East Falkland. From a quick initial squint at the only small-scale chart in existence of that stretch of coastline this bay, more akin to a narrow inlet, appeared to suit our special needs very well. Nevertheless, to avoid the inevitable, and understandable, island-wide suspicion that would emanate from the ship's crew, Campa Menta Bay had to be a part of a longer-term plan and thus wait its turn for inspection.

Once settled into our 'condemned-for-human-habitation-in-1918-and-again-in-1945 wooden-hutted camp' at Moody Brook, a few miles to the west of Stanley, and with *Forrest's* inherited patrol programme underway, we could take stock. Part of that stock was to slowly alter *Forrest's* long-planned itinerary to cover not only the training of the settlement volunteers by one of our two-man training teams, but also to visit as many beaches as possible. The overt cover was that I was compiling my guide in order to encourage more yachtsmen to the Islands. This innocent hobby was met with approval by the Islanders, but not so His Excellency the Governor and Commander-in-Chief (HE), who forcibly believed that I should have remained permanently in Stanley on military duties. On the other hand, had he and his subjects known that I was 'reporting back' to Defence Intelligence 4 (DI4) in the MOD, where worldwide beach reports are - or certainly were - kept, there would have been the most unhelpful rumours that an invasion was imminent. Despite HE's public strictures I refused to change my decision.

While I was keen to fill my guide with yacht cruising-type information, it is also clear that what a yachtsman looks for in a safe anchorage, with a good, accessible 'run ashore' is very much what a landing craft cox'n also needs in order to put his 'embarked force' or 'cargo' ashore as dry as possible. As the inshore waters had been barely surveyed since the 1830s, the chances for impact hydrography were high and welcome, for thus there was never any doubt about the obstruction's existence - and precise position.

At the end of my thirteen-month tour I had amassed about 1,000 black and white photographs of beaches, bays and headlands, plus a 120-page A4 notebook full of sketches and hand-drawn charts with soundings. I had also annotated the few existing Admiralty charts, mostly engraved in the 1830s. On arriving home I sent the whole package to the Chief Hydrographer at Taunton, only to receive the reply: '*These notes and charts are the amateur jottings of an itinerant yachtsman and are of no interest to this department.*'

I could live happily with that rejection slip and so began compiling what was eventually to be called *Falkland Islands Shores* for private publication, and that would have been that, had it not been for General Galtieri in 1982, when my notes were suddenly classified 'Secret' as they became useful for planning the British re-invasion.

Chapter 9

A Winter's Cruise among the Falkland Islands

An oxymoron or viable proposition?

Published originally in the Royal Navy Association's Journal of Spring 1979 as a navigator's view of sailing these waters, in an attempt to show that they do not deserve the poor reputation they have.

Admiralty Chart 1354A should be consulted along with South America Pilot Volume II.

There are many members of the Royal Naval Sailing Association who will have visited these remote islands during various tours of duty in HM ships. There are some members who would have called in just to Stanley, or even sailed past for warmer climates after rounding the Horn. But are there any who have done either and have regretted they missed the opportunity to stay and explore in a small vessel? Very sadly, I doubt it, for the islands have a reputation they do not deserve. It is certain the weather is always unpredictable, the areas where yachtsman would wish to explore (with due respect to the hydrographic department) are poorly charted, there are no shore facilities, and they are a long way from home.

However they have a beauty of their own. Thankfully, there are no marinas (indeed there are no other yachts); there are plenty of sparsely chartered places for the adventurous to explore, certain that they will be the first yachtsman to do so; the wildlife and scenery are unbelievable; food and fresh water plentiful; there is an abundance of creeks and inlets to shelter in; there will always be an incredibly hospitable welcome in the outlying settlements, and navigation is made a little easier for the timid by the abundance of kelp. I would be a fool to paint too rosy a picture, for there are considerable dangers and difficulties in navigation. The tides can run strongly and have a set of rules seemingly known only to themselves. Often the weather is cool and windy but there are wonderful periods of warmth and calm.

The journey I'm about to describe was one of many I've made in a 150-ton motor vessel, the MV *Forrest*, skippered by a seaman, Captain Jack Sollis, with immense local knowledge. This journey was made as part of my military duties in the islands, but for the purposes of this essay, I have viewed the passages from a yachtsman's position and intend compiling a guide on the off-chance that future round-the-world yachtsmen and women might be persuaded to stop a little longer here. The weather was not typical for a winter's passage, but it did happen and shows that even in winter, enjoyable cruises can be made.

From my log:

27 May 1978. Port Stephens in West Falkland. Barometer 38.10 and steady. A clear ice blue sky to the east. Not a breath of wind. Ice on the decks. Although I have thought before that the islands are beautiful, these thoughts must now be surpassed by my feelings this morning.

We had spent the night at anchor off the little wooden jetty used for shipping out the wool clip. Dinner had been eaten ashore with the Robertson family and had included roast hogget, cooked to taste like the best lamb available in England. All mutton in the islands is cooked so expertly that one often wonders about the age of the 'lamb' sold to us back home. The meal had been well-rounded off by a comfortable armchair in front of a roaring peat fire, the best part of a bottle of Drambuie between three of us, and long tales of sheep ranching on the 183,000-acre estate. The coastline alone of this one settlement being well over a thousand miles.

We weighed anchor at 0800 hours and headed east towards the entrance of Port Stephens harbour about eight miles away. There was not a ripple on the surface of the loch, except those made by the gentoo penguins 'porpoising' away from their rookeries in search of the tiny, shrimp-like crustacean, krill. The only other creatures about at that time were the 'puffing pigs' known more formally as Commerson's Dolphin or, to be really precise, as *Cephalorhynchus Commersonalii*. They are about 4 feet long and found only in the Falkland Islands and the Straits of Magellan. The other dolphin found around the Islands is the Peals Dolphin (*Legenorhynchus Australis*) which is 6 feet long and differently marked.

The bird life around the vessel was typical and consisted of a selection of wandering and black-browed albatross, rock shags (a slightly more colourful version of the common cormorant); kelp and dolphin gulls, kelp pigeons and the great petrel known as 'stinkers'. The shags are particularly stupid birds. Being so inquisitive they often forget to flap their wings as they turn their heads to watch the ship glide past beneath them. They will then fall into the rigging and tumble to the deck, where they shake their heads in puzzlement before diving overboard.

Once clear of the loch we turned westwards around Stevens Bluff at the entrance to Ten Shilling Bay and set a course to pass west of Castle Rock. There's a small tide race off Castle Rock, in which many large ugly looking jellyfish were wallowing. The black-browed albatrosses were feeding unremittingly on these revolting creatures and as we steamed through a flock of twenty, they were so gorged, that without the help of any surface wind, they were unable to take off. They paddled and flapped at great speed across the water till their exertions made them regurgitate. Freed from the heavyweight of food they soared effortlessly into the sky, before turning back as if to reproach the vessel for disturbing an otherwise peaceful breakfast. I knew how they felt and went below for home-made mutton sausages and curried, pickled penguin eggs.

Castle Rock is as one would expect - only more so. The approach from the south-east is unspectacular but the view from the west opens up a remarkable sight of what could easily be a man-made structure with towers at each end, battlements and even the appearance of a portcullis, where the ocean has forced its ways through the complete structure over the years. The rock is steep-to, and thus is not marked by long streamers of kelp at its base. This kelp marking is vital for safe navigation throughout the archipelago. There is less kelp in West Falklands than East Falklands, as generally, the coast is steeper-to. However, the absence of kelp does not necessarily indicate a safe passage, for in strong tidal streams it 'runs under' and cannot be seen.

We headed towards the east end of Bird Island, aptly named, but from a downwind position more appropriate names would spring to mind. It was on this island that the British 360-ton barque *Herald* was wrecked on 12 August 1885, outward bound from Liverpool to Valpariso. Even in these days of tidal predictions, the tides need careful watching. The coasts of these islands are littered with the remains of ships that fell foul of these treacherous currents.

To starboard, the coastline to the east of Stephens Peak is one long ridge of rocky outcrops known as the Indian Village. It certainly resembles a large colony of tents and wigwams. In the early morning mist and with a little imagination, one could hear the cries of the redskins and watch wisps of smoke curling up into the icy-blue sky. The effect was most eerie. Now the sun was beginning to appear over the hills north of Cape Meredith, and with it a little light breeze was creeping in from the east. We headed for the mist-shrouded Rodney Bluff ten miles to the north-west. The tides, here, follow the coast at 2-3 knots but are badly influenced by strong westerly winds which force them to remain east-going even after the turn. This day there were no problems and everything behaved as ordained in the Admiralty pilot.

This stretch of coastline is all steep-to and there are no off-lying dangers, nor is there any kelp to warn of the approach of land, as would be found in shallower waters, but in good visibility navigation is straightforward. There are no lights outside Stanley and so night passage-making should be confined to radar-equipped yachts or bright moonlit nights. [This was written before the advent of GPS.] Oddly enough, some of the best times to see kelp is during a star-lit night, providing the sea is reasonably flat, for it shines with an unmistakable sheen. Kelp is remarkable stuff. Many of the beaches are guarded by great kelp patches through which it is sometimes possible to sail down or up-tide (but not necessarily motor) without much hindrance, nevertheless choosing a zigzag route between the individual clumps is advised. Behind these natural breakwaters a yacht can shelter even though the prevailing wind and sea may be running straight in. It seems to have very much the same effect as oil on the surface of the water. Kelp grows on rocky patches and care must be exercised when approaching it, for it grows to great lengths thus its surface position may not be over the danger it marks. Providing it has not 'run under' it is easy to tell which way the tide runs, and therefore where the danger lies.

One mile east of Rodney Bluff is High Bluff, and behind this, further east, lies Rodney Cove itself. This is one of the few ideal bolt holes for a yacht in bad weather along this stretch of the coastline. Kelp stretches out either side of the entrance, forming a narrow passage into a good anchorage over sand in about five fathoms. There are a number of rocks at the head of the cove but these are well kelp-marked and do not run under at any state of the tide. The kelp at the entrance protects the anchorage in all but the most severe south-easterly storms.

Rodney Bluff is a prominent, striated headland very dark against the grassy down hinterland. We altered course to starboard in order to pass between Sea Dog Island and Cape Orford. This is a useful dodge if a passage is required into Queen Charlotte Bay, for the tides run strongly out through the Smiley Channel, north of Sea Dog Island. Sea Dog Pass is well marked by kelp that does not run under, as contrary to expectations, the tides sweep past to the north. The flood tide sets south-west in the Smiley Channel, where it can run at 7 knots, with a westerly wind this produces a vicious race.

Once in Smiley Channel, we altered course for the Horse Block Rock five miles north-north-west. This is one of the most fascinating rock formations in the archipelago. Unfortunately no description in the 'Admiralty pilot' does it justice. Certainly when viewed from the south, it appears to be a simple, tall stack 220 feet high, but from any other aspect it resembles an enormous Scotty dog. This day was a perfect day for landing on his rear, offside hoof, but sadly (I had become addicted to landing on obscure rocks and islands in the Falklands) we had a time problem as we were due at Beaver Island to deliver stores and mail and for what turned out to be another memorable lunch. We were obliged to leave the Horse Block Rock to starboard as the water between it and the mainland had not been surveyed. [In 2003 I navigated a 70-foot sloop here and found plenty of water.]

Our next passage was Tea Channel between Tea and Weddell Island. The entrance is two cables wide and well-marked by kelp at slack water. It is advisable to keep to the west side of the channel to avoid a large pack of kelp (over deep water), although the whole entrance is safe. The tide floods to the north through Tea Channel and we entered against a weak, ebb tide. Knob Island should be left to the westward, although this is not obligatory, but there is more sea room to the east for a yacht facing contrary winds.

Staats Island, to the west of Tea Island, is the home of the Guanaco, a llama-type beast which has been allowed to run wild. A visit ashore here would be an interesting diversion, but beware, anchoring in the kelp-sheltered cove on the north-east corner of the island, and particularly, beware of the Guanaco which have been known to attack humans.

I wished that we had had time to explore French Harbour to the east but noted it for further attention in the summer when we shall be carrying the Bosun sailing dinghy. It is believed to be an excellent yacht harbour.

We left Governor Island to port passing between it and an unnamed tussock island. This is Stick in the Mud Channel, named as such for some reason that I was unable to 'fathom' as there is plenty of water. It might have been something to do with contrary winds, so a yacht should be prepared to motor through.

However the same navigational rules apply as for Tea Channel, for the sides are well marked at slack water. The flood tide (to the north) can run at 12 knots so this is definitely a passage to be made only with absolute confidence in the accuracy of one's tidal calculation. The pass is one cable wide and except for the tides, there are no other problems. Incidentally, if making for Beaver Island from the south, do not attempt the channel between Beaver Island and Governor Island for there is no water.

The same applies to the channel between Staats and Tea Island. Governor Channel is probably the best channel, but even here it is advisable to wait for a fair tide.

Turning west around Governor Island a yacht must keep to the north of a small islet off the north of Governor Island, which appears to be unattached to the main island – but it is not! This pass is steep-to and well-marked by kelp. If you have a moment, heave-to and send the dinghy ashore for mussels.

A note of warning about tussock islands. Tussock is a large, bushy shrub with long spiky leaves, the bulbs of which can be eaten. The plants grow together in great profusion to 6 or 7 feet, but the problem is not when walking ashore, although this can be difficult enough. When whole islands are covered with tussock and viewed from a distance, they resemble palm-covered atolls such as are found in the Pacific. Consequently the islands seem to be very much further away than they really are. This can be dangerous and after about 3,000 miles of cruising the islands I am still caught out by this illusion.

We turned west around the unnamed tussock island and immediately left the main tidal stream. The tides in Beaver Sound are weak and do not force the kelp to run under. We steamed up the sound towards the settlement at the head, to find ourselves landlocked in a peaceful anchorage off the jetty and in three fathoms over a sandy bottom. The edges of this sound are well marked by kelp and so all clear water is safe. The jetty is ideal for lying alongside (in a yacht up to 20 tons) the rise and fall being about 14 feet. At low water, a yacht could lean against the end of the jetty on hard, level sand to carry out repairs or scrub the bottom. This is one of the better jetties in the islands for doing this, as not many offer these natural facilities.

I went ashore to meet Mr and Mrs Felton. Luckily, I had been warned of the welcome we would receive and was certainly not disappointed. Lunch was inevitably roast lamb and when in the islands you are offered lamb, it really is the real thing. Vi Felton is an expert with her peat stove, surpassed only by Tony's expertise with his wine locker. We followed the lamb with freshly made rhubarb crumble and thick cream scooped out of a full two-gallon plastic, washing up bowl. Visitors (as well as Royal Marines!) are given the full treatment, including a seemingly endless supply of home-made black currant rum. Sadly we couldn't stay long, as it was necessary to reach New Island before dusk, and so with sincere promises to stay the night next time, we embarked in the rubber dinghy to return to *Forrest*.

The passage out of the sound is straightforward providing the kelp is avoided. We kept to the north side, leaving a small tussock island to starboard and a larger island off the north side of the entrance to port. This is Rookery Island and is next to another unnamed tussock island. Except in the brightest sunlight, tussock bogs, with few exceptions, are very dark.

There are rocks off these islands but they are kelp-marked at all stages of the tide. The final turn to the north is around the southern end of a narrow island which runs north-south to the south of Peak Point. Three cables to the east of this island is a prominent kelp patch covering shallow rocks. However a passage may be found between this patch and the unnamed 'north-south' island. From here the passage north between Beaver and the two Channel Islands is opened up and now New Island could be seen about seven miles away. This passage should only be attempted with a fair tide. Kelp is run under here, except the large patch just mentioned. At the north end of the passage are the twin Colliers. From the south they resemble two fingers raised in eternal salute to those who dare approach their domain. They are easily identified from a distance and can be safely closed and passed on either hand, allowing a clear berth of one cable.

A course of 330°T takes one across Grey Channel to the entrance of New Island harbour. To port could be seen the distinctive line of rocks guarding the channel's western entrance. These are the Seal Rocks which stretch for over a mile, forcing the flood and ebb tides into dangerous races at either end. If it is necessary to pass between Beaver and New Island it is advisable to use the northern passage at slack water. This is the end with the strongest tides but it is also the safest from the navigational point of view.

A yacht should approach New Island's South Harbour between Coffin Island and the main island. This pass has at least a depth of twelve fathoms, while its edges are well marked by kelp at all states of the tide. On the beach one and a half miles to the west of Coffin Island is an old whaling station with the wreck of the Scottish 1,800-ton steel, fully-rigged ship the *Glengowen* which in 1895, was burnt out in Stanley harbour and towed to New Island. If caught in a south-westerly gale (the only unsafe quarter), an alternative anchorage can be found in this little bay.

We anchored off the jetty in 20 feet of water, near the head of the harbour in good stiff mud for this jetty can only be used by small craft. In easterly winds a swell builds up in South Harbour and, as mentioned, if the wind increases from the south-west, then it would be best to move to the whaling station bay.

On the beach at the head of the bay there is a fascinating vessel, *Protector*. She was a Canadian minesweeper from the last world war that was sailed down to become a sealer in the 1950s. She is reasonably intact with her engine and deck fittings. A climb aboard for those interested in ships' construction is well worthwhile. Also on the beach is a ship's lifeboat from the *Glendowen*, which I found much more interesting. Badly hogged after years lying ashore, but I think it might just be possible to resurrect her. There is also a pulling dory from the whaling days in remarkably good condition.

New Island is one of the main breeding grounds for the black-browed albatross. They nest among the rock hopper penguin rookeries, on little hummocks of mud with a hollow crown. At this time of year, both the albatross and penguins were away and due to return for the October breeding season.

These western islands are the scene of many wrecks over the last two centuries. Here is a small selection: In October 1854 the British 340-ton brig *Giacus* was wrecked on Governor Island. The *Yarra Yarra*, a British 1,246-ton barque was wrecked on Beaver Island cliffs in April 1885. The *Francis*, a whaling brig from London, was wrecked on New Island in February 1842. The *River Derwent*, a 500-ton barque from Liverpool, was wrecked on New Island in August 1867.

Sadly this is far from being the full list of casualties for this very small part of the archipelago, but it gives some idea how, over the years, the Falkland Islands came to be regarded as a place for sailing ships to avoid or treat with great care. The dangers are no less now, but modern aids and knowledge give today's sailing skipper a great advantage over his predecessors. The islands are part of our heritage as a seafaring nation. They are more than worthy of a visit by the modern adventurous yachtsman or woman, who could not fail to come away with an even greater admiration for the manner in which the old sailing ships were handled. For every ship that ended her days in the Falklands, there are many more who safely navigated the islands without mishap.

Chapter 10

The Falkland Islands: A Retrospective, 1978-1979

In September 2002 I was asked by the then monthly newspaper *All at Sea* to write an article called The Falklands War, A Retrospective. This is it:

Although it is twenty years since victory in the Falklands I'm still asked if it was worthwhile and I still answer with a resounding 'Yes!'.

This conviction was reinforced recently by a visit to the Islands to lay a wreath in memory of six crew members from one of my landing craft that had been bombed and sunk on 8 June 1982. In June this year (2002) I found a well-balanced, self-confident population that had not existed before 1982 which, when coupled to a growing sophistication, emphasised my pre-war view that the islanders and their then dormant attributes would be, have been and remain, worth fighting for. This vibrancy is not the result of the recent injection of money from fishing licences but a mere determination to repay for the sacrifices made. It may be little comfort to the bereaved but it is clear, to me, that no one died in vain.

The other question I am asked is, 'Why?' This is more complicated to answer because of the then government's willingness to let the islands go by default while suppressing the warnings from those of us then serving 'down south'.

It is not generally known that Mr Callaghan's administration prevented the Islands being taken, or certainly being threatened, in the late 1970s through the dispatch of a timely but small naval force. Something that Mrs Thatcher could also have done had she been so minded and had her defence secretary agreed.

The paradox is that she, having 'allowed' the islands to be invaded, had the courage, after being embarrassed into changing her mind, to regain them. Yet before that reversal and once the *fait accompli* of invasion, so longed for by the Foreign and Commonwealth Office, had been confirmed she was persuaded by her defeatist Defence Secretary, supported by the chiefs of the army and the Royal Air Force, that direct action was, by then, too difficult. And that would have been that but for the First Sea Lord, Admiral Sir Henry Leach who, not concerning himself with flawed, introspective diplomacy, suggesting otherwise. The rest we know.

When asked to attend this year's commemorations, I dusted off my charts for a private pilgrimage to the beaches and bays that had meant so much to me. So it was, that three days before the formal events, I stood in the driving snow and howling winds while allowing my mind to be swept back - not to the diplomatic intrigues in which I had been embroiled, but to the practicalities of my work when commanding the tiny Royal Marines garrison between 1978 and 1979.

In those days, the forty-four Royal Marines of Naval Party 8901 were not a viable defence, but merely a 'Foreign Office sponsored' presence, for on invasion (it was always 'when and where' not 'if'), our duty was to rush into the countryside to play guerrilla warfare. Clearly a task set by some FCO mandarin who had never seen this unforgiving country of 'dragon-backed mountains', or squelched through the peat bogs, or tripped across the ankle-breaking stone runs in an austral winter (or summer come to that).

However, sense of a sort eventually prevailed. and so I had arrived in 1978 with orders to fight the Argentines, and thus in theory, force them to sit back and think while we 'bought three weeks bargaining time in the United Nations'.

As a tripwire we were expendable, and thus by our very demise, Britain would have an excuse to mount a counter invasion. This was militarily possible, then, but politically improbable, and an action likely to make our deaths rather pointless, as the Governor insisted on repeating. The role of a tripwire is not an enjoyable one! Nevertheless, that was the new plan and it was my job to ensure that it was in place for my successors.

I asked for more marines. I asked for defence stores and weapons, I asked for new accommodation to replace that which had been condemned in 1918 and again in 1945, and I began looking at beaches.

Knowing the Argentine Navy's order of battle, coupled with its capabilities, it was not difficult to assess how and where they would land, and what would be their immediate and their ultimate objectives. Surveying the beaches closest to Stanley confirmed that they were suitable for an amphibious invasion, and this allowed me to select the areas that demanded our strongest defence. The less easy task was to find a beach to which a small party of 'non-combatant' marines would make their way after secretly observing and assessing the initial Argentine assault. From this pre-prepared and pre-provisioned hide, they would communicate with home, and on the assumption that there would be a re-invasion (we had to think positively), it was onto this beach that they would guide the preliminary Special Boat Service reconnaissance party.

Before arriving in the islands my research had revealed that very little was known of the coastline and that what was known was in the head of Jack Sollis, the local civilian captain of the Royal Marines' 150-ton patrol vessel, MV *Forrest*. At that time my aim was to record as much as I could for the innocent purpose of enticing members of the various yacht clubs of which I was then a member, to come and cruise the archipelago. That, on average over any twelve-month period, only three yachts visited Stanley – and none visited the rest of the Falklands – was no deterrence to my desire to advertise the stunning but unknown beauty that lay to the west of the capital's waterfront. Using Jack's experience I embarked on this self-imposed task. There was, of course, an ulterior motive.

Campa Menta Bay on the north coast of East Falklands was chosen as the one 'military' beach and so it was in the cliffs to the west of its entrance that we hid the 'stay behind' party's bits and pieces. To allay any suspicions, all other beaches received the same intensity of 'military' interest, for by and large, the conditions required by yachts and minor landing craft are similar. Thus when sketching, sounding and photographing I studied the beaches from both points of view, which was just as well for immediately tongues began to wag.

The problem was how to explain what I was doing – and why – to the governor, the islanders, and naturally to the few Argentine residents. To say that I was surveying for personal reasons would satisfy the islanders and provoke no supplementary questions, but would anger the governor. Yet to explain that I was surveying in expectation of a British re-invasion would alert the Argentines (no bad thing for them to surmise that we would return) and disturb the governor (already worried about the islanders' morale), while exposing myself to severe cross-examination from all directions. To offer different reasons, depending on who was listening, would lead to accusations of complicity by the very people whose help I needed, the Islanders themselves. Whatever my decision (and it was the 'personal hobby' one that I took), I was bound to upset the governor and this I did.

There are about 15,000 miles of coastline covering roughly 900 islands and by the end of the year I had amassed over 150 pages of notes, a thousand photographs, drawn one hundred of my own charts, and annotated the official ones that had all been first engraved in the mid-1800s.

On my return, I offered everything to the Chief Hydrographer of the Royal Navy and while not expecting much enthusiasm the rejection slip was remarkably abrupt: *These are the amateur jottings of an itinerant yachtsman and are of no interest to this department.* Amateur they may have been, but they did fill in quite a few blank patches.

Summoned to advise the amphibious commanders in 1982 my 'amateur jottings', and amusingly, not those offered by the hydrographic office, were studied intensely in the search for primary assault beaches: San Carlos (the best compromise), Berkeley Sound (nautically acceptable but too close to Stanley), Salvador Waters (militarily good, nautically poor), Fox Bay (would require a second amphibious assault across Falkland Sound), Fitzroy and Bluff Cove together (nautically poor but close to Stanley), were all candidates, while others were marked for smaller operations.

As the Task Force approached the Islands through April and May 1982, I began to worry about the accuracy of my jottings, and yet I only found it necessary to 'lie' twice! Although I knew them to be useful for our purposes during the amphibious landings, I swore that both Volunteer Bay and Carcass Island were useless for their proposed roles. One was home to the only king penguin colony, while the second was the finest of nature reserves. I could not bring myself to, in effect, recommend the destruction of either.

Three final thoughts crossed my mind: it had all been a labour of love that should never have been useful in war; if we had had a more robust government before 1982 my notes would, happily, not have been used, and while some have kindly dubbed me the 'Falklands expert' this is not true - the beaches and inshore waters, yes to a certain extent, but if I was asked to name a mountain or valley I would have to remain silent.

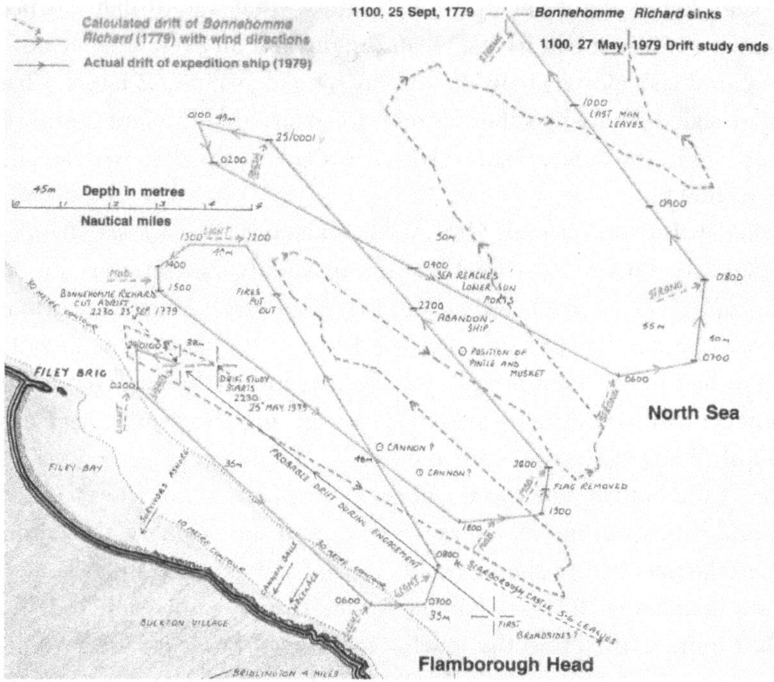

Drift study produced for the search for the *Bonnehomme Richard*

Chapter 11

The First *Black Velvet*

Written by invitation for the Hurley 24 Owners Association in 1980.

In 1973, Jonathan Mason was the managing director of Hurley's in Plymouth. He was a friend of mine and suggested that Hurley build the smallest boat acceptable for the two-handed Round Britain and Ireland race (RB&I) and the Observer Single-handed Transatlantic Race (OSTAR). In those days the shortest, acceptable, length was 24 feet. Now it is rather more.

Black Velvet was built of GRP (glass reinforced plastic) and exhibited at the London boat show in January 1974. She had no engine, so extra weight in the keel was made up of heavy chain which could be removed. I regret I cannot remember the weight. I had one large 'Admiralty sweep' on board with which I could scull her at about one-and-a-half knots - that was all that was needed. Although *in extremis* I did have a small dinghy and an even smaller outboard which I could lash alongside in the dinghy to give us about 2 knots. I had the fore hatch sealed shut when she was built to ensure that the fore cabin was the one dry place in the boat in bad weather. Not always the case with small, boat hatches of that era.

During spring of that year, Hurley was taken over by an asset stripper and rumours reached my wife, while I was in the Mediterranean, that they would be taking *Black Velvet* back and selling her as an asset. Determined that this should not happen, Patricia paid a crane driver in Plymouth's Millbay Docks a fiver and had her lifted onto a Royal Marines lorry (she had chatted up the duty officer), and the vessel was swiftly driven into the nearby barracks and hidden until I returned from the Med.

When I did return, the asset strippers complained that they hadn't been able to find the vessel but as the race was due to start shortly, they did agree to let her take part before she was sold. Thus, I sailed in the smallest and only engineless boat in the 1974 two-handed Round Britain and Ireland race. Almost at the last minute, my crew, the much-experienced Sergeant Gerry Norman, was offered the place of skipper in another equally small yacht. With pleasure I let him go and searched for a replacement.

As expected, we were last into Cork, the first of four compulsory, forty-eight hour stops where, because of the IRA threat, all 'service-crewed' boats had to anchor off, with no crew allowed ashore. Damn silly, as it only marked us out. During this time Clare Francis filled my water tank with Guinness, an action we did not discover until after sailing for Barra. By this stage my new crew had proved totally unsuitable, and agreed (it was his idea) that I would manage all the sailing during the four legs, and when I was ashore he would clean, maintain and complete all the chores during the compulsory stops. This even meant cooking and washing up every meal.

Off the north-west coast of Ireland, we hit a series of northerly gales during which my ailing crew finally had a total, emotional collapse. I decided to turn direct for Plymouth, from where I sailed with two crew, Roger Dillon (shortly of the Royal Cruising Club) and one other to meet the fleet at Lowestoft, they having rounded Muckle Flugga.

Here I met two other yachts that had also retired and transited the Caledonian Canal, so we 'established' (with the Royal Western Yacht Club's permission) the 'Round South Britain race'. The three of us set off but two retired somewhere along the south coast and I came on single-handed to Plymouth. In the end I had sailed nearly as many miles as if I had gone round the top. On the way though, we had a spot of bother with the Royal Yacht off Cowes at 0300 one morning, when my 'very temporary' crew picked up in Gosport (to allow me some sleep who I then dropped off at Weymouth), fired a starting cannon at her in salute. We were instantly lit up by a searchlight and warned off by the police, while I slept, innocently, below.

After all that was over *Black Velvet* was badly damaged while on her exposed mooring by a runaway barge in a gale. At the time the boat builder had called in the receiver and was being sued for bankruptcy. Also at that time, I received a call from the then, I think, boat-builder's accountant, suggesting that if I appeared at a certain pub with £2,000 in notes in my pocket, then she would be mine. As I had not been allowed to move *Black Velvet*, despite warning the receiver of a possible danger, he agreed for the damage to be repaired at his cost. It was during that arrangement that this dodgy offer was made. As I was not sure that it was legal I telephoned Sir Kenneth Cork (of Cork Gully) himself over the weekend. He was not amused at being disturbed, but in the end offered the boat to me for the same amount. As this was a bargain I took it.

I then sailed her extensively around the south coast and out into the Atlantic, achieving many more than the average miles for a comparable boat of her size. During the Queen's Silver Jubilee in 1977 I entered and won the West Country division of the Royal Thames Yacht Club Silver Jubilee race. *Black Velvet* was the smallest boat nationwide and, on return to Plymouth, had sailed over 100 miles in the 24 hours of non-stop gales while others (everyone larger and some even Royal Navy sail-training vessels) sheltered within Plymouth Sound. We received a very fine engraved decanter.

In about 1980 I had an engine fitted (a useless Vire of almost a minus amount of horsepower) and then sold her to one of my Royal Marines sergeants at Poole. Almost immediately after the sale she broke her moorings and ended up stranded on the beach at the top end of Poole Harbour. Thankfully she was not damaged other than a few minor superficial scratches.

After that I'm afraid I lost touch but did see her for sale at Cobbs Quay in Poole one or two years ago. I believe the present owner is up for membership of the Royal Yacht Squadron, which will make it the second time she has appeared on the club's list.

And that's about it - except to say that in all the gales that I have weathered at sea I was as happy in *Black Velvet* as I have been in many much larger vessels. The motion was often uncomfortable of course but we never seemed to be in any danger as she simple rode over everything. She was a cracking little boat in which both my children sailed within days of being born (indeed, before they were born) and in which they cut their first nautical teeth.

I am afraid this is slightly in note form but gives the main essence of my time with her. I was sad to see her go but life had to move on as the family grew.

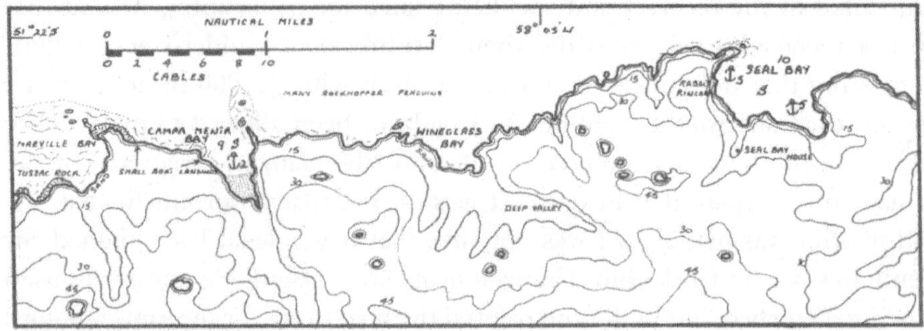

Chart of Campa Menta Bay.

Chapter 12

The First Kiss - A Narrowboat on the Four Counties Ring

First published in the Royal Cruising Club's *Roving Commissions*, 1986

I doubt if *Shutlinsloe* has ever been described in *Roving Commissions* for she is a 58-feet long canal barge - or narrowboat - of uncertain age, with a maximum beam of about 6 feet and a draught of about 3 feet 6 inches. Vague as these dimensions are they assume, on a canal, a much greater significance than would be normal to a deepwater sailor. Regrettably, she has no sails at all, but is powered under normal conditions by an enormous diesel engine of undetermined make and horsepower. *In extremis* she is propelled by the combined pull of four children on tow ropes and two men with barge poles. Incidentally, I should never refer to one of these 'accessories' in a derisory manner again, as they really are useful for extraction from awkward and - usually - well-witnessed situations.

The advice in the handbook was quite clear and needed no elaboration: '*Working a lock is like your first kiss - until you've done it no amount of reading about it beforehand can quite prepare you for the experience*'. Whether or not I can remember my first kiss is my secret, but I certainly remember my first lock; it was April 1986 and the author of the above was not far wrong. What puzzled us was why the preoccupation with locks? Our first one-and-three-quarter mile tunnel was a far more emotional event for which there was no descriptive warning. Which, on reflection, was probably just as well!

On returning from three months working with open-landing and raiding craft in north Norway, I had naively assumed that the Easter holidays would have been arranged, without my involvement for somewhere warm and uncomplicated. However, 1986 was different, for I had been returned home, twice, with double pneumonia. This departure from the normal was to continue through April, with the hiring, *in absentia*, of *Shutlinsloe* during a snap every bit as cold as the weather I had just left at 70° N. Ice every day on the decks is standard in the Arctic, but surely not on the Trent and Mersey.

The aim was to join forces with great friends, Mike and Lizzie Shuttleworth and their two sons, then circumnavigate the Four Counties Ring which, very roughly, takes in part of West Staffordshire, Shropshire, the Potteries and the West Midlands: a simple 'aquatic amusement' considered just-the-job for a convalescing cruising man, and very much in line with that quote from the earlier aims of the RCC. My godfather (Lieutenant Colonel Pat Phibbs, RCC) always advised me, that due to the vagaries of wind and tide, sailing craft have destinations, not times of arrival. Our first mistake was to assume that these restrictions would not apply on the canals. How wrong we were.

Wind certainly affected our progress as did locks although, sadly, not one lock keeper's daughter disturbed our passage. Opening hours of canal-side pubs also dictated our rate of progress more than the most contrary winds, let alone 'man and dog – overboard' three times. These were facts that we had not considered when making out or itinerary. When all this was coupled with manoeuvring a 58-feet long 'barge' along a canal 15 feet wide and in a 30-knot crosswind at only 3 knots, with a keel clearance of 6 inches it is amazing that we completed our voyage at all. But we did and along the way learnt a large number of new skills at handing craft in adverse conditions. What we expected to be a simple holiday turned out to be a remarkable saga of unexpected nautical and social problems and is to be recommended to anyone who thinks he or she has learned all there is to know about seamanship.

The very first words in the log for 5 April were '*Snow forecast*' followed by a strange comment about wanting to pack the dinghy, anchor and mountains of food. All quite unnecessary, but old habits die hard. The previous night, that remarkable small boat sailor, Frank Dye, had listened to a lecture I had given locally in support of the RNLI and afterwards, had answered dozens of questions about the coming week. It was one of his craft that we were hiring and so the advice he gave us was, as expected, invaluable. Thousands of totally inexperienced people hire narrowboats throughout the year without batting an eyelid – his problem was people like us who knew too much and who tried to be too clever.

On arriving at Frank's boatyard on the Macclesfield Canal, any concern we might have had disappeared instantly. The vessel was spotless and very well equipped with eight bunks, two heads – each with a hot shower – and a modern galley. A spacious saloon forward led through French windows to the bows, which formed a large, sheltered, private space for sunbathing – about the only facility we did not use. In the nautical department, she was fitted with plenty of berthing ropes and mooring stakes along with windlass handles for working the locks, oilskins, boarding planks, water hose, lifebelts, life jackets and, of course, the two vital barge poles. All we needed to do was hoist the RCC burgee in the bows, buy a copy of Pearson's *Canal Companion for the Four Counties Ring* and head for our first lock.

Jack, Frank's right-hand man, came with us as instructor for our first kiss (sorry - lock). This is not usually necessary with first timers but he had already worked out that we were different and would need careful guidance. Our trepidation on approaching the first of one hundred or so locks must have puzzled the long-suffering Jack but he was perfect in his politeness and patience. I must now confess that it turned out to be a slight anti-climax for it was all too simple, requiring very little pre-planning or effort and when it was all over left us feeling, 'Is that all there is to it?'

However, like kissing, experience is everything and usually means increasing enjoyment. Before long, our locking procedures turned into a finely practised and hugely enjoyable art. As with kissing, so I'm told, every look was different, the last lock was always the best while the next lock was eagerly awaited; without them it would have been a very two-dimensional journey both geographically and emotionally

The first night was spent at the North Portal of the Harecastle Tunnel. We arrived in a snowstorm just in time, we thought, to catch the last convoy through before nightfall but, as the log reveals, it was not like that:

1730. Alongside tow path at entrance to tunnel. Keeper refused a massive bribe to let us through. Another narrowboat appeared and engaged in furious argument. Turned out to be next week's keeper who was just sorting out a private feud. They both told us there was nowhere to moor.

Kidsgrove therefore had the distinction of being our first 'port'. It was nearly the last. Euphoria at working out our first solo lock evaporated at the bottom of a 60 feet deep, concrete cutting where daylight hardly penetrated. We had only the snowflakes to comfort us. A recce was planned to the nearest pub so run-ashore clothes, money, dogs and children were gathered for a full-scale assault on the local.

Evening. Ashore to The Bluebell pub where no dogs or children were allowed and a distinct feeling that, had it had not been Saturday night, it would have been no women - ours left on their own accord. Despite being left behind Mike and I felt a little out of place and so, following the quickest pint of our lives, we returned for a delicious chilli con carne, a glass of port and bed.

Where were all the fun-loving establishments of the brochures, the lawns sweeping down to the towpath rejoicing in the cries of the young, their mothers, their elder sisters and their dogs? We didn't realise it then, but the Harecastle Tunnel was more than a man-made obstacle, it was a genuine watershed of social significance for us holidaying, barge people.

This was the second tunnel built beneath Harecastle Hill and was dug by Thomas Telford in 1827 alongside Brindley's earlier one of 1777, the entrance of which can still be seen as a marvellous testimony to the skills of 200 years before. The original method of propulsion was for the crew to lie on their backs and walk the barge with their feet on the roof, for the one and three-quarter miles. Rather strangely, 'normal pedestrians are expressly prohibited from using the tunnel', a rule which must have been made as the result of some unbelievable attempt to walk since there is no towpath and it is haunted.

The tunnel is not for the squeamish nor the claustrophobic. *Pearson's Canal Guide* (as invaluable as the RCC's Pilotage Foundation's *North Atlantic Crossing Guide*) even gives British Rail information, for those unable to take the strain of the ghosts, a dripping roof only two feet above one's head, or the knowledge that the tunnel was closed for four years in the 1970s because of roof falls. However, despite the trauma of passing 100 feet or so below Kidsgrove, not far enough away in our opinion at the time, we emerged at last into the world of the British Waterways advertisements and my log was able to take on a happier style:

Sailing through the back streets of the Potteries is every bit as fascinating as gliding through the wonderful stillness of the country which is full of nothing but nature at her finest. Moorhens, Canada geese, mallard, voles, water rats, kingfishers: there's something different around every bend and every lock and bridge has its own character in peculiarity.

The children are already into inventing highly imaginative and probably dangerous games which usually involve hanging sloth-like from the bridges as the bow passed beneath and then dropping into the cockpit. As the narrowboat is almost impossible to steer astern they would have to keep hanging there if they did not drop on time. There is also an 'aeronautical' version of pooh sticks which involves hurling objects over the bridge and trying to catch them on the other side. I must add that this was only over deserted farm bridges connecting empty fields.

Oddly, on this stretch, we seldom saw another human being either in the towns or in the country. We had entered a world in which our narrowboat was the only source of human life and it was very satisfying. Once, when the canal did pass close to a motorway, we realised that an existence we had left two days earlier was already alien. A policeman even waved at us from his blue-flashing Ford Granada, 50 feet above, and I raised my gin in salute for the poor chap was escorting a very slow-moving yacht on a lorry.

The Trent and Mersey Canal passes through Stoke and the heart of the Potteries – which was the reason for building it. Historians of architecture would find this stretch fascinating, but it was difficult to keep the children interested, for they preferred to remain below in the warmth playing 'racing demon', and only rushed on deck as we passed what must be the largest collection of lavatories in the world. There were thousands upon thousands of them, all individually wrapped in polythene, waiting for transport to almost every port on earth. Of greater educational importance was the Wedgwood factory, a two-minute walk from Trentham Lock, but I'm ashamed to say that, after the sight of the loo mountain, any further interest in pottery by the young had quickly waned.

The Stoke flight of locks produced our first nautical problem when our narrowboat became well and truly jammed between a block of wood on one side and a hefty milk crate on the other. The children were summoned to flood and then empty the lock, an evolution that only succeeded in torturing the topsides and rubbing strake. We still could not move horizontally but we did have the up-to-now dormant bargepoles. The crate was reduced to splinters and we were on our way to lock 36.

1040. Lock 36 is jammed by a piece of jetsam with us on the outside. Towed the gates open with the bow warp – interesting, with Hamish (my 12-year-old son) on the helm 58 feet away and all adults leaning on the lock bar.

1100. Last lock for a mile or so, under a crossroads. Fascinating stuff this. Locking beats sail changing or reefing any day! Moored beneath motorway for a visit to the shops.

An attempt to eat lunch in three different pubs between Stoke and Milford produced a very rare collapse of morale which, for once, was instigated by the adult male members of the crew. This was still not quite the canal (as far as the pubs were concerned) of the brochures although as it happened, we were not to be embarrassed in this respect again. The Trent and Mersey canal was, to us, the 'dry' stretch. We were not to know it but once we turned onto the 'Staffs and Worcs' at Great Hayward the watershed would be crossed once and for all. Maybe we were just unlucky. We were certainly unlucky with the weather as we were still sailing through intermittent snow showers.

1430. First of the Milford locks. Very cold.
1530. Through the Stone locks. Snowing.
1630. More locks. Still snowing and now blowing.
1640. Heavy snow. This may not qualify for the Tilman Award but it is cold enough (–2°C which, with this wind is the equivalent of –22°C).
1800. Aground starboard bank with Force 7 on the port quarter. Snowing. All hands, rather unwillingly as we appeared to them to be safely moored, summed on deck to push off fore and aft.

This was not the first, nor the last, time that we learnt a new lesson in craft handing and 'canalmanship'. In this case I was at the helm in full Arctic clothing attempting to steer a straight course (important at sea but vital on a canal) down a 20-feet-wide lane with a 58-feet barge in 30 knots of crosswind. I failed. For some time I thought that I had the procedure weighed off. The bows would be crabbing along the port hand bank about three feet off, with the stern just clear of the opposite bank and the engine revolutions set for the maximum permitted speed of 4 knots. It was a fine balance but it seemed to work. The amusements would occur on approaching a bridge where the clearance each side was under one foot. The trick was to know exactly when to straighten up - too soon and the barge would be flat alongside the leeward bank, or too late and the RCC burgee would be impaled into some innocent farmer on the windward tow path. It was also the quickest way of having one's tot stopped by the watch below. On this occasion, the stern smelt the ground, full revs failed to produce the power and the bows swung to starboard.

There was a silver lining to this cloud. By the time we were free, it was too late to make any further than the village of Westona, a mile or so to the south-east, not that we had much choice in the direction we could steer. As a result we moored close to the Saracen's Head pub. Now here was a real canal pub which is thoroughly recommended. We didn't eat as the girls had spent the blizzard preparing a magnificent meal below. All the same, the welcome was worth a two-minute walk, and please forgive us, the pork scratchings were out of this world, even for those of us who are not expert in that sort of food. They were made by the local butcher and considered one of the culinary highlights of the week.

7 April 0730. Ice on the decks but no wind. What a beautiful country this is.
Never seen from a motorway and seldom from a country lane.
0940. Arrived great Haywood. Moored to 'water ship' alongside the Anglo
Welsh Boat Co. As always everything is laid on and very convenient.

Great Haywood is the junction of the Trent and Mersey, and the Staffordshire and Worcestershire canals, and as with many canal intersections, marks a dramatic change in scenery, as well as methods and principles of construction. In this case it also marks the beginning of a particularly beautiful stretch of water. The 'Staffs and Worcs' (built by Brindley and completed in 1772) soon opens out into the reed-edged Tixall Wide, which actually bears no relation to a canal. Several theories exist about its origins. One is that it was built as an artificial lake to calm the dubious owner of nearby Tixall Hall. There are certainly other examples of this procedure, often in the form of elaborate bridges and cuttings. Either way it is a magnificent haven for wildlife.

Here we confirmed, once again, that despite the weather, we had chosen the best time of the year for our first attempt at the British canals. We had seen less than a handful of other narrowboats; the birds were beginning to nest; the pubs were almost empty and we never once had to queue at a lock, or worse still, at a flight of locks.

Our locking procedures were now close to perfection. On sighting the lock the crew would be summoned, and the three boys and one girl would grab a windlass handle each, leap to the tow path and run ahead. The gate would be open by the time we arrived, and while one half of the team closed the gate behind us, the other would operate the sluices. The first team would then run around to open the exit gate. The time from entry to exit was down to two and a half minutes (but why hurry a kiss?) for an average rise or fall of 6 to 8 feet. Even the log became lyrical about the whole thing, although I'm not sure that Colonel Pat would have totally approved.

Coming up to a lock, all you can see is the gate ahead of the bows, often
under a bridge with absolutely no apparent headroom, in fact a blank wall.
Once we had sunk the eight or so feet, the downstream gates would open like
a theatre curtain revealing a new stage set – and it really was different. Each
time we felt like clapping the set designer. The lock gates are drawn apart by
willing children to reveal a new scene of meadows and overhanging willows
or beeches, with the canal curving away around the bend to new and hidden

surprises. I'm used to dollops of cold sea water polluting my gin but there's nothing more harmful here than the odd pussy willow or catkin.

7 April 1400. Passed up through Deptmore Lock. To me this is the archetype of locks. But no lock keeper's daughter yet to be seen. Conifers lining the lock by the whitewashed cottage in the middle of fields. Tame mallard helping with the gates! Very cold, rain and sleet.

1730. Moored alongside the Anchor Inn at Cross Green. All ashore for excellent steaks and a friendly, noisy atmosphere. Turned in at 2230.

At Autherley Junction we turned hard-a-starboard into the Shropshire Union Canal, and again a whole new environment. The canal cuts into Staffordshire with long straight stretches through grand, deep cuttings giving way, in a few yards on the edge of a hill, to breathtaking embankments 100 feet or so above the surrounding, Lilliputian countryside far below. Thomas Telford, the builder, preferred to cut and fill rather than follow the contours. This contouring method, favoured by other canal builders, produced many locks rising and falling only a few feet at a time. To us though, the Shropshire Union was notable for two things: over forty-four years of sailing I have, thank God, only known one man-overboard emergency, and that was when I fell in from a 49-feet yawl while practicing for the 1970 two-handed Round Britain and Ireland race. In one day on the Four Counties Ring we had two men and one dog over the side. The dog misjudged her return from a walk ashore and simply belly-flopped into the canal; quickly recovered, a little surprised but not harmed. The second was Hamish, who missed his footing when returning from working a lock. Emergency action was simple, engine immediately to stop, a long arm and one dripping laughing boy below to a hot shower and dry clothes, in time for the next lock.

The final emergency was slightly different. Mike and younger son Ashton were alone on the upper deck while we rested below from our watches and the weather. The door leading aft to the tiller position was bolted on the inside to stop it blowing open in the strong northerly winds.

1300. Moored alongside the Navigation Inn (Gnosall Heath) which sold draught Guinness. After lunch, sailed for Market Drayton. Suddenly woken from afternoon kip by the door being rattled very hard by Ashton who was trying to tell the watch below that 'Daddy has fallen overboard'. I rushed on deck to find this seemed to be only partially true as 'Daddy' was walking nonchalantly along the towpath about half a cable astern while carrying the ship's mop. We slowed down and as he got closer, we could see that he was soaking from head to toe – he had simply waded ashore and decided to take a walk, as he knew we would stop at the next lock. For some reason he had been washing down the top sides when he slipped. We got him below and I took over the helm and promptly ran the barge aground. I'd been watching our wake for no more than five seconds as I thought about the possible dangers if there had been the usual summer traffic.

The concentration required for motoring along a canal is more than that needed when 'running down the trades' and is taking a little getting used to.

There's always a fine balance between depth of water, width of the canal, revs on the engine, therefore not breaking the speed limit, or making a breaking wave astern, yet having enough power to overcome the ground suction effects while maintaining steerage way. Thank goodness we have the canals almost to ourselves.

That night we spent moored at Market Drayton after dropping down the flight at Tyrley Wharf. These flights were outstanding and transiting them in good order required quite a discipline. The children, usually led by the youngest, my daughter Hermione, took charge while Lizzie and Patricia handled the warps; the men considered it important to be at the tiller for these evolutions! Heaven knows how long the flights would have taken without our small army of youngsters, and this was probably the main lesson learned – never attempt this sport (for that is what it was to us) without fit young children.

The morning at Market Drayton brought home one of the few unpleasant aspects of barge life. That is, if one insists on mooring near civilization, usually for a pub or restaurant. Dogs are a hazard, for it is a sad fact that the tow paths around any village or town are the obvious places where dog owners wish to walk their pets. The result is unpleasant and sadly universal. Conversely, Market Drayton also confirmed all that is fun about barge life. Unlike some yachtsmen, unless members of the same club, bargees do not jealously guard their piece of water and, without exception, have generally warm greetings and offers of help for each other be they amateur or professional.

There are many who still live on and make their living by the canals, and they are more than tolerant of their fellow travellers, whether they are inexperienced or just plain stupid. Even at our most incompetent we were never aware of critics leaning on their tillers commenting in barely suppressed voices. Everyone is united with their love of the canals and its inhabitants. It really was most refreshing, and if I was to single out anybody for praise, it would have to be the employees of the British Waterways Board. Some seasonal staff of south coast harbours and their governing local councils should take a lesson. Not once were we moved on or told 'You can't moor there' or asked for mooring fees. Apart from Kidsgrove, it was all smiles and help throughout.

9 April 0830. After a long walk for papers and milk we slipped under motor. Not that we have a choice!

The constantly changing scenery altered from lush meadows to deep, deep cuttings, from overhung, narrow 'ditches' to high-flying aqueducts or embankments; from ornate private bridges built to placate landowners, to modern motorway-style underpasses. Here on the canals, the pace of life was slow and gentle, producing a wonderfully friendly relationship between perfect strangers, which is not so often found elsewhere. The final flight of locks (for the Tailyour family) was at Oldham. From the top of the flight we could see the village laid out far ahead and below in a fascinating diorama. More and more detail, and life, became visible as we crept closer and closer in both horizontal and vertical planes, while the fifteen locks over a mile and a half produced exhausted children and grateful parents. Luckily at the bottom was a traditional canal pub which welcomed us with open arms and a delicious lunch. The landlord was clearly used to the sight with which we presented him, but it was also a sad occasion as we had to leave. Patricia's magisterial duties called. For once how nice it was that my military obligations were not to blame for the shortening of the holiday.

The final log entry reads:

A memorable four days with many lessons in seamanship and craft-handling relearned. Definitely a new experience and in such delightful company. Next year we might expand our horizons and try French kissing!

The rest of the year followed the normal path of Channel/Biscay cruising with the minimum use of an engine (and no marinas or barge poles) but for four glorious, cold days I had sampled a fascinating style of seamanship that, on reflection, I wish I had tried years earlier. Many of the mistakes I made were elementary and very humbling and I'm certain I came away a better seaman for that.

Chapter 13

Her First, My Last: The Norwegian Arctic

Published in the Royal Cruising Club's *Roving Commissions,*1988. A similar article, *Arctic Notebook*, was published in the American magazine *Ocean Navigator*.

Judge no Ice 'till Crossed, nor Ale 'till Drunk, nor Maid 'till Bedded.

It was a perfectly normal morning. Minus 15°C with a 10-knot southerly wind. I pulled out a small plastic chart from inside my shirt and calculated the wind chill to be -32°C. The sky was black but for the Aurora Borealis hanging in electric-blue, moving curtains above the northern skyline. A full moon had skirted the horizon of mountains throughout the previous twenty-four hours. The time was 1045 and it was a Saturday morning in late January 1988. My position was 68° 50'.1 N; 16° 19'.2 E.

The freshening wind from the head of Kasfjorden, five miles north-west of Harstad, blowing across the warmer water (all things are relative for the water was actually -1°C) swirled away in wisps of low-lying Arctic sea smoke, increasing in density towards the open and warmer sea. Good to capture on canvas or camera but devilish for navigation.

Dawn and dusk together were due in about an hour; the colours thrown across the otherwise black and white landscape of dramatic mountains and blue-black fjords would be brief and sensational. I checked my camera snug inside two warm sleeping bags.

There should be nothing unusual about cruising the Norwegian Arctic in January. We sail in the dark and some sail in the Arctic, but not many do both at the same time. I had had little choice and now it was my thirteenth and last winter. At least it was to be my last operating small, open landing and raiding craft in support of the Royal Marines' 3 Commando Brigade.

In celebration, I wanted to test my military experience under sail to see if there was any peacetime relevance to our work and, conversely, to study of what use this more relaxed medium might be able to offer the service in time of tension. Through the fortuitous intervention of a fellow Royal Marine stationed in Harstad, I had shipped out a small, green, gaff cutter in one of my larger landing craft. Immediately on arrival, *Larusanne* was spirited away from her new owner to a small ice-bound marina where, given a weekend of fitting out followed by some single-handed sea-time, she would be presented in a less *déshabillé* state to her owner.

I had sailed at 2100 the night before. One of the advantages of working in the Arctic winter is that there is no rush to complete a task before sunset - and anchored at 0430. Nevertheless, it is imperative to be aware of how late in the day it can become.

This black and white coastline, known as the Rock Rampart, is bounded by the Vesterålen and Lofoton Islands that splay 170 miles south-west to north-east out from Harstad. The area is well explored in summer, when despite being north of the Arctic Circle, sunbathing and swimming are regular pastimes.

The attraction of these off-lying islands, apart from the outstanding scenery and remarkable passages and anchorages, is the large expanse of sheltered water among them and in inland from them. This is an area of deep and narrow fjords, sheer cliffs, gently sloping coastal snowfields, benign tides, small villages and snug bolt holes for a winter yachtsman. To me the ultimate attraction was that in thirteen years I only saw two other yachts between January and April.

Over the years we had learnt that the noon-time dark is far more fascinating and challenging than the midnight sun and, this is important - there are no mosquitoes in the winter.

However this challenge is not as dramatic as it might seem for there is a remarkable degree of light from the moon, stars, the Northern Lights and, closer to home, civilisation. Unlike the wilder parts of Scotland, the coasts of north Norway are well populated so it is quite normal to find the fjords edged with streetlights. These and domestic lights can confuse the navigator but, by and large, as with many other coastal areas, navigation in the dark can be much easier. Not least because in summer the lighthouses look similar: small, white, wooden, conical structures, but in the winter their different light characteristics are more easily identified.

Larusanne nodded gently alongside the small ice 'wall' a few inches thick. The brittle-frozen fenders were still effective although during the night they had punctured. A heavy-duty plank, weighted along one edge, was already firmly on the list of extra equipment to be acquired. I could have moored to the village jetty, but as shoreside facilities are sparse I saw little point. On the eastern shore, vertical cliffs had offered a secure mooring but that was nothing unusual. I could have anchored, but in common with many fjords, the depths were either too deep or over smooth, glaciated rocks, offering poor, or no, holding ground. I turned in after shaving, for beards encourage moisture and thus frostbite then slept, fully clothed, inside two sleeping bags with zips at opposite sides. The cabin temperature was 20°C below freezing.

On the morrow it was my first full day alone with *Larusanne* and time to teach her many of the drills and procedures that had become second nature in powered military craft.

I undressed to the two inner-most layers of clothing, ready for the heat of cooking a large breakfast that would constitute the first of the 6,000 calories necessary in every twenty-four hours in the Arctic. I rinsed out four vacuum flasks for the hot, sweet, blackcurrant drink that would supplement the many bars of chocolate and packets of glucose tablets during the rest of the day. The water tank had frozen solid, room for expansion had been left on *Larusanne*'s arrival, but there was plenty of fresh snow outside. The whiskey bottles stayed, grudgingly, in their locker, for even I recognised the dangers of alcohol in the extreme cold.

Before sailing it had taken nearly half an hour to dress, adhering to the well-established principle of many layers of lightweight clothing, topped by a loose waterproof outer for wet conditions. That way it is much easier to control the body heat and prevent one of the great dangers – sweat. Sweat condenses into the clothing when warm and then freezes when re-exposed to the cold. Dry snow, unless removed by a small stiff brush before going below, melts into the fabric and then refreezes when back on the upper deck. The cold is not by itself dangerous, but the damp most certainly is.

The only source of heat when not cooking was a single candle. It ensured that while there was a welcome temperature difference compared with the outside, this was minimal. It also ensured that I would not sweat nor would I have to waste time and energy – more sweat – taking off and putting on clothes every time I nipped in or out of the cabin. On deck it was the same. I wrapped up well when static but removed a certain number of layers to carry out arduous tasks. Survival and living are synonymous in the Arctic.

The problem areas are the head, hands, feet and teeth. As it was damp on deck, I wore a cotton Arab *shemagh* wound around my head, which gave ideal protection from the boom and yet dried easily in my sleeping bag at night. I also carried an Arctic wolf fur hat with a peak and ear flaps, which was indispensable in extreme cold when all moisture had been frozen out of the air. On my feet I wore a pair of over-sized, thick-soled, reindeer skin boots with three pairs of socks, two of loop-stitched wool over a thin cotton pair next to the skin.

I had avoided the fur-lined boots on sale for they were difficult to dry once wet inside. Three pairs of gloves were stuffed into pockets: a rubber polka-dot pair for handling bare metal fittings, a fur-lined pair for normal working, and a large pair of industrial rubber ones for hauling on wet lines and halyards. Teeth? Fillings contract in the cold, colder than an ice cream, and can fall out. It is sensible to have them checked in advance.

The same principle applied to much of the upper deck. The cold renders many materials brittle and fragile, but the real danger is caused by moisture seeping into working parts and then refreezing.

I made a note to purchase anti-freeze grease from a local garage for smearing over snap shackles, spring hanks, rigging screws and seacocks whose interiors do not freeze as the sea temperature, unless beset in ice, is about plus 6°C. Depending on salinity and depth, sea water freezes at about -2°C. Canvas covers (PVC degrades in the cold) would be needed for the larger upper deck fittings such as winches, foredeck gear and rigging screws. A can of anti-waxing additives for the diesel fuel was vital as were spare water-pump impellers.

It is best to remove the water pump's rubber impellers if stopping for some time. My Royal Marines' rigid raiding craft cox'ns would sleep with their outboard motor carburettors in their sleeping bags, but this might not always be practical - or pleasant! Necessity once forced me to run the 8hp diesel without a water pump and at quarter revs. With the air temperature in the cabin below -10°C it operated faultlessly. I also started the engine every hour or so to keep some residue heat in the system.

Breakfast over and the flasks topped up, I hung a variable-focus mini-Maglite torch around my neck alongside the rubber-encircled hand bearing compass, both guaranteed to operate if kept warm, wound the *shemagh* tighter around my head and ears, donned the upper layers of waterproof clothing and climbed into the dark. Dawn - or dusk - was adding perspective and the slightest touch of colour to the horizon.

With the wind still off the ice I knew I would be safe. The floes that littered the fjord would have trapped us had the wind been onshore and small yachts cannot break their way out even if the ice is as thin as a quarter of an inch.

It was too dark to record this first overnight mooring with the camera. so I filled a pack with my watercolour paints and brushes, clipped a pair of Norwegian army cross-country skis to my Royal Marines-issue 'ski-march' boots, and set off for the shore. It is possible to moor, unknowingly, to an ice island, as the intertidal zone could be a mass of broken ice. Normally this might not matter, but it would cause a considerable delay in seeking help in an emergency. A man can walk on sea ice (softer and more yielding than freshwater ice) when it is above two inches thick, but it is easier and safer to use skis. If a stream runs under the snow into a fjord, then thicker and safer freshwater ice will be encountered. Under these conditions the intertidal zone is usually impassable.

It was too cold for watercolour painting so I sketched the scene in pencil before recovering two anchors frozen into the ice. I had dug holes for the flukes and then filled them with seawater, which froze quickly to encapsulate the moorings. A few minutes of chipping and I had recovered all the ground-tackle to the fore deck. The engine was started to give it some warmth rather than to give us way through the water and all plain sail was hoisted.

A propeller guard and rudder stops were added to the list as a maverick floe had formed a solid obstruction beneath the transom, soon dislodged by a stout boathook.

The passage north-west was straightforward with just one flashing light seven miles distant as a guide. The sector lights, so common in Norway, are very useful for fixes as they dovetail into each other. Without juggling frozen parallel rulers in the cockpit, accurate position lines can be obtained from two or three lights simultaneously as one crosses from one coloured sector to another.

GPS would have been useful on the approaches to the coast, but, I was told, of limited value in the deep-sided fjords. It was not missed. Decca would be recommended and knowing nothing of the owner's circumstances, I debated whether or not to suggest a radar. In the near permanent dark it could be useful, especially when lights are obscured by snowfalls or white-outs, while the difficult-to-spot spar buoys might, anyway, have been removed by the seas, floes or even trawlers. However, radar can be a two-edged weapon. The shore contours are often altered by ice and on one memorable occasion my landing craft veered suddenly to starboard while in confined waters, only to discover that the echo was caused by the head of a cormorant that, according to the radar, had the right of way!

Norwegian charts are issued by their admiralty and sold in licenced bookshops. The scale is usually 1:50,000 except for harbour plans and narrow passages. They are descriptive and easy to read by torchlight but can become out of date quickly. Small bridges linking the numerous islands appear, even before Notices to Mariners have had time to catch up, as I know from a spectacular example of impact hydrography at 0200 in the middle of a thick and unexpected blizzard.

Ordnance Survey 1:50,000 maps are good for seafarers, for not only are they to the same scale as the charts, but they show many typographical features (such as contours) that are not otherwise marked. They also indicate, rather more clearly, the recommended anchorages - but not navigational marks or lights. I made a note to buy the Royal Norwegian Automobile Club (KNA) and the Norwegian Automobile Association (NAF) guides.

I added to the list a further miscellany of items I knew we would need. The stout plank would also be useful for the widely spaced uprights of the local jetties; a stiff brush for removing snow from the deck; a long heavy-duty boat hook with spike as well as hook for pushing ice floes away from the bows and stern gear; thermal jackets for the engine and battery (removed when running!); electrical spares for every fitting especially the plastic and rubber ones and, in addition to the standard VHF, a Nordic mobile telephone system. This is much more likely to be answered from the bottom of a fjord in an emergency and can instantly be connected to the coastguard or Norwegian life-saving service which, in these parts, has its headquarters at Bodø to the south. The wind backed to the north-west, the sea smoke lessened and there was peace and utter silence.

To the south, and to the west and east, the coastal lights emphasised civilization and were no comfort. It was exactly what I wanted to escape. The moon was bright through a curtain of electrons, while the mountains were clear and two-toned black and dark grey with a hint of pink at their very peaks. The sea was visible where it reflected distant lights while the wind-chill increased as we swung to the north, remaining on a close reach around the headland. I'd never been afloat in the Arctic without noise, so the unexpected quiet was an additional attraction.

By and large the winds follow the direction of the fjords, suggesting a beat or run except when in the widest areas. Katabatic winds are the real menace, but a study of the 'land maps' shows the likely trouble areas. These occur when cold air that has collected in a hanging valley is nudged over the edge by a gentle offshore breeze. This mass of air falls rapidly to sea level where it bomb bursts in every direction. Williwaws in other parts of the world have the same effect but without the shocking cold.

The spray slicing across the port bow took on the expected malignancy. Settling *Larusanne* on a steady course, I hopped below and within a few moments had donned the all-in-one, buoyant, padded suit given to me by a Norwegian friend some winters before. Although waterproof it had many zips for ventilation which could be opened on a down-wind side to forestall a build-up of moisture. I fitted double-lensed goggles over my eyes and with an air temperature well below -2°C, flying ice was the next hurdle.

Before returning to the cockpit I carried out the first of many trips to the mast to work the running rigging. This was important to prevent ice forming in the sheaves which could effectively lock the sails in place. Apart from that, lumps of ice falling from 30 feet can hurt!

I turned to the chart to check the course for Harstad, eight hours sailing away if the wind stayed in the northerly sector. A white-tailed sea eagle meandered slowly overhead while rafts of eider duck splashed their way across the bows. All in all it was turning into a pretty normal day – for an Arctic winter – and *Larusanne* was clearly enjoying it as much as her skipper. Now all we had to do was persuade her owner how worthwhile his decision had been. It wouldn't be difficult.

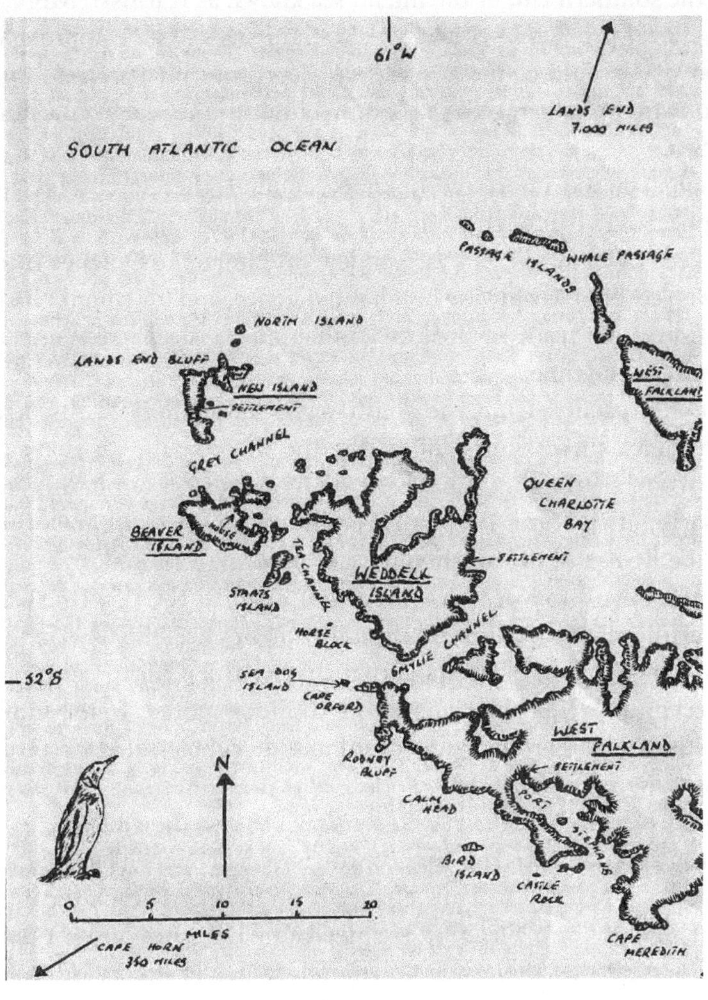

Chapter 14

Karin Plaza Beach Recce, 1994

While serving in the Republic of Serbian Krajina (RSK) as a European Community monitor, I found myself, by chance, able to carry out a beach reconnaissance (of sorts) of Serbia's only outlet to the Mediterranean.

One of our patrol's planned stops for the day was the small town of Karin Plaza, at the southern end of the inland sea known as Karinsko More, in order to discuss local problems with the civic dignitaries. As we approached what in happier days would count as a seaside resort, our interpretress for the day described it to me as being Serbia's only outlet to the sea, even calling it the Serbian Sea.

'As such,' she was interested to know, 'could it, therefore, serve any use as a trading harbour? Is it deep enough? Could ocean-going ships unload here?'

I was keen to know too, as was, I hoped, my contact in Defence Intelligence 4 (DI4) who covered worldwide beach intelligence, and for whom I had worked on and off over the years, regardless of what other tasks I was being employed to undertake at the time.

As we approached from the south-west, six artillery shells, fired from Croatia in quick succession, exploded in the water about a quarter of a mile from the town, sending up plumes of sunlit spray and reminding us - quite unnecessarily - that Karin Plaza was very much on the front line of the tussle between the RSK and the neighbouring Croatia.

With the town's mayor's shattered roof open to the sky, courtesy of the Croatian artillery, we met him and the only school's headmistress in the latter's temporary house. Karin Plaza (modern maps now call it Karin Gornji) had been shelled recently, forcing the teacher to move into another house immediately opposite his own, across the narrow and muddy rubble-filled street. Here the damage was more liveable with.

From my diary: *They received 20 artillery shells on Sunday night.*

Towards the end of this meeting, at which we had by then been joined by the chief of police, I realised that any chance of an informal beach reconnaissance was about to slip away. Pleading the need to have a pee and on being told, as I had guessed, that there was no running water in the house, I suggested

I walked down to the beach. This was agreed on the strict understanding that I had a police escort.

Walking across the sand towards the tideline, I tried to estimate the weight-bearing properties of the dry sand above the high-water mark. At the water's edge I took off my socks and shoes, rolled up my trousers and waded in up to thigh-height, to begin what was probably the longest pee in Serbian medical history. All the while, I was digging the sand with my toes while attempting to gauge the underwater gradient and 'trafficability' properties. Finished, eventually, I turned towards the shore, and it was not until then that I noticed that my escort was a United Nation's Argentine policeman wearing what I took to be 'Malvinas' war medals. Being given to spontaneous laughter I was suddenly convulsed for here was an Argentine veteran guarding me while I conducted a covert beach reconnaissance on someone else's shore. In broken English I was asked what I found so amusing but I didn't have the heart to tell him.

On our return to our HQ in the RSK's capital Knin, I included a brief beach reconnaissance statement in our Daily Report to Brussels. Later that night in the privacy of my hotel bedroom I compiled a more comprehensive document for DI4 and the SIS. This is paraphrased here from a rather more comprehensive and detailed report:

> *The possibilities of the RSK using the beach at Karin Plaza as a loading/unloading port were investigated.*
>
> *Due to the lack of permission to visit the neck of the 'Serbian Sea' and the inadvisability of conducting an overt survey, only an outline impression was obtained: however it is thought that, at a future date, this may be useful as a starting point for a more detailed study. Naturally, it was not possible to cross the front line to ascertain the suitability of the sea approaches beyond Ribenica.*
>
> *Currently this 'harbour' would appear to be the only potential outlet to the open sea available to the RSK and although it is never likely to be suitable for heavy traffic it might be considered feasible for landing craft of a substantial size: yet even this assumption must contain strong caveats as, for instance, the dimensions (and particularly the clearance) of the bridge over the Ribenica Kanal are unknown at present.*

The ECMM HQ in Brussels made no acknowledgement, whereas DI4 and the SIS were both most grateful.

Chapter 15

Escape Plans from Croatia, 1994

Between 1993 and 1994 I was employed by the Foreign and Commonwealth Office (FCO) and on an ad hoc basis, by the Secret Intelligence Service, for duties first in the Republic of Serbian Krajina (RSK) then, subsequently, at Split, to cover Croatia's Dalmatian Coast. Life was such that when in Knin, the RSK's capital, members of my small, international team were regarded as spies for Croatia, and when in Split, as spies for the Serbs. Due then to the pending attack by Croatia against the RSK and thus the certainty of Serb reprisals, coupled with a formal and personal FCO warning that my own life was in danger, I felt it prudent to prepare escape plans for my team of myself plus one Dutchman, one Frenchman, one Irishman and a Dane.

While our colleagues in Knin brushed off their non-existent evacuation plans it was sensible that I did the same for Team Split. Given enough warning we had two options. The one I preferred, naturally, was to take one of the yachts I had already earmarked in the marina and sail across the Adriatic to an Italian port…or hop along the coast to the Headquarters of the British Forces in the Former Republic of Yugoslavia, at Divulje where, I doubted, we would be made welcome in what would be the middle of a serious drama.

The second option was to go by road to Divulje Barracks but I reckoned we would need more notice than was likely for that move and, to add a complication, we could not go in our European Community Monitoring Mission's white-painted car. A local taxi was out of the question. I considered earmarking and cold-starting a civilian car from the hotel car park, or hiring one in advance - but could we guarantee that it would be 'free' at no notice and who would pay! So it was back to the maritime option by 'stealing' a yacht as my diary entry explains:

Must see the marina dock master and ask to look over the most suitable candidate by pretending I might like to buy it. I already have one in mind. It strikes me that any yacht owner will be happy for a sale under the current circumstances. What I need to know is how to get on board, where the sails might be kept (assuming they are not already bent on - or, even, ashore) and how to start the engine. Will she have enough fuel and so on? The nearest largish Italian port with an established marina is Pescara at 114 nautical miles, although San Benedetto del Tronto is a touch closer. Both are a twenty-four hour sail away given a fair breeze.

As it happened, during one of my walks around Split's marinas my eye had been caught by a beautiful, traditionally designed and built, wooden yawl of about 36 feet in length. Unlike almost all of the other vessels moored in their untidy berths this one seemed to have been maintained; at least, she had not been allowed to fall into total disrepair. My initial thought had been to seek out her owner and ask if he would like a weekend crew but as the threats to our own existence became greater, I decided that it was best not to give an inkling of my ulterior motive.

At last, and with the final vestiges of Lekeu's behaviour behind us (a Belgian rogue monitor whose behaviour had been causing considerable alarm not only to us but to the Croatian authorities before he was sacked) I was able to turn my ideas for escape into action. Calling on Captain Maroje Moroević, the Split Marina's harbour master and, by happy chance, the Foreign Port Representative in Croatia for the Royal Cruising Club, I learned that the 36-feet yawl that I had in mind had been abandoned three years earlier by her owner, who had not been seen since. He had been, according to Moroević, one of the intelligentsia that had fled the country, probably never to return. As a member of the RCC I felt it right to take the harbourmaster into my confidence and was met, not only with understanding, but a guided tour of the vessel that included the 'secret' place where a spare set of keys would be kept. Moroević also instructed me on starting the engine. The fuel tank was about a third full and thus offered a fair range should we have to motor much of the way. The state of the diesel after so long lying undisturbed in the tank had to be an acceptable risk. The sailing side of affairs I could work out for myself.

Encouragingly, Captain Moroević believed that if the vessel were to be left in a safe Italian port she might yet be reunited with her owner. He was, therefore, happy to be a party to this scheme.

In the end I resigned from the FCO in disgust at being ordered to falsify my daily reports for Brussels and so my liaison with the beautiful *Eloise* never took place – very sadly!

Chapter 16

Bordeaux Revisited, 1995

Take a detailed look at British Admiralty chart number 2916 then think of a December night in 1942. As you do so, imagine yourself in a two-man, canvas canoe, laden with limpet mines, Benzedrine tablets and a silk escape map. Feel the sharp needles on your cheek as spray, thrown up from a paddle, instantly turns to ice. Peer through the darkness and seek, in vain, for the extinguished navigational lights, while pondering the next mile (of a total of over ninety) along one of Europe's strongest-running river estuaries patrolled, then, by the continent's most belligerent nation.

Now flash forward to July 1995 and a 12-ton gaff cutter with hot showers, a fully equipped galley, a bulging drinks cupboard, and a crew of two middle-aged men and three teenage girls - plus one lucky lad of similar vintage - as it forges upriver and you might wonder what connects these disparate journeys. The clue is in the chart's title: '*La Gironde*'. This mighty, muddy estuary leads, via the River Garonne, to the docks of Bordeaux where, in darker days, the expression 'Cockleshell Heroes' entered British naval history, the humble canoe was confirmed as a weapon of war, and Lieutenant Colonel 'Blondie' Hasler's name came to prominence in connection with small boats.

At 1917 on 7 December 1942, His Majesty's Submarine *Tuna* surfaced in a dead-reckoning position of 45°21'.8N; 1°14'.1 W, fourteen and a half miles south-by-west of Corduan island that lies at the entrance to the Gironde Estuary. Before the Biscay waters had begun to sluice from beneath the boat's upper-deck casing, six canoes were being manhandled into the fresh air. The flimsy hull of one was ripped in the hatch and immediately passed back below while the remainder were hoisted into the water by a makeshift crane fixed to the 4-inch gun barrel. With five canoes safely away the captain, Lieutenant Dick Raikes, DSO, Royal Navy, wrote in his log:

2003. Operation [Frankton] completed.... Waved au revoir to a magnificent bunch of black-faced villains...proceeded on main motors...towards the western horizon while the ten Royal Marines paddled northwards towards an uncertain future.

That future included five nights of paddling, broken only by breaks during the winter daylight, the placing of limpet mines on as many merchant ships as they could find alongside Bordeaux's docks, followed by a proposed – but unplanned – escape overland to Gibraltar: providing they could meet up with the French Resistance in Ruffec, a small town 90 miles to the north. Only four men would survive the operation and only two would reach home, while their six colleagues would be drowned or executed.

By the summer of 1995 I could no longer delay following the route that the canoeists had taken, for to write Blondie's biography convincingly, I needed to see for myself the natural dangers that they had faced. I could only imagine those imposed by the enemy. Nowadays the significance of the Gironde and the two rivers, the Garonne and Dordogne, that lead into it is clear, but then, the waterway's importance beyond the vineyards was known only to a few Germans, Japanese and Britons, as civilian blockade runners secretly ran a gauntlet to the Far East carrying specialist machinery and returning with raw materials such as rubber.

These ships had to be stopped and Blondie's 1942 plan for using canoes was the most acceptable method. Blocking the estuary was ineffective – yet, paradoxically, the haphazard RAF mining was to give the submarine's captain the greatest headache. The risk to civilians from equally imprecise bombing was unacceptable. It was a task that had quickly reached Combined Operations Headquarters' 'too difficult' pile – but it had also reached Blondie's fertile mind.

The 1995 plan was to use *Black Velvet*, my 12-ton gaff cutter, to follow the route, photograph the canoeists' stopping points from seaward, invite retired members of the French Resistance to a party on board while at Bordeaux, and visit the *Conservatoire International Plaisance de Bordeaux* where there is a section devoted to Blondie's war and peacetime exploits. By doing all this I hoped to gain an understanding of the difficulties that had faced his team during Operation Frankton.

My own team joined at La Rochelle on 14 July 1995. The Bastille celebrations inevitably delayed our start but as the weather was settled and we had time in hand, they were also a welcome addition to the crew-bonding process. The unexpectedly slow sail south was in contrast to the excitement of the previous evening's 'storming of the Bastille'. The lack of wind ensured that we did not arrive off the northern entrance to the Gironde, and what (in authentic deference to the buoyed channel's earlier mines) we called the 'swept channel', until early evening. Sadly this was too late to continue south to make *Tuna*'s 1942 surfaced position in daylight. As an 'agent' had been organised by the

British Consulate in Bordeaux to meet us at Port Bloc on the southern arm of the estuary's entrance, we turned into the small marina. He was to offer navigational advice on approaching Blondie's daytime hides by water, but we also wanted to visit the Atlantic-facing beach close by, where two marines had prematurely landed after their canoe had capsized in the tide race over the Banc du Gros Terrier, one mile offshore.

There was though, no agent as Peter Seldon, the other adult, and I sipped our 'identifying' double Pastis at the agreed rendezvous – but, never mind, for I am rarely embarrassed about running aground (which we had done during the approach thus delaying the meeting – indeed the probable reason for missing it) in the interests of exploring, or what I call 'impact-hydrography – so we returned to an undergraduate-style, pasta supper, an early night and our own interpretations of the estuary's muddy bank's peculiarities.

On the morrow, using ex-Argentine night vision goggles and under motor, we caught the last of the considerable ebb and were well on our way by the start of the flood at 0315. We were now in 'Blondie territory' and on the exact route he had taken before dawn on 8 December 1942. Even the German Navy's anti-submarine *chasseurs* that had provided many of his alarms were at anchor a few cables offshore in the guise of darkened – but innocent – merchant ships. We slipped past them and headed for the mole off Le Verdon – where a canoe had gone missing – as Blondie had done, passing the position where the crew of a third canoe – capsized off Pointe de Grave – had been released to swim ashore after a gruelling and time-consuming tow. Reflectively, we raised a glass of whisky in their memory, for neither marine had survived.

The two remaining canoes made their first landfall at Pointe aux Oiseaux on the west bank – now eroded to non-existence. I had visited by car and knew there was nothing to be gained by sending the dinghy ashore, especially as there was a mile of mud to cross. Blondie's men had discovered this as they dragged their canoes seawards after dusk on 8 December, leaving telltale marks before the rising waters kindly obliterated them. Still in the dark, we made for the centre of the 'swept' channel with the tide and *Black Velvet*'s diesel engine (known affectionately as 'Mr Perkins' as it was made by the Perkins Marine engine company) giving us more than 10 knots over the ground.' This was exhilarating stuff, provided we did not want to stop – which we did – and although 4 knots is the highest rate tabulated on the chart, it was never less than this throughout our passage and often rather more. On one occasion we stemmed the tide alongside a buoy but couldn't keep abreast of it and slowly made our way stern-first towards Bordeaux - thus, no doubt, causing a little confusion with our navigation lights.

The estuary was hostile enough to a 12-ton yacht 'strengthened for ice' (strengthened for tree-trunks would have been more appropriate) and we didn't have to keep an eye out for the enemy, nor did we only have to travel by night, so what then of the problems facing a canoe in mid-winter? Our collective minds were often silenced by these sobering thoughts.

Blondie's next stopping place had been a ditch half a mile south of Port des Callonges on the east bank. By car, I had found and photographed the precise spot where he had lain with his three companions and their two canoes throughout 9 December, so even had the tide allowed, there was little need to go ashore.

Abreast of Pauillac, the tide having risen appreciably, we left the main channel to head east. The mud banks had begun to disappear, dawn was breaking and a wonderful low mist covered the river's surface. Rising above this sea smoke and sweeping inland across the gentle slopes were the vineyards of the Medoc, with their immaculate chateaux, regimented neatness and sense of old order. The beauty of the hour had given us new navigational courage, so we aimed to pass between Île de Patiras and Vasard de Beychevelle, as had the Cockleshell Heroes half a century before - they with their 6-inch draught and us with our six feet. The islands remain largely uninhabited and mostly unchanged since those days when the marines searched the reed-encumbered banks for hiding places. These were the same mud walls topped by rushes that, we know from Blondie's descriptions, 'cracked like pistol shots' as the canoes were dragged into their temporary sanctuaries.

But we were swept past with no chance of anchoring until, opposite Ile Nouvelle, we returned to the west and the Haut Medoc, joining the deep water opposite the Chenal de Despartins. Two and half miles further south, Blondie had chosen the right fork that passes west of Île Verte, but the chart (and my own road visit) showed there was now no exit, even for canoes, at the southern end of this narrowing passage.

On the apex of the junction between the Dordogne and the Garonne rivers sits the Elf oil refinery, the point at which the Gironde ceases to exist and the rivers begin. The deep-water channel narrows here and took us closer to the shore than I preferred; certainly closer than Blondie, anxious to avoid the anti-shipping gun emplacements (which are still visible) would have considered prudent, yet beyond the buoyed channel, alarming eddies and overfalls reminded him – and us – of other unseen dangers that lurked below. We had no choice over which route to take whereas he had had to choose the lesser of two fearful evils and that cannot have been easy.

Passing east of Île Verte (now named Île Cazeau) we photographed the concrete remains of the German gun position close to which Blondie had hidden during the penultimate day before his attack. Motionless in their canoes in the middle of the southernmost field, the men had spent the daylight hours within one hundred yards of the Germans. Again we raised a glass to their determination to take the war to the enemy, deep in his own territory, armed only with limpet mines and cold courage.

From here onwards the east bank is now ruined by industry, whereas the Haut Medoc remains studiously unspoilt for this is an idyllic place, where the passing of time is noted only by the lifecycle of the grape.

On arrival at Bordeaux our instructions were to enter the covered U-boat pens under full sail – including squares'l – but approaching the outer basin at the wrong state of tide was no more possible for us as it had been for a submarine, so we motored at a quarter of a knot over the ground back to the marina where we reported to our new 'agent', Daniel Charles. A Belgian, and then, director of the *Conservatoire International Plaisance de Bordeaux*, he told us that the Resistance workers had received no invitations from the consulate which, rather surprisingly, did not inhibit the staff from saying that they would still come and drink our duty-free. (The French Resistance had been made up of those noble and courageous French men and women who not only fought against the German occupation but who also helped escaping allied personnel to reach the comparative security of Spain, or better still, a Royal Navy Motor Gun Boat off a North Brittany beach or even an army Lysander aircraft in a field). The consulate staff were rather put out when, instead, we accepted a private tour of the *Conservatoire*, where most exhibits are afloat and in full working order, including Blondie's box-sided, experimental sloop Sumner in which he and Bridget – his then bride – had entered the first two-handed round Britain race that he had established. (Later renamed the two-handed round Britain and Ireland race.) This amazing museum – shrine almost – of yachting and boating, hopes that one day Blondie's equally experimental, junk-rigged yacht *Jester* may too, end her time here.

Four days later, after a hideous seven-hour passage into short, almost vertical seas, heaped-up by a strong, adverse, northerly wind, we were safely – and thankfully – alongside at Royan. Despite a 7-knot tide under us and Mr Perkins at maximum revolutions we had been stopped over the ground for long periods and while, to us, that was certainly not funny if we were to carry the tide, to Blondie's team a similar situation might have incurred capture and death. We though, were fortunate and eventually able to relax for the first time since entering the estuary and its rivers for such had been the worrying effect of a permanent current faster than *Black Velvet*'s cruising speed, especially when alongside at Bordeaux with the stern and rudder facing into it every six hours. Here we took stock of the expedition. Frankly, unlike Blondie's operation in which he and his remaining three colleagues had damaged or sunk six ships, our aim had only partially been met for we had visited no hiding places, we had passed through no tide races and we had met no Resistance workers; yet I had learned much about the Gironde itself and my admiration for Blondie as a wartime leader and navigator was further enhanced.

However we may also have found a flaw in even his meticulous planning, for before we both started neither of us had any idea of the freshwater content of the tidal Gironde and the Garonne – even on the flood – and had given it no thought until, in our case, when moored at Bordeaux, I noticed by chance that *Black Velvet* drew two inches more than usual. I took a measurement there and again at Royan, where she was back to her marks – after allowance had been made for a serious cargo of fine wines at 'plonk' prices having been embarked while upriver.

Over the months before departure, Blondie had measured the draught of his canoes to the nearest one-sixteenth of an inch, in order to balance equipment carried against drag and thus speed: experiments that had even involved the amount of wartime lavatory paper to be embarked – thick as a board and heavy too – when the precise number of sheets was calculated, 'practised' and finally ordained. If he had known of the Gironde's freshwater effect, his canoes might have carried even less. As for us, we certainly had had our own worries but wetted-surface area and an alert enemy were not among them. Nor had either of us met our respective agents first time, and while that was disappointing for us, it was nearly a tragedy for him at the start of his three-month overland escape with his one remaining companion.

Chapter 17

Lieutenant Colonel Herbert George 'Blondie' Hasler. DSO, OBE, RM.

...that fascinating combination of man of action who is also a man of ideas, capable of high self-dedication where action and ideas meet.

Thus wrote Douglas Phillips-Birt in 1960 for his publication *British Ocean Racing*. Equally relevant was Agur when he uttered his Confession of Faith in Proverbs 30:

There be three things which are too wonderful for me, yea, four which I know not:
The way of an eagle in the air;
The way of a serpent upon a rock;
The way of a ship in the midst of the sea;
And the way of a man with a maid.

Unlike Agur, Blondie - the 'man of action and ideas'- made it his business to know the ways and means of these four things, despite some (the last in particular) taking a little longer than others.

Blondie Hasler was a direct contemporary of my father's in the United Kingdom's pre-war Royal Marines - then a comparatively carefree existence when they cruised together in their various, small, (very second hand) gaff cutters. Hasler's involvement with small boats continued throughout the conflict, initially in landing craft during the Narvik campaign and then by experimenting - first with explosive motorboats and eventually canoes prior to the 'Cockleshell Heroes' raid on enemy shipping at Bordeaux. As the war in Europe dragged to a close, Hasler moved to Ceylon where his Royal Marines used canoes, carried to the enemy coast by Catalina aircraft, to harry the enemy during the Burma campaign.

When peace was resumed, and as a direct result of his wartime boat-work, Hasler was medically discharged from military service, but any sadness he might have felt was mitigated by the freedom that now allowed his imaginative brain a far wider range for inventive thought.

Post-war, I sailed with Hasler and was able to watch this unique mariner in action, thus I can confirm Lucas Philips's perfect summing up of Hasler's unspoken philosophy that he describes in his book *Cockleshell Heroes*. Although written of Hasler's wartime exploits, it also presages the introduction of three of his most enduring inventions: *Jester* and her junk-rig; the servo-pendulum self-steering gear, and the Observer Single-handed Transatlantic Race or OSTAR. Phillips-Birt further wrote:

The impulse of the moving waters was in his veins. Together with this passion went an ardour for contriving and devising things. He was not content to accept things ready-made but worked them out for himself, and they had to pass every test. He was fascinated by 'all trades, their gear and tackle and trim'. He loved making things with his own hands, from the beginning up, and to whatever problem he turned – whether it was… the rig of a dinghy… the diet needed for a long cruise – he devoted to it an intensity and singleness of purpose that was not satisfied with any ready-offered solution but impelled him to probe the smallest details of invention…. All this means that Hasler was, and remained, very much an individualist; in both senses of the term, he liked to paddle his own canoe.

Hasler's 'creative' nautical character had been cast since very early childhood in a number of home-built sailing craft, but in 1935, it was more firmly established when he sailed single-handed from Plymouth to Portsmouth along England's south coast in a 12-feet open dinghy he called *Trivia*. Two months later he returned single-handed to Plymouth. By the standards of the day – and even those of today – these were noteworthy cruises and widely reported in the yachting press.

With the war in the Far East at last over, the purchase, in November 1945, of the '30-square metre' *Tre Sang* marked the first step in Hasler's civilian life. Despite cynical belief from the Royal Ocean Racing Club's hardened skippers that the '30 squares' with 'their toothpick hulls, low freeboard and tiny rags for sails, were only suitable for the Solent', Hasler determined to prove that the very hull shape was, in empirical practice, 'perfect for climbing every sea rather than smashing its way through them'. By the end of 1946, and against all the pundits' predictions *Tre Sang*, 'sailed by men of iron', had won the RORC's Class II Championship. Nevertheless, Hasler believed that this was only a start, for in his reactionary view, it was not winning that counted but efficiency. Now he had the experience to proceed 'with the exciting work of developing the sailing vessels of the future that will have an automatic means of reducing sail area so that an absurd amount of mast and rigging is not left standing to support a very small area of canvas'.

Among many slowly fermenting ideas, Hasler began designing self-steering systems in order that a better look-out could be maintained, while also applying creative thought to such items as revolving Perspex hoods for enclosed cockpits, self-tailing winches, halyards and sheets leading to a central position, and even the diet to ensure healthy, oceanic voyaging. Hasler, who did nothing for his own aggrandisement, was thinking only of making success easier for others to obtain through more efficient designs. Better handling conditions at sea and greater comfort made for less energy wastage over a long voyage and this, he argued, made for superior alertness and thus enhanced safety.

Hasler's newly built, 25-feet *Jester* became his workhorse and was originally fitted with a Ljungstrom lapwing before he settled on the junk rig, together with the revolving pram hood over a central hatch - no cockpit - into which all lines led, a whipstaff tiller and a prototype of his servo-blade steering gear. These were all revolutionary departures from the accepted norm described by the renowned marine architect, Angus Primrose, as 'the only radical advance in yacht design this century'. But how to market his ideas and spread the word? Of course - declare a race across the Atlantic single-handed, non-stop then gauge the public interest.

So it was that Hasler's standing in the nautical world was further enhanced in 1960 with the OSTAR in which he finished second across the line in New York. But what pleased him most was that four of the five competitors were in yachts under 30 feet in length - and all finished. In 1964, the second OSTAR gave Hasler even more pleasure for it was won by the French sailor and fellow innovator, Éric Tabarley, in a yacht especially designed for the event. To Hasler this was the most significant sign of success.

When in 1966, Hasler instigated the first two-handed round Britain (and Ireland - was added later) race, his fame as an innovator and inventor was at its height and with this and the continuing OSTARs came larger, faster vessels - many now multi-hulled - whose steering gears had to match these increases in size, configuration and performance. In 1970 when I entered the heavy-displacement, 49-feet wooden *Speedwell of Cremyll* for that year's two-handed round-Britain race, Hasler was faced with developing his most powerful steering gear to date. Adding to the complication was her yawl rig and wheel steering. I remember well the intense trouble he took to ensure that the length of the servo blade was precisely correct, shaving off a quarter of an inch at a time, to guarantee he reached the exact length for maximum performance. It was a master class in excellence where short cuts and second best were unheard of.

This perfection extended to his views on personal safety and what the French, on an associated subject, have called the 'purity of the act'. Thus it is unsurprising, that in 1967, Hasler had proposed that radio transmitters be prohibited in his forthcoming races because calling for help in mid-ocean would bring discredit on the event and that it would be more seemly for the entrant to 'die like a gentleman'. He was not entirely joking, although I suspect the nuances of that statement would be lost on the current generation of single-handed skippers, a good many of whom are less than self-sufficient when accepting transmitted advice on weather, navigation, routing and medical matters. Of course, none of this is bad as technology and communications become more refined – and cheaper – but it is a far cry from Hasler's original dream of self-sufficiency and thus genuine, personal achievement.

Hasler's two races now spawned almost every subsequent single-handed and fully crewed oceanic event. Indeed, the first round-the-world race (the Whitbread) was invented among his round-Britain skippers, myself included, while we sat out a gale in Barra in the Outer Hebrides in 1970. The spirit of those heady, pioneering days lives on in myriad oceanic races but not so with the current 'original single-handed trans-Atlantic race' (as it is now known) because, despite its title, there is little 'original' about the current event, even though it includes a Jester-class. Vessels under 27 feet are no longer allowed to enter and those that do are required to pay a considerable entrance fee. Closer to Hasler's original concept is the more recent annual Jester Challenge for Corinthian vessels under 30 feet in length. This is based on his Series Two race that he had proposed to replace the OSTAR if over-aggressive sponsorship and 'the nannies' skewed his original idea, which they were doing.

HRH Prince Philip succinctly summed up Hasler's achievements when he wrote in 1998:

Anyone with a passing interest in yachts and yachting will have heard of 'Blondie' 'Hasler but…there was more to his life than Tre Sang, Jester, *ocean racing, self-steering gear, junk rig and reefing systems. His lifelong passion was small boats…What became famous as the 'Cockleshell Heroes' raid on German shipping in Bordeaux could only have been conceived and led by someone with a deep understanding of – and faith in – small boats.*

'Blondie' shared the inventor's perception that there must be a better way of doing practical things but he also seemed to be able to conjure original ideas from his restless and far-seeing mind. Add to that, prolific author, portrait painter, cartoonist, musician, gifted amateur hydrographer and diligent searcher for the Lock Ness Monster... [made him] one of the great characters of this century.

I wonder how many of today's yachtsmen, yachtswomen and members of the Special Boat Service have any idea that much of what they now take for granted when they put to sea or don a pair of swim fins and goggles began life on Blondie Hasler's drawing board?

Page from my notebook covering North Falkland Sound and San Carlos Waters drawn in 1978

Chapter 18

Collision Regulations and Single-handed Watchkeeping

There has been much controversy over single-handed sailing and the collision regulations. The following is paraphrased from my book *Blondie* (Leo Cooper, 1998) and encapsulates Hasler's views on the subject.

When writing the biography of Lieutenant Colonel 'Blondie' Hasler (founder of modern, single-handed ocean racing), in one of the appendices I was obliged to discuss his view on watchkeeping while sailing single-handed. This is it:

Watchkeeping when single-handed is an emotional subject, and although, in theory, covered by Rule 5 of the 1972 International Regulations for the Prevention of Collision at Sea, this can be open to subjective interpretation. The rule firmly states:

Every vessel shall at all times maintain a proper lookout by sight and hearing as well as by all available means appropriate in the prevailing circumstances and conditions so as to make a full appraisal of the situation and the risk of collision.

There is no doubt that a single-handed yachtsman cannot, to the letter of the law, keep a proper lookout at all times and thus the business of such ocean races could be brought into question. There continues to be much correspondence on the subject in the nautical press and within such bodies as the Royal Institute of Navigation, and it is not the intention to enter the debate here. However it is appropriate to mention the subject and to offer an interpretation of Blondie's views.

His opinion suggested that Rule 5 was not, purposefully, specific enough for it does not make it clear whether one man is required to be on watch the whole time as a lookout and nothing else, or whether this one man might also be steering, navigating, shaking his relief while also carrying out all the other duties required on the bridge or in the cockpit. 'A proper lookout by sight and sound', he stated by way of example, 'cannot be kept through the windows of a wheelhouse in pouring rain and with internal machinery running.' He then continued by emphasising that an experienced single-hander can maintain full mental and physical efficiency for an unlimited number of days, without ever sleeping for more than twenty minutes at a time. 'Catnaps often for as little as half a minute taken at frequent intervals throughout the twenty-four hour period enable him to deal efficiently with collision risks in congested waters.'

It is also possible for the lone yachtsman to 'keep a lookout' through the use of radar detecting devices that alert him to a ship's radar at, at least, horizon distance. The alarm device on his own radar (should he have one) which every two minutes (if he so set it) switches on, takes a look, and if nothing has changed or no new echo is detected, switches of for another two minutes.

It has often been argued, convincingly, that an experienced single-hander can keep a better lookout from his open, exposed cockpit than can many a steamer's bridge team - often also one man - from the all-too-snug confines of a wheelhouse with other distractions. The heavy reliance on a radar set, on which very few, small yachts show up in a heavy sea or normal ocean swell is unreliable. But it is too easy to become embroiled in an 'us and them' argument when there are plenty of examples on both sides of foolhardiness, crass stupidity and unprofessionalism.

The degree of vigilance which is necessary for a single-hander must, with common sense, be related to the probability of encountering another vessel and in the open ocean a degree of relaxation is justified especially in unrestricted waters where it is the duty of a power-driven vessel to give way to sail - although the 'right of way' vessel also has a legal duty to prevent collision. Nevertheless it would be a foolish yachtsman who relied on that 'let out' clause for his own safety.

Despite not being covered by the law it is, too, recognised, perhaps unofficially that except in the case of the large French entries in two of the single-handed trans-Atlantic races a yacht will cause negligible damage to an ocean-going, power-driven vessel, and consequently the risk to the single-hander is entirely his own affair - and that lay at the heart of Blondie's opinion.

Nevertheless the 'nannies' (as he called them) continue to use the 'proper lookout at all times' argument to support their view that single-handed, ocean sailing should be outlawed. However, for the above and other reasons, the International Association of Institutes of Navigation believes that single-handed ocean racing should not be banned - and there, currently, the situation thankfully, remains.

Chapter 19

Me and My 'Chum'

First published in the Royal Cruising Club's *Roving Commissions* in 1996

Last year *Black Velvet* attempted, once again, to earn her keep with a pelagic trip to the Wilson's Triangle, whose apex is roughly one hundred or so miles to the south-west of the Isles of Scilly. Not for the first time we failed to see the elusive Wilson's petrel but the four-day expedition had given me much thought towards how we should approach the problem next time.

Just a brief reminder, if I may. *Black Velvet*'s primary purpose is to take 'oligers, 'ographers' and 'ologists, of whatever persuasion, to sea in order to study their chosen subject. If, as in this case, they are ornithologists then we are obliged to carry five 4-gallon drums of 'chum' to entice the birds alongside in their hundreds and in a very few minutes. Chum is second-hand fish-and-chip fat in which we suspend the less attractive remains of Plymouth's fish market and this year, as an experiment, we added handfuls of popcorn. 'Chumming' is best conducted in Force 3 or less so we can get the ship to within inches of the birds as they peck at the corn. The offal, we discovered, tends to sink and may well be discarded altogether in the future.

This year the Devon Wildlife Trust (DWT) - with whom I have had a long-standing arrangement - booked us for five weekends of pelagic voyages into the Western Approaches, but sadly (from, I have to admit, the financial point of view) this was cut to just one.

Four 'birders' met us at the Falmouth Yacht Marina after dinner on 8 August. They too had listened to that evening's shipping forecast, prompting the familiar question, 'Is your boat seaworthy?' The fact that she is certificated by the Board of Transport as a commercial sailing vessel did not really satisfy them but knowing that we had GPS did. I didn't have the heart to tell them that we seldom use it as I believe that radar and a sextant are far more useful. Following our first such voyage a year or so ago, the DWT had told me that the 'birders' were not convinced that I knew where we were and thus they could no longer employ me unless I had a GPS. Reluctantly I fitted one.

The well-known West Country yachtsman, Peter Seldon, was crew this year, as son Hamish, was sailing in somebody else's yacht. We sailed at 0500 on 9 August as I wanted to get away in advance of what I knew would be another poor 0555 forecast, in order to be well offshore before the birders knew what was about to hit them. I also planned to get at least one 'chumming' session under our belts (for less exotic inshore birds) in case they decided to cancel. It was important that any such decision came from them and was not seen to be the fault of *Black Velvet* or her afterguard. As the BBC offered winds from the south-west at Force 6, Peter and I knew that we would be in for an interesting time, with a foretaste of what was to come as soon as we cleared the Lizard. Although this year's crew were not sick, as to a man and woman, last year's had been, they were not made of such stern stuff. A cockpit conference was convened.

Peter and I suggested that we should push on towards the Triangle, chumming as we went, before making another decision at dusk. Nevertheless, by sunset our four passengers felt that enough was enough particularly as they had recorded six birds that they had never seen before, at least not closer than half a mile. The consensus was that to flog all night against a rising wind and sea (bad for chumming anyway) on the chance that they might, but only might, see one extra bird – the Wilson's petrel – was not what they were paying for. Actually, I thought it was, but that was not the point. 'Could we,' they asked, 'anchor for the night and come out again in the morning?' This was their decision and Peter and I were happy to accept it. The trouble with the Triangle on a four-day trip is that the whole of the first twenty-four hours is spent getting there, two days are then spent waiting for the 'willies' to turn up (none did last year), and the fourth day is spent rushing back with no time to look at the coastal wildlife or to chum elsewhere.

But already on this voyage we had tabulated thirteen Mediterranean shearwaters, more than twenty Manx shearwaters, one sooty shearwater, fifty-four storm petrels, one Sabine's gull, two great skuas, and the rest, which even I could identify. Late that night we picked up a buoy in the Helford and while the birders discussed the day, Peter and I sat in the cockpit with a whisky and, knowing the morrow would be even worse, devised a foul-weather plan with the hope of selling it to the team below.

One look at the morning's winds and rain convinced even the most ardent that it was an 'estuary day' and so with relief from the afterguard that our paying guests didn't want to cancel altogether, we set off for the relative calm of the Fal, where they immediately photographed little egrets, buzzards, a seal and a heron. I refrained from making shooting gestures towards the heron and the buzzard, both of which have proliferated to the point that neither are welcome at home on the farm; the damage they do to the trout, the pheasant poults and mallard ducklings is dreadful. At the moment the birders were happy and that was what mattered. (Incidentally, I do not shoot the protected birds but nor do I encourage them.)

That afternoon we put the 'crew' ashore while I tidied the boat expecting a disgruntled return. Not a bit of it. We were dealing with enthusiasts and if pelagic birds were out then butterflies were in. They claimed to have photographed a 'clouded white' (usually only found in north America) that had satisfied them beyond my belief and so passed a most pleasant evening at anchor above King Harry Ferry.

A pre-dawn start into a moderate sea but less wind brought us to the third day's first chumming position, ten miles south of the Lizard where we handed the sails. The usual drill is to heave-to and while fore-reaching at a knot or so, pour the chum steadily over the lee rail. When it has spread for a few hundred yards we drift down through the broadening slick and then tack back to repeat the procedure. The slick gets longer and wider as it slowly dissipates and thus less and less attractive – it is of course vegetable oil supplied by the Devon Wildlife Trust itself. We can conduct the whole process under sail but that takes time and, when tacking, means leaving the slick at its edges, much to the birders' frustration so, regrettably, the engine is used.

Even so, there is much jilling around which can look suspicious to other seafarers. So much so that a deep-sea trawler, on whom we had been keeping an eye for she was surrounded by birds, hauled his nets and steamed across. Not knowing his intentions we followed each other's sterns like a pair of dogs so that, in our case, we could keep within his 'flock'. Clearly, he thought we were up to no good for leaflets recently issued to West Country skippers – pleasure and commercial – by Customs and Excise had warned of yachts behaving exactly as we were. Understandably unconvinced that we were studying the feeding habits of seabirds, which was our excuse over Channel 6, the trawler slowly steamed away, but all the while keeping us under surveillance. I am now obtaining a huge code flag Delta ('Keep clear of me for I am manoeuvring with difficulty') unless someone can come up with a two-letter group that more accurately describes our behaviour.

With all chum expended, it was too late for the cliffs. This was a pity for I felt that we had not offered the birders all the possible options but my tales of ravens and peregrine falcons, not to say the Cornish chuff, provoked promises that they would return.

In fact the main lesson of this year is that we should not advertise, specifically, a voyage to the Wilson's Triangle, but instead, a mixture of ocean, cliffs and estuaries depending on the weather - with the occasional butterfly thrown in.

Although this year's birders did not go home empty-handed, I felt at the time that they might have been short-changed, for by coincidence, that was the one weekend of the year when the DWT hires the *Scillonian* (the Isles of Scilly ferry) for a trip to the Triangle. However while we were watching six 'new' species the *Scillionian*'s team had spent observing three Wilson's petrels, at a great distance, and nothing else. Four-hundred cramped, unhappy and very seasick birders had returned to Penzance more than disappointed. Our team, in their letter of thanks and in retrospect, believed that we had had the better deal.

But Peter and I did even better for during our return to Plymouth; we passed between Nare Head and Gull Rock then hove-to to watch six ravens cavorting very close alongside. Neither of us are bird watchers in the accepted sense, but it was all great fun and we had learnt much from the experts about a form of wildlife we tend to take for granted. Our understanding that there is no such animal as a sea gull was confirmed, that the skua is the bullyboy of the oceans is true and that storm petrels love popcorn.

Next year, at long last, *Black Velvet* will be helping another form of 'ologist, for two glaciologist's have agreed to hire her for their work in east Greenland. This is what she was commissioned to do and should be even more fun.

Tussac bogs

Chapter 20

Why Envy the Immortal Gods?

First published in the Royal Cruising Club's *Roving Commission*, 1997

When one has good wine,
A graceful boat,
A maiden's love,
Why envy the immortal gods?

So wrote the Chinese poet Li T'ai Po in the seventh century AD. Despite the maiden's absence I envied nobody this summer – not even the gods – for the truth is I fell in love again, this time with another set of islands, in another hemisphere, but with the same equally capricious, not to say downright eccentric, weather.

In 1993, my third *Black Velvet* was 'strengthened for ice' around the waterline and painted black. I had wanted, rather grandly, a wooden hull but she was moulded in glass reinforced plastic. As much of my youth had been spent varnishing and caulking our Bristol Channel Pilot Cutter *Olga*, the reduced maintenance was welcome, yet tradition remained with the gaff-rig, spruce spars, three sextants, towed Walker log and a hand lead-line. Otherwise *Black Velvet* displaced 12 tons in the 'light' condition, was 42 feet overall (including a 7-feet-long bowsprit) and drew 6 feet, although with 3 tons of climbers' crampons she plunged four and a half inches below her marks. She was briefly commercially certificated, but I now prefer my own views of what constitutes a seaworthy vessel and on what I should spend my limited budget. Also in my view, some of the certificated requirements were downright dangerous while others were totally impractical for such a small vessel.

Her reason for living was to take 'ologers, 'ographers or 'ologists to places they could not otherwise visit, and in this duty she has suffered, patiently, hundreds of hours in the North Atlantic waiting for the elusive Wilson's petrel as ornithologists, sustained only by a mysterious enthusiasm were, simultaneously, being copiously sick while staring through gyrating and too-powerful binoculars.

Then, in 1997, the two-handed race to Iceland was inaugurated, before which I asked a fellow skipper under what burgee she intended sailing, 'None!' she replied, 'Too much weight and windage.' I pointed aloft at my 600 yards of rigging and below at skis, sledges, 210 man days of food and duty-free. She grinned. At least she was fun. Another competitor, prior to the 1999 two-handed round Britain and Ireland race, publicly accused me of 'wasting everyone's time by not entering to win' and if that was not enough, for being 'irresponsibly ignorant' of the tensile strengths of my halyards and sailcloth. She was in her early twenties and I in my mid-fifties with then, over 150,000 miles under my safety harness.

As explained, *Black Velvet* usually plied her trade carrying environmentalists to places they would not otherwise be able to reach. But for nine glorious weeks in 1997 she unexpectedly, took my son Hamish and me to Iceland's uninhabited Vestirdir - a round journey of about 3,500 miles.

We started this odyssey from Plymouth on 7 June in 40 knots of wind, by taking part in the Reykjavik Yacht Club/Royal Western Yacht Club's two-handed race to Iceland, which for us, was a feeder for our main event of that year, which was to land and support a three-man climbing party in Greenland's unsurveyed Depotfjord at 66° 06'N; 35° 45' W. The sea ice or *storis* should have started to thin around June before breaking up with August's heavier seas, but in July 1997 there were 9/10ths of ice guarding the coast throughout the summer.

The mountaineers had wanted to be the first to 'knock-off' three peaks inland from a tributary of the Knud Rasmussen Gletscher that empties into Depotfjord. Studying aerial photographs they had chosen what seemed to be a nearby, promising anchorage from where *Black Velvet* would act as 'base camp'. The approach soundings to the fjord end with a depth of 127 fathoms, 30 miles offshore, from where on in, it was a blank chart - and polar bear country. The climbers had chosen peaks that had not, knowingly, been visited before but as the only chart was suspiciously free of inshore soundings (and, anyway, was on a scale of 1:400,000) the chances for what I call 'impact hydrography' were real.

Preparation for the expected storis was much the same as for any cruise but included poles for fending off ice-flows; a sacrificial, rubber dinghy, a wooden, folding dinghy and, obligatorily, a 12-bore shotgun with polar bear shot that we had to buy in Reykjavik. We also carried a .22 rifle for dogwatch sports rather than for killing.

I had applied for permission to visit Greenland, a procedure that required us to share scientific information and to confirm that my insurance covered reimbursement to the Danish Government of DKK 500,000 in case of rescue.

In strong winds *Black Velvet* sails under jib and triple-reefed main but that heads'l was then un-trustworthy so a new one had been made – and, to prove that I do know, it was of 8.4 oz cloth. We set storm sails or any combination of a reefed main, main tops'l, stays'l, jib, jib tops'l and squares'l, this latter with one row of reefing points.

The engine was overhauled by the Plymouth Sailing School and the wind instruments by Waypoint One. The stern gland was re-packed, the underwater fittings (plus spare propeller) checked, and I fitted four new 90 amp/hour batteries.

The seventeen-day 'first leg' northwards included drifting around the Fastnet before running south-westerly for thirty hours streaming warps and rolling like blazes off the west of Ireland:

11 June, 0615. Wet and windy. NE F. 7. Occasional sea across deck. 0700. F.6–8. Handed jib to deck – wind too strong for furling gear...1000. Sea increasing. Tried to set storm jib but not possible unless in stops. Should have thought of this earlier. Wind gusting F.9. Towing warps. 1200. Noon to noon 149' in wrong direction. Now under bare poles as enough windage with 600 yards of rigging! 12 June. 0415...We are not going to win this race...13 June. Heading for Bantry Bay to wait favourable winds. The aim is to get to Reykjavik with no damage and ready for the next, more difficult, phase of the operation.

We failed to land on Rockall to pay our respects to its temporary inhabitants from Greenpeace and finally motored the last 300 miles in a flat calm, to arrive at a deserted Reykjavik Yacht Club in the pouring rain. This enforced use of the engine was, of necessity, to get us in before the climbers' aeroplane, but we had already, and unwittingly, disqualified ourselves from the race by embarking bananas and a case of Guinness in Bantry Bay. It was here that we had licked a few wounds, including a mutinous Calor gas solenoid which was painstakingly brought to heel by Hamish who, preferring self-help, effected the repair with a few deftly cut slivers of metal from a tin of new potatoes.

The day before the mountaineers arrived in Reykjavik, the meteorological office produced their latest ice charts showing between 6 and 8/10ths of ice to within 60 miles of Iceland's north-west corner and nothing less than 6/10ths to the south of Angmassalik - and from there to Cape Farewell as much as 9/10ths. We always knew it was an optimistic hope that the ice would clear early in the year but now there were distinct signs that it would not clear at all, at least not down to 3 or 4/10ths, the thickest I was prepared to attempt without the danger of becoming 'trapped'.

We were in good company for the French yacht *Nosy Bé* was, too, waiting her chance as Bruno Calle and his lovely companion, Caterine, were heading for Disco Island, off Greenland's west coast to overwinter.

With the climbers aboard and accepting that Depotfjord by sea was out we adjourned to the nearby very Irish pub, to agree, that as we now had a week free, it would be better to spend it sailing; if not to Depotfjord then at least as far as the ice, to take some 'macho shots' alongside a flow or two. After that, the climbers would fly to Kulusuk (Angmassalik's nearest airport) and thence to the icecap by helicopter. Stores (including our massive 27-feet-long squares'l yard) that we would not now need as depot ship, were landed and we took our departure for the Arctic Circle and the *storis* at 0800 on 3 July. In a wonderful quartering sea we sailed towards Snæfulsness Peninsula, slipping easily into *Black Velvet*'s idiosyncratic watchkeeping system whose aim is to ensure corporate harmony through three periods in every 24 hours when all are on watch during the natural divisions between night and day, forenoon and afternoon. Nobody felt cheated of sleep while we usually celebrated some spurious event with a tot.

Unfortunately Iceland's weather is no less tormenting than the English Channel's. As the wind veered to the north-west - our course - and increased beneath an angry and lowering cloud base, pierced by the very tip of the silhouetted Stapafell volcano, two of the three climbers succumbed. The third, a Royal Navy doctor and long-standing friend who did not wish to climb alone, asked that we find some shelter - preferably about 500 miles up a fjord! While I silently debated this request, the scene reminded me chillingly of a Hitchcock film: everything - sea, sky and land - was painted in a wide variation of the colour grey.

In fact I chose Grindavik, east of the notorious Reykjanes headland, despite no charts on a scale less than 1:300,000 and the knowledge that the port was closed, except one hour either side of high water due to dredging. We turned and ran downhill, rolling hideously which seemed to suit the mountaineers, who now began calling for soup, then encouragingly, for brandy.

As we approached to one and a half miles off Reykjanes's rocks in an onshore, near gale, the linkage 'twixt wheel and rudder came adrift; at least that is what Hamish, on watch at the time, assumed. He woke me with the quiet but urgent news: 'Don't tell the climbers but I think we have a bit of a situation!'

The naval doctor, sharing the watch, looked on while Hamish with commendable composure rigged the emergency tiller as though it was a minor dog-watch evolution. With rather less tranquillity (out-of-sight and not having to pretend otherwise), I scrabbled around a never-visited portion of the bilges, abaft the engine, with a torch in my teeth trying to see what had happened and once established, looking for the absent nut and washer.

Happily the dreaded cape missed its opportunity, and shortly afterwards we were able to enter Grindavik's marvellous bolthole under the precise guidance of the harbourmaster on the foreshore with his handheld VHF. The Blue Lagoon's sulphurous waters, two monkfish bartered for three cans of Tesco beer, and one day of enforced idleness while the winds moderated, had even the climbers itching to return to sea. We still had time to use up so the next Time Passing Measure was a visit to Hvalfjordhur – Whale Fjord – where the Second World War naval base, HMS *Baldu III* (for the forming of Arctic convoys) can still be visited at Hvitness and where Hamish and the doctor slept ashore on the 'haunted' island of Hvammsey (64°22'.5N, 21°33'.2W). We lay to 70 feet of cable off Hvammsvik's north-western beach drinking whisky through a still, almost sunlit, midnight.

By 0600 the wind had shifted through 180° and was now onshore. While we still had plenty of water, soundings suggested we should sail, or at least shift our anchorage, before the ebbing half tide. I hoisted the Blue Peter for the shore party to return. Two further defects now manifested themselves; the gear box would not engage 'ahead' and the windlass's innards jammed. Unlike the gas solenoid and the steering linkage, neither was a serious problem for we had a light breeze – although our arrival back in Reykjavik might be delayed – and five pairs of strong arms. Once out into the main fjord, the wind, as perverse as ever, changed again forcing us to beat the twenty or so miles. In fact, with the propeller trailing at about 3 knots the gear box did engage, and so despite the absence of the expected Force 5 from astern, we were able to make our ETA.

Hamish mended the windlass – better than before – by drilling a deeper recess for a retaining pin (clearly a design fault), and thanks to an obliging insurance company, a spare part for the gearbox was flown in the next day from

Germany. We had prodded some unfortunate creature on the way up the fjord while the engine idled, in gear, as the batteries were charged. At the time I had thought nothing of it, except to acknowledge a slight nudge and change in pitch that had lasted a few seconds. I hope the denizen's wound healed as quickly as our machine. With the earlier collapse of the self-steering motor (a sealed-for-life component), that too was replaced via airmail and under guarantee, these were our only defects Plymouth to Plymouth. We carried a spare propeller, but thankfully, never needed it.

Incidentally, we never listened to a forecast; sailing when prudent and anchoring when we felt otherwise. Our experience was, that if in doubt about an anchorage and the likelihood of williwaws, we would head offshore where, although the winds could be strong, there was seldom much weight to the seas.

We arrived back at the Reykjavik Yacht Club on 8 July. The climbers flew the next day, and after repairs, the two of us were free to set off once more for the *storis*. By 12 July we had just ten days before rendezvousing with the shore party down from their Greenland hills, exchanging their kit, putting them on an aeroplane home and restowing for our journey to the Faeroes. This was not long to achieve the new aim, which was to sail to the ice-edge 'for trials' before accepting the challenge in the RCC Pilot: '*There are six fjords to the east of Skutulsfjordur, shown without soundings...*' They would make interesting exploring.

At midnight we again approached the Snæfulsness icecap, around which Hamish had walked during our first weekend in Iceland as a form of recce, should we need to put in to Arnastapi on the south coast or Olasvik on the north. Magnificent in the last of the dying sun's rays (or first of the rising sun's?) and soft breezes - how the climbers would have enjoyed this - while to port and starboard, whales breached amid pink and white depth charges of spray.

The next day we were becalmed and while supposedly in a hurry, it was too beautiful a day to allow Mr Perkins to disturb it, so Hamish fished for cod; we had steaks for lunch, fish cakes for supper and pâté until Reykjavik! That evening (Sunday 13 July) we were again crashing along in a Force 4 north-easter, which (apart from the fine, freezing drizzle) was perfect for the nearest reported ice north-west of Vestfirdir.

Now the wind-chill factor crept below freezing for the first time and as we approached the line at 24° 50'W it was time to brief King Neptune on his latest recruit, lying off-watch below. The King and His retinue (always with a capital 'H' in honour of his status) board ships when they cross the equator, or the Arctic or Antarctic Circles, to enrol newcomers to His watery kingdom. Without such endorsement, written on an elaborate scroll, a sailor who falls overboard will be easy prey to sharks and whales. So at the precise moment (17.23) Hamish was woken by the foghorn. Leaping to the hatch he found nobody in the cockpit but a bearded and bedraggled (more than was intended) Lord of the Seven Seas (impersonated by the skipper) climbing up from the bobstay clutching a bottle of rum and a scroll; unfortunately the trident didn't make it onto the foredeck. As a first-timer to the Arctic Hamish was, at least, spared the usual indignities that normally attend such occasions!

Once suitably enrolled, and after His Majesty's blessing and departure, we agreed that *Black Velvet* should continue for the ice. Obligingly, a wonderful example of 'iceblink' now lined the western horizon with three, upside-down icebergs suspended in it. Beautiful though these were, it was clear it would still take considerable time to reach them through the *storis*, and with a beat back, this meant less time for exploring. The unsurveyed fjords beckoned more strongly and we tacked round for Isafjardhardjup (66°15'N, 23°15W).

The wind chill had dropped to -20°C but we had the right clothes while we kept the cabin at the outside, ambient temperature. Only when peacefully at anchor would we have any form of artificial heating to warm the saloon - and we were better off for that ruling.

Isafjardhardjup is easy to enter and with such beguiling beauty it's not always so easy to leave. Beyond its safe, 12-mile-wide entrance exists a variety of scenery, a glacier, a small, spotless town for provisions, wildflowers in great profusion, seals, swans, red phalarope - and the rest. It is not unknown for it to be iced-up in winter (a few years before one hungry polar bear walked ashore here) and has nine and a half uncharted fjords leading off it, including those mentioned in the RCC pilot.

Deciding to visit Isafjordur (66°03'N,23°07'W) before setting off for the unknown we anchored at 0715 on 14 July in 30 feet to the west of the town, having motored the last mile or so through the narrow passage between the *eyri* (the terminal moraine on which much of the town is built) and the eastern side. The bottom here was thick mud and excellent holding ground, although it is also sheltered and unaffected by any swell, sea or passing wash. Hamish took the washing ashore - a chore he relished (twice) once he discovered that the laundry maid was young, blonde and even by Iceland's high standards, very attractive - and we sailed the next morning having taken on no provisions but doubly complete with clean clothes!

All around, mist-shrouded, cloud-bisected mountains of great grandeur towered over their fjords, benign looking, but doubtless capricious, while the mythological Greek god of the winds, *Aeolus*, rejoiced with us as we set all five fair-weather sails to catch the zephyrs towards Isafjardhardjup's northern shore in blazing - yes blazing - sunshine. The south-eastern fjords mentioned in the pilot had taken second place to those that lead off Jokulfjord, itself an offshoot of Isafjardhardjup. We were bound instead for first Leirufjödur and the Drangajokul glacier, before attempting to survey Hrafnsfjordur, Lonafjordur and the upper reaches of Veioileysufjordur. As we turned for Leirufjödur's entrance the water turned milky from Drangajokull's meltwaters reducing the underwater visibility to nil. This was a pity, for the entrance is guarded by a terminal moraine along which (as we soon discovered) are dotted huge house-sized rocks.

Although preferring to anchor we picked up onc of two lonely mooring buoys to see if they were suitable; by their size and well-kept appearance they were. That evening Hamish walked ashore to the western edge of the Drangajokull - a longer walk than he anticipated - and returned after midnight clean from a shower beneath a fall of meltwater. Later we were to be told that the glacier has actually advanced over 2,000 feet in the last three years; global warming has yet to reach Vestirdir.

The next day we sailed first for Lonafjordur (66°16'N, 22°33'W) for no other reason than it has the prettiest shape. Safely across the bar on a three-part transit chosen from the chart we continued on this course until just short of the Lonanupur peninsula.

With no soundings to guide us we initiated a routine for the future. Hamish sat at the chart table with the radar's 'distance off' cursor switched on, the echo sounder calibrated to the waterline, the tide tables for Reykjavik, a matrix of tidal differences, and a blank piece of paper. On deck I moved *Black Velvet* forward in a series of short slow bursts with one of the two dinghies alongside loaded with the 'armed' lead line and a 10-feet sounding pole. The mains'l was hoisted with two reefs, regardless of how little wind there might be, to allow for any sudden williwaw and the jib (the stays'l was too low-cut for any forward visibility) was ready for instant furling on the modern Wykham-Martin with an endless line.

About one hundred soundings later we had circumnavigated the fjord as close as we could to its edges (even closer in the dinghy) and established five good-looking anchorages. It was the end of a wonderful, fulfilling day as we headed back down our transit - safely negotiated - into Leirufjödur. The reason for returning rather than staying at anchor elsewhere was a very sparky and attractive German girl (plus her boyfriend and kayak) to whom we had made a promise. We would act as safety craft while they explored the fields of flowers before lifting them to Hesteyrarfjordur (66° 20'N, 22°49'W) and the summer foot ferry to Isafjordur and their motor car.

The next morning we sailed for the upper reaches of Veioilsufjordur (66°20'N, 22°40'W) to find two useful anchorages, before giving Hrafnsfjordur. (66° 15'N, 22° 26'W) the same treatment. Ironically, we did not survey our base fjord as carefully for on our fourth pass and with three feet below the keel registering on the echo sounder, we hit a rock in the entrance.

An unexpected mist had, within about 30 seconds, obscured the distant transit marks on our approach, and coupled with an almost certain (but previously untabulated) magnetic anomaly on the moraine, we had swung, unknowingly, in a gentle arc to starboard. As soon as were off, by both of us swinging out to port on the end of the boom, Hamish took the dinghy ahead, and over the obstruction with the sounding pole. When the mist cleared it was obvious that we were about 1 cable off the transit, but not quite as far to the east as the rock marked on the chart. All this indicates that the deepest part of the bar is very narrow; probably further west and, like the back of a dragon, has peaks and troughs along much of its length. I suggest a certain amount of luck is needed to pass over a trough.

Hrafnsfjordur was another unknown quantity which we had entered against a cold, easterly wind, lowering visibility and occasional driving, bitter drizzle. It was also very late in the day after hours of close navigation (and another spectacular example of impact hydrography) since dawn. We were both tired, and perhaps should not have entered the fjord at all, although the sail back out was most exhilarating. Apart from the enticing lack of charted soundings, it is not really an interesting fjord.

An abiding impression was the lack of jetsam and only the occasional piece of flotsam - usually at the tops of the fjords where a tree trunk might be beached. Among other memories are the thousands of ice patches across the slopes and mountains representing every possible shape - many beautiful, some erotic, others accurate in their impression of a country or a well-known figure (Paddington Bear was particularly lifelike!) - all making fixing rather more easy and fun. One of the great joys was switching off the GPS and relying, more accurately, on visual observations, the radar, the sounding lead and pole, the dinghy and Hamish's horizontal sextant angles.

Having dropped the kayakers to a lament on Hamish's pipes at Hesteryi, we reluctantly sailed for the south, calling first at the dying village of Flatyeyri (66° 02'. N, 23°31'W) in Onundarfjodir, just for fun - and water. Hamish (whose second name is Patrick) had his 24th birthday on 21 July so we pushed quickly on to Patreksfjordur to celebrate there. On our way in, well after midnight, we stuck our nose into Vatneyri's noisome inner harbour and were quickly driven out by the smell. We had not planned to stop anyway, so in a flat calm we motored to the very head of Osafjordur, passing beautiful sand dunes to starboard. Here we lay to our anchor in what was, without doubt, the most stunning haven of them all.

The next morning, after Hamish's birthday shower beneath the seven-stepped waterfall, we held our noses and refuelled in Vatneyri while I baked my first (and last) chocolate birthday cake. It was not a success! Having telephoned home, we managed, quite without planning, to exchange a one-litre bottle of duty-free whisky for fifty-three gallons of diesel using only my four Icelandic words - *Tak* (thank you), *Nei* (no), *Jao* (yes) and Whisky (let's have a party). Quite who lost out I'm not sure. We achieved an amazing bargain; the tanker driver was ecstatic and the amount of fuel was less than his monthly spillage allowance. In truth, we had offered a credit card but the driver had 'forgotten his machine'!

Making, sadly, for Reykjavik, we sailed into the thickest of fogs off Blakknes and an increasing southerly wind. By the time we were 'on finals' the next day, the approach was out of the question and so sought a perfect spot off the hamlet of Alfsnes (66°11'N,22°46'W) where we anchored at 0140 on 23 July to both the Admiralty Pattern and CQR anchors. In one gust of about 55 knots we even went full astern on the engine just to test the bottom and as we didn't move an inch slept soundly without standing anchor watches.

By 0800 the wind had moderated a little, allowing us to enjoy a cracking sail into Reykjavik harbour where we moored, for the last time, among the RYC's friendly yachts. Due to an unscheduled recall to England, my part was now over and on 26 July I left *Black Velvet* in Hamish's hands, happy that he would look after her impeccably. He did and to drive the point home, arrived in Plymouth at the precise hour that we agreed - without a blemish and in time for the next crew of whale-watchers the following day.

I said at the beginning that I envied nobody, but during my last evening in Reykjavik, two maidens (plus two men) had joined *Black Velvet* from England. Before them lay the Westmanyear Islands in glorious sunshine, the Faeroes in mist, a landing on Sula Sgeir in thick fog, Corryvrecken, drying out alongside in Whitehaven to offload the fifteen pairs of climbing boots, Howth and the Helford. As I left at 0400 to catch my flight home I envied them all.

Chapter 21

L'homage à Éric Tabarly, 1998

It is arguable that without Blondie Hasler's Single-handed Transatlantic race, the name of Éric Tabarly would not have sprung to prominence in the international sailing world. Thus France would have been denied the discovery of a new national sport in which she continues to dominate. Certainly Blondie considered Éric's win in the second Observer Single-handed Transatlantic Race (OSTAR) vital for the future of his races, epitomising as it did, precisely what it was that he wanted his races to achieve. The twin, crowning glories as far as Blondie was concerned, were that Éric was a Frenchman and that he had designed *Pen Duick* especially for the race.

Shortly after the start of the 1998 Blondie-invented, two-handed round Britain race, we learnt of Éric's death off the Welsh coast from his beautiful, one-hundred-year-old Fifer - another *Pen Duick*. By coincidence, *Black Velvet* was sheltering in the Helford waiting for the tide and wind to turn favourable when the news came through, and while this was not in itself a reason for abandoning the race, other factors combined to ensure that when we did eventually make the Lizard we kept on heading south. Camaret was our first port of call to purchase a French courtesy ensign - left ashore in preference for an Irish tricolour - and to grab a glance at the local press, from which we learned that a memorial service for Éric Tabarly would be held in the Rade de Brest on Sunday 21 June. This meant a four-day wait in the area but it was an occasion that we felt it was our duty to attend. Éric had been an honorary member of the Royal Western Yacht Club (RWYC) so a telephone call confirmed that we should represent the Club afloat.

In the event, *Black Velvet* was the only British yacht present in the Anse de Poulmic. Having deciphered the instructions and charts from the local papers, we anchored, as instructed, off the *Ecole Naval de Lanveoc-Poulmic*'s esplanade under the Royal Cruising Club's burgee. Now we had to fashion a RWYC burgee (also, to my shame, left behind) out of a predominantly blue Missions to Seaman's pennant long ago presented by the Rev Donald Peyton Jones. Peter Seldon and I were pretty certain PJ would not mind the transformation his pennant was to undergo, with blue, felt-tipped pen, a cut up and stitched in place white handkerchief for the 'crown', typewriter erasing fluid and yellow and red dye markers! The result, though I say it myself, was very impressive, and at the mast head, looked as good as the real thing. (It currently hangs in the RWYC's clubhouse.)

It was a stunningly beautiful day and a day of great emotional pride for the French people. President Chirac with Jacqueline Tabarly and her daughter began the ceremonies at eleven o'clock with a simple but huge open-air mass for invited guests ashore, conducted by the Bishop to the French Armed Forces. Loudspeakers conveyed the service to the many yachts anchored close offshore, among which, in impressive but ghostly silence, the French Navy's twin tops'l schooners, *L'Etoille* and *La Belle Poule* in company with Éric's *Pen Duicks II* and *VI* tacked, reached and ran in the light zephyrs. No motors were allowed for, as the newspapers had ordered us, 'Nobody drives a motor bicycle through a church'.

Shortly after noon, the VIPs were transferred by presidential barge through the huge fleet, further offshore, of all shapes, sizes, rigs and means of propulsion, to embark in the destroyer *De Grasse*. Ensigns were lowered in salute as she sounded her mournful siren to begin a lengthy silence, during which only the lapping of bow waves from over 500 vessels could be heard as they stemmed the tide astern of the destroyer's crowded quarterdeck – from which numerous wreaths and bouquets of flowers were strewn to drift rather poignantly through the fleet.

A six-gun salute ended the formal ceremonies and was the signal for thousands of men, women and children, who unrehearsed and unplanned, now been manning yards and decks in silence, before breaking out their sails for an impromptu sail past along the warship's starboard side, watched by the family and official mourners. The gentle airs, as though part of the schedule, quickly developed into a useful, stiff breeze.

Black Velvet had played her part, and after numerous television interviews conducted with some difficulty over the taffrail to microphones held on the ends of boat hooks, we took off for the open sea at nearly our maximum speed, once more under the RCC's distinctive burgee. The only Blue Ensign had been appreciated and much remarked upon by the French press.

The whole day was, as Monday's French papers claimed, *Le Testement d'un Marine Legende*. We were proud to have represented not only Éric's British yacht club but, as it had turned out, the British yachting community as a whole. For Peter and me the beauty and significance were emphasised by the modesty of the arrangements: an attribute in perfect harmony with the great seaman of our age (because of his humility, probably the greatest of our age) that we had all come to honour.

Chapter 22

High Latitude Meandering - and a Bothersome Return Home

What follows is the basis of an illustrated lecture given to the Royal Yacht Squadron in 2001.

Even cruising should have a purpose and meandering is not one of them; at least, that was my view until the summer of 2001.

'Hearing of other people's gales is boring.' Actually one's own gales can be pretty boring if the vessel is well-found, the crew fit, competent, not sick, and vitally, there is plenty of sea room and nobody else to get in the way. There is often not much that one can do until conditions moderate (I'm talking about cruising), other than go below for a gin, or snuggle in a corner of the cockpit with a good book and a pipe. Paradoxically, calms, by their frustrating effect on one's sanity, can be less attractive than a full-blown blast, and for that reason I have often advocated that the BBC should issue light-wind warnings as well as those for gales: *Now attention all shipping, there are warnings of calms in the following sea areas....*

My son-in-law, Rolfe Oostra, was a 'known' Australian climber who started life as a Dutchman, and with my daughter (a diver and underwater photographer) then established 'Double O Explorations' (now '360 Expeditions') whose aim was to film adventures in seldom-visited places.

With the approach of a sixtieth birthday and after thirty-two 'gap years' with the Royal Marines - often in open boats, in the Norwegian Arctic, in winter - it had been my intention to head south at last, but *Black Velvet*'s reason for existence was to take 'ologers, 'ologists and 'ographers to places that they could not afford to reach, or simply, to where there was no alternative transport.

During the austral spring of 2000 in Byron Bay - the hippy capital of Australia where I felt strangely at home - Rolfe and I discussed the world's out-of-the-way places and concluded that Double O Explorations' first film should be a reasonably simple adventure, conducted from within our own resources. *Black Velvet*, the ideal platform for this inaugural attempt, was offered and accepted before we had even decided the destination. However, the east coast of Greenland was eventually chosen, for I possessed the charts and aerial photographs from a previous attempt to land climbers into Depotfjord at 66° 06N; 35° 45 W.

Thus at 1020 on the morning of 4 June 2001, *Black Velvet* slipped from her Plymouth moorings with 'four souls on board'. Three were Australians – under thirty and unversed in the ways of a small ship at sea. Rolfe had gathered Marcus (climber and cameraman) and Dave (climber and crocodile breeder in Queensland, but crocodile hunter in Zimbabwe). Nick (an English climber) would join in Reykjavik. The only serious expenses had been three months of food and duty free. We also carried a broadcast-standard camera, pulks, ice axes, ropes, crampons, firearms and polar bear ammunition (to be bought in Reykjavik). The ship was down on her marks by the expected four and a half inches and all was well.

As is my custom with a new crew, the first night at sea was spent at anchor off Looe, following a day of safety drills and instructions. The climbers were quick learners, strong and resourceful – but I cooked the first meal just to set the culinary standards.

It is bad manners to sail past Ireland without calling in, and as Dingle seemed the natural point of departure for Iceland, we made a short detour to see Fungi – the very male dolphin – and a number of other friends more able to join us for a whisky. With some strength of will we stayed just the one night and were soon charging through the Blaskets with a following breeze, a clear sky and a plan to climb Rockall from the dinghy. However, as we lunged through that rock's surrounding bright-azure waters, bad weather, deeper into the Atlantic, forestalled our amphibious aspirations with a vanguard of deep swells. Instead, we sailed close enough to study almost every handhold up a crack that diagonally bisects the east-facing cliff.

We started the cruise with a Force 9 and we ended it with a Force 9, and a thoroughly unpleasant, 20-mile thrash towards Reykjavik against cold, steep, breaking seas with windage from *Black Velvet*'s 600 yards of rigging not helping. The alternative would have been to heave-to or run seawards but the crew, anxious to stretch their crampons, rejected the idea and I gave in. We were welcomed by two customs officers who considered three visits necessary to sample the bonded stores, and who then complained that I had locked away too much… and gave me permission to break the seal they had attached in the first place. They let us turn-in at 0430, more tired than had we remained at sea.

As soon as the customs-induced hangover had been slept-off, we plugged into the internet via the Reykjavik Yacht Club's computer. Icelandic weather forecasts are of little more use than a sea-eagle with vertigo, but the ice reports are accurate and constantly updated. Nevertheless, the news was bad and no matter how much spin we put on things, nor how much index error we applied, it would be good luck that would get us through the sea ice, or storis, to the Greenland coast and not bad luck that would keep us away. As a week's delay would do no harm, the climbers decided to practice on Iceland's highest peaks, while I transformed *Black Velvet*'s cabins (aka an Australian student squat) back to civilisation, before plotting and re-plotting the ice edge and the individual icebergs reported to be beset in it. At one stage the pack was within 20 miles of the north-west corner of Iceland and from there to the Greenland coast it was as thick as 9/10ths. There were often even early in the season – a series of leads along the coast but still separated from the open ocean by some two or three hundred miles of impenetrable *storis*.

The east Greenland storis usually starts to melt northwards from Cape Farewell by the end of July, but it can break early to form polynyas, yet this is often a false dawn for it can just as easily be blown back inshore – and there lies the danger for a small sailing vessel. It is best to wait for the permanent melt.

Time for Plan B. Forget Depotsund, the climbers would fly into Angmmassalik. To help us in the decision-making, Jõn (Commodore of the Reykjavik Yacht Club), introduced us to Olav Haraldson (Member of Parliament for the Progressive Party), and his son Harald – a remarkable team that had completed the only unsupported, father and son walk to the South Pole. Harald had also completed a solo, unsupported walk to the North Pole and a crossing of the Greenland icecap. Understanding the financial implications of near-penniless mountaineers flying to Angmmassalik, they pointed out that to get to any half-decent (and preferably unconquered peaks) a vastly expensive helicopter flight inland would also be necessary. 'Had we considered a Plan C?' they wondered.

If not, our distinguished visitors suggested that we should forget southern Greenland – all the nearer peaks had been climbed anyway – and look further north. Round the saloon table we pondered this while the Icelanders, both on mobile telephones, dialled furiously and I swear that at one point they included each other on a five-way conference call.

We hadn't considered a Plan C but that was now the chosen option. For marginally more money, Icelandair would lift the team to Scoresbysund (the largest fjord in the world), from where it could be pulled into the Liverpool

Range of largely unclimbed peaks by dog and sledge teams – and these obvious attractions won the day. The flight dates would give them the opportunity to practice on Iceland's highest mountain (7,000+ feet) while I sat, blissfully alone (and no longer in an overcrowded Aussie-style squat!) for a few days, in Reykjavik's alternating cold fog and warm sunshine.

This decision threw up one or two extra administrative details. First, we had been joined by a fourth climber, Nick Curtis-Raleigh, another wiry, superbly fit English mountaineer, and by another yachtsman, Fergus Kemlo, who was a jovial, Tigger-type character. He would have helped man the ship, had we remained in the logistic support role. The Scoresbysund option now gave me time to survey the five remaining uncharted fjords of north-west Iceland. (In 1997 my son, Hamish and I 'did' the penultimate batch of four.) Secondly, Harald's perceived wisdom confirmed the need for heavier shot for the 12-bore, for a greater chance of a first-time kill against a polar bear and the nearly as dangerous musk ox which roam Scoresbysund's hinterland. Thirdly, there were no land maps available in Iceland that covered the expedition's new area. But a visit to the local chart depot allowed for some rough forward-planning. Fourthly we needed to reassess the food (carried from England) which we would need to land for what had become a three week, (now) unsupported expedition.

As it happened, Fergus was suddenly offered a journalistic job in London that required him to fly back almost before he had arrived. So, once the climbing team of four had flown, I was on my own again and happy for that. But – and it was a significant 'but' – single-handed surveying of uncharted areas is one thing in calmer tropical climates, but among Iceland's fjords, with a dodgy echo sounder, even dodgier steering gear and unreliable weather forecasts, it was quite a different matter.

Plans A and B had allowed for two weeks ashore for the mountaineers with *Black Velvet* in reasonably close proximity. But now, I for one was glad that I would not be living for this extended time on pot noodles, pasta, porridge and Mars Bars. So, just to rub it in, I re-stocked the fridge with the only food that could almost be regarded as cheap – smoked salmon – and pondered my immediate future.

Although I could make the nearest of the north-western fjords single-handed in forty-eight hours or so of hard, sleepless, coastal sailing, it would be more fun and I would probably visit more places, with a companion. Two telephone calls later and Mark – a retired Royal Navy friend of mine – was on his way from Kent with the simple instruction to bring newspapers and whiskey. After a welcoming pint of Guinness in the distinctly un-Icelandic pub, The Dubliner, we sailed on 12 July into light winds to negotiate the numerous patches of 'magnetic variations are reported here' that guard the north-western approaches to Reykjavik. Our first landfall was off Malarif and Svötuloft, dominated by the twin peaks of the Snaefulsness icecap and the ominous-looking extinct volcano of Stapafell.

During the crossing we were entertained by a school of white-sided dolphins and watched numerous whales breaching, but it was slow process with our destination never seemingly drawing any closer. Visible for 60 miles, it took a long time to reach Stapafell's shadow. Now the winds were kinder to us in strength if not in direction, and with short breaking seas, it was important to keep our eyes peeled for the bergy-bits and growlers that can lie many miles downwind of icebergs. The western horizon was clear with occasional hints of iceblink but no sign of the three icebergs reported to be about 30 miles off the coast. I called a coast radio station to be told that the bergs had, unusually, reached so far across the Denmark Strait that they had left the south-going East Greenland Current and joined the warmer Irminger Current which travels north and east around the top of Iceland. If we wanted a photocall of *Black Velvet* among those white, unstable cliffs we were into a stern chase and one we would probably not win, so we began to meander.

As Mark had never sailed north of the Arctic Circle, we decided to head for the nearest ice edge, aiming to cross the Circle at about 24° 40' W. It was cold now, with a wind-chill in the −20°Cs and spray to match. *Black Velvet* has two heating systems but I refused to use either at sea, relying instead on a single candle to take the chill off the saloon. Only when at anchor – and expecting to be so for more than two hours – will I switch on the warmth and thus avoid sweating when below to be followed by frostbite on deck.

At the appropriate moment King Neptune came on board via the bobstay, clutching a bottle of rum, and once Mark had obtained the mandatory permission to enter Neptune's icy domain, the monarch retraced His steps leaving us free to meander 'without let or hindrance through' His watery kingdom.

As His visit had had us both on deck, we took the opportunity of this chance encounter to initiate a planning conference. Hove-to for half an hour (suddenly, like sailing on silk) we savoured our monarch's generous offering while studying the charts. Though the ice edge was only a day's sailing away the attractions of deserted fjords were more compelling in the time available. I had visited the fjords that lead off the north side of Isafjardardjup – the Jökulfirdir –

during an earlier voyage, and anyway, they were now upwind. So we let the sails draw for Sugandafjördhur, but not yet in need of human company, simply took a sample of the anchorage's seabed (fine, volcanic grit) and eased the sheets for Onundarfjördhur – the next fjord south where I had once spent a peaceful night. We put our nose in far enough to get a feel for the place and headed onwards. I had never visited Dyrafjördur, but as the chart showed a tantalising blank patch at its head, we swung gently south-east and equidistant between the stunning, towering, crater rims and vast hanging valleys that line each side and headed for the twin, pyramid peaks standing sentinel above the opposing bank of the upper reaches. It was, I remarked in the log, perfection.

On the south coast of this steep-sided fjord nestles the small, trading village of Thingeyri and its tiny, enclosed harbour which, despite exchanging waves with two very pretty girls, we bypassed, (honestly!) so that *Black Velvet* could enter, once again, her uncharted element and allow me to write, '*Damn the nannies who tell me it is irresponsible to sail in unsurveyed waters – for who will rescue you when you hit a rock?', is their dank opinion. Who indeed! And if nobody had done it in the first place, we would still be standing on a river bank wondering why on earth we had hollowed out our tree trunk.*

We surveyed as far as the depths allowed. Despite having been repaired in Reykjavik, the echo sounder was again useless, yet the armed lead line gave us a much more accurate reading, and of course, a proper feel for the bottom, which seemed to have a large number of house-sized boulders littering it. We didn't drop the huge Admiralty Pattern anchor that I use in such places, but eventually drifted back towards the open sea via a final wave to the shore-side attractions. (You still have to believe me!)

A gaze through the binoculars at Arnarfjördur suggested nothing interesting, so we scudded southwards, cutting across a viscous and sudden easterly gale under triple-reefed main and small jib. On then to Patreksfjördur, one of the most peaceful, safe and beautiful of Iceland's north-western fjords. Summer weather is never bad – or good – for long, and this previously visited fjord did not disappoint, for soon the remote, windswept sand dunes opened up to starboard. Ahead lay tall, steep mountain slopes; some nurturing the last of the winter snows, others decked in a profusion of wildflowers and green grasses waving a welcome – Mexican-style – above the shoreline.

Waterfalls cascaded. The wind gusted to Force 6. The wind died. The wind blew from the west and from the east. The sun set and the sun rose in one movement, and at 0200 on 17 July we moored to a fishing vessel in Vatneyri on the fjord's northern coast and slept.

Patreksfjördur, as it likes to be called (after its host fjord) is a busy village that exists for no purpose other than fishing, but one where the inhabitants are friendly to rare visitors. To prove it, I was summoned ashore by an elderly gentleman who spoke no English but who indicated that, in celebration of the first British yacht to lie alongside one of his trawlers, I was to choose as many turbot as I wished from a fish box.

This new day was ideal for a drift further inland while a cod lay gently poaching in white wine. One of the turbot would wait until supper. Patreksfjördur opens into an expanse of protected water with steep hills to the north and gentle plains and dunes to the south. It is true that the winds here can whistle down the mountainsides but the ice in the upper reaches has usually melted by high summer, and the 'katabatics' are less in evidence than further north.

Mark's father had served in Arctic convoys and had spoken often of Hvalfjördur where they had formed up, so we decided to push on southwards for the remains of the stone frigate, HMS *Baldur III*, which lie towards the top of 'whalefjord'; a passage enlivened by head winds and driving drizzle that had Mr Perkins taking a lengthy watch. Although benign-looking when compared to others, and with no local icecap or snowfields, Hvalfjördur, with its sudden and lengthy squalls, has a cantankerous reputation. Now, with dark storm clouds, heavy with water, tumbling dramatically down the slopes, we decided to frap all sails and motor the whole length. Little remains of the naval base except a crumbling jetty and, back from the beach, piles of stones. We circled where once picket boats and supply barges had lumbered 'tween shore and ships, and we imagined, with ease, the fjord full of fussy escort corvettes, busy destroyers, important cruisers and slow, ponderous, brave merchant ships. Those had been terrible days and with the weather matching our sombre mood, we decided not to spend the night in that foreboding place, but to head for Reykjavik – which we reached at 0730 after a cracking sail.

Next day the climbers returned in time for a celebratory dinner that I had fixed in advance. The retired gunboat *Thor*, scourge of the Royal Navy in the Cod Wars of the 1970s, and now a friendly restaurant, lay half a cable from *Black Velvet*'s berth.

Good bet! The climbers had arrived back exactly as planned, giving them time for a shower before being led the few yards to *Thor*. As their only food for the previous weeks had been, pasta, dry porridge mixed with melted snow, and milk powder followed by Snickers bars, the sight of a pre-laden table – with chairs – was serious stuff. *Thor*'s chef had worked marvels across four courses of turbot (courtesy of *Black Velvet* being befriended by the Patreksfjordhur fisherman), a selection of smoked and cured Icelandic fish and meats, roast puffin for the main course, and a pudding whose details I forget (it was getting on in the evening), except that it, too, was very rich. There had not been one inch of spaghetti in sight.

Eventually, we all, including the cook and waitresses, returned to *Black Velvet*'s cabin and the port decanter to enjoy a number of extras for all had been entranced, not only by the climbers' charms, but also by their endeavours. It was time to drag out the charts and listen in awe.

The shore party had climbed seven peaks, most of which they believed to have been previously unvisited, and had returned in good order, clutching hours of video tape with which they hoped to establish themselves as documentary film makers of the earth's wilder places. They had landed on Constable Point's rough airstrip (20 nautical miles inside Hurry Inlet) and then transferred via helicopter to the settlement of Scoresbysund itself, from where they trekked northwards towards the mountains that make up Roscoe Bjerge and Liverpool Land. Seven peaks surrendered to their ice axes, many of which, they believe, had not succumbed before – the highest being 4,840 feet above sea level – and they had climbed each from just about sea level. Gradually they had made their way clockwise through the range to Kolding Fjord and the sea at Gletcher Bugt, taking in any peak that was either challenging or (they convinced themselves) had not seen a crampon since time began. Although claiming to be glad not to have seen any polar bears – nor the equally feared musk ox – the retrospective disappointment decreased as the decanter's level lowered.

The climbing had been testing and certainly enlivened by a few falls, but their greatest concern had been the six-day trek to get help that had been necessary. Neither they nor *Black Velvet* had long-range communications – nor had we wanted them, for our collective view was, and remains, that there is far too much reliance on outside help and advice these days, and achievements are diminished for that.

The party continued on deck through the dusk/dawn light until it was considered – at 0430 – that the nightclubs would now be sufficiently lively to be worth a visit. I bade everyone farewell and returned to my own whisky at a price I prefer, and to reflect on the unqualified success of the climbing phase, with some fantastic footage to back up the claim. My own surveying phase had too, been successful, despite being curtailed by faulty – yet brand new – Raytheon/ Autohelm instruments. Knowing that equipment is still under warranty is no good five miles up an uncharted Icelandic fjord! At least we had been spared – by careful use of the lead line – any 'impact hydrography'. Now all we had to do was to restow *Black Velvet* and get her and her embarked axes, crampons, ropes and sledges safely back to Plymouth.

On the morrow, Mark and three of the mountaineers flew home, leaving me and Dave (the crocodile man) to transport the crampons back to Plymouth. As with descending from a peak, the journey home in a sailing vessel can sometimes be the most hazardous part of an expedition. There is probably some wear and tear (there was); some relaxing as the home port nears (there should have been), and especially in my case, a reason for haste that can cloud judgements. My son, Hamish, was due to be married to Claire in the middle of August and I had promised the 'Home Secretary' that I would be back three weeks in advance – at the very latest.

During a telephone call home I had commented – foolishly, for yachts have destinations not times of arrival – that I would call again when off the Irish coast (thank God that country had the safety sense to keep its coast radio stations open for 'normal' traffic, and not force yachtsmen to purchase shorter-range, mobile telephones), which I trusted would be within six days and would then give a rough estimate of our ETA off Plymouth breakwater. If you want to make God (or Murphy – depending on your religion) smirk, tell him your plans.

I warned Dave – the one remaining mountaineer and now sole crew member – that just because it was the return journey, there was no guarantee that it would be easy, but as a climber, he was well aware that down-climbing to base camp usually produces the greatest dangers. Yet I fell for my own optimism, and had we known what lay ahead, I might not have been so euphoric on the telephone home before sailing into a stunning morning of moderate north-west winds forecast as far as Ireland.

The wild slide, downwind to the Reykjaness peninsula, was good stuff, and as we finally cleared the island, our hopes for the predicted fast passage were high. Usually I am happy to dally at sea 'for as long as it takes' while concocting any excuse to avoid using the engine or bashing to windward. This time though, the impending marriage and my promise to arrive three weeks in advance was very much against my own nautical inclination, to cloud every decision. Although sometimes frightened by nature, I am never more so than by the 'Home Secretary'!

A further, but suddenly brief, good omen was a near simultaneous sun and moon sight at 2200 on 26 July, and despite their altitudes being respectively, a mere 0°15'.4 and 11°51'.5, it was from this last visual fix that I took our departure as the cloud closed in and the wind backed to 145°. Our course-to-make-good was 145°.

The next day it all started to go wrong. At 0300 we handed the stays'l and pulled down two reefs in the main. The glass was falling gently, it was raining. Full of self-pity, I wrote in the log, '*Why, when BV wants to go south-east, do we have the only south-easterly gale of the season.*' The problem wasn't, at that moment, the wind direction, but with well-over twelve tons on a 28-feet waterline, short seas stop *Black Velvet,* so until the swell lengthened, we were doomed to stand almost stationary over the ocean bed.

In practice, in order to gain as much sea room as possible for the future, we began by reaching westward until the increasing seas put paid to that idea. It would have been better if we had headed eastward, but north-north-east was the closest we could have made, and that was towards the coastline that even power-driven vessels avoid.

The seas, now more gale-like and solid, began sweeping the decks and filling the cockpit, with one having the nerve to remove the inflatable dan-buoy, but with commendable tact leaving alone the EPIRB (emergency beacon) alongside it. I put out an 'all stations' call in case it had been activated while under water but received no reply.

With the wind a steady southerly Force 9 it was time to head north and stream warps. The seas were heavy now, and although longer, had developed an ominous steepness - we could not beat into them, even with trys'l and engine, and it was now too dangerous to reach across.

With over 100 miles of sea room, I was initially happy with this decision and as we paid out every warp that came to hand, a peace of mind prevailed - that calmness that comes after making a safety-enhancing decision at sea.

This state did not last long for we continued closing the coast too fast. With no sign of a serious moderation, or, of more importance, a change in direction, I began a series of military-style 'appreciations of the situation'. These depressions often take ten days to pass or fill as they come up against the Arctic high, and at over 2 knots (we couldn't go slower even with additional drogues made out of three canvas buckets), we were becoming poorly placed. The only two safe courses were more than 50° either side of our enforced track. The westward (Reykjavik) option was dismissed, not just for the likely sea conditions off Reykjanes - bad enough in normal conditions but horrendous in a Force 9 - but because, once back in our berth, I would have had to leave the boat and fly home. To the east lay the worst of all lee shores and no safe haven. In fact, either option meant bringing the seas onto a quarter and we had already witnessed that danger. The only alternative was to head for Heimaey in the Vestmannaeyjar Islands, but this too had its problems for steering a set course, stern first under warps in dangerous breaking seas and 50-plus knots of wind, is not a precise art.

Other factors entered the 'appreciation'. Both the gear box and steering linkage (we prepared the emergency rudder stock and tiller) were becoming unreliable and would force us to request a tow as we swept past the harbour entrance. The Icelandic sailing instructions, though, suggested that in the current weather conditions, no vessel was likely to put to sea – 'especially for a *Black Velvet*' I thought – and the mainland's leeward coast lay just five miles, or two terrifying hours, beyond.

We were in no immediate danger, providing I could keep the speed low, but as time crept on my worries increased. We could aim for nowhere but Heimaey and if we missed the one-mile-wide gap between it and the off-lying island of Bjarnarey, the situation would become bleak – very bleak indeed, and suddenly.

Then, with twelve short hours to go, the wind veered as the glass began a steady rise. Force 9 was reached only in gusts, with intermediate 'calms' of just Force 6. We had been let off the hook. With relief I ordered the warps to be brought inboard, the heavy weather jib and half the stays'l to be set, and a course made for Barra Head. We had been at sea for four days and were still less than a day's sailing from Reykjavik.

That evening, with the two headsails pulling like oxen, we crashed across a confused sea with the bowsprit spearing into the breaking crests while the glass began another slide. We were being thrown around quite hideously but were making some easting and would shortly have all the sea room we needed, as far even as Spitsbergen. At 0430 the next morning and with the barometric pressure at 995 but with only a Force 7 from the south-west, we had our first proper meal. Nevertheless, more and dirtier weather was on its way, and I said so in the log. An hour later the glass rose by one millibar – enough to raise morale by the same minute amount – but it was a brief respite, for the wind now increased to gusts of 55 knots while backing to due south. We had not made enough easting.

Thus a passage that had begun well now gave me the most anxiety in a cruising career that stretched back to 1946. Morale had been at its peak, for we had sailed with an excellent forecast, expected to last us to Ireland, but things soon became out of hand. The chicken I had been marinating for supper was bad (we had lamb cutlets, instead of salmonella) and the wind backed and rose to a steady Force 9 – perversely doing so once we had transited the narrow passage between the Reykjaness peninsula and the offlying islands through which there was no return in an onshore gale. Forced to tow warps once again and prepare for the worst, our precious sea room had been swallowed up, until quite suddenly, a last-minute veer saved the day and allowed us, with much discomfort, to crash south-eastwards in a frantic attempt to clear the coast. Now - blast it - a southerly Force 10 to 11 took charge.

'Sea anchor?' muttered the climber, face down in *Heavy Weather Sailing*.

'Yes,' I replied, 'but we don't have one.'

To Dave this was akin to climbing without ropes. 'We'll make one out of the trys'l,' I tried.

He remained unimpressed although the improvisation was apparently, 'Good enough for the bush!' And that was good enough for both of us.

The cone of danger northwards subtended an angle of fifty degrees either side of the track down which we were now drifting, and yet we could only deviate by a few of those degrees for the odds of being rolled were shortening by the minute.

The next few hours were not funny and I thought it proper to say so, ending with the opinion that 'there are no atheists on the battlefield or in a Force 11'.

'I don't know about that, mate. All I do know is that if nature doesn't kill you, it toughens you and I guess we are about to be toughened!' Being an Australian he used rather more colourful words but had made his point.

What I did not add was that southerly gales here can last ten days if their depression, passing north through the Denmark Strait, butts into an equally resolute Arctic high.

No matter what we streamed over the bows I had not been able to reduce *Black Velvet*'s progress to below 2 knots until, at the end of the first twenty-four hours, we had lost over half our precious safety margin, and I had, frankly, run out of options to guarantee our eventual survival. The 200 miles of Iceland's southern coast that stretched, equidistant either side of our now-northerly track, possessed no safe havens, even in settled weather.

I resorted to making an 'all ships' call every half an hour - not to ask for help, I add quickly, but to see if someone could foretell a wind shift. Nobody answered. I wrote in the log, '*I have run out of options, it is now up to the Almighty!*' About the only positive action I could take - more for moral purposes rather any serious expectation it would work - was to prepare both bow anchors, a hefty CQR and an even heftier Admiralty pattern anchor, for lowering to their extreme as we closed the coast.

With a few terrifying hours to go we were spared the indignity of beaching in the horrendous surf by the most welcome wind shift I have ever experienced, and although the seas were now threatening by their confusion rather than their size, we were able to make a course for the Hebrides (where a full, northerly gale did actually help us for once), and, from there an unplanned meander, with only one small-scale chart, into the Irish Sea.

Howth, as expected, proved amusing – but it was On! On! to the wedding via an adverse Force 8 off the Tusker Rock, until finally – finally – we were able to lay a course for the Longships light or lamp post, as we called them in my youth. By then though, the engine had sucked air due to the violent rolling – which didn't matter much as both the gear box and self-steering motor had died. We had long since resorted to hand-steering, which, together with the lead line, sextant and Walker log, never let us down. I wrote, *I don't know why I bother with this modern rubbish'. The truth is, when things get really awkward, I don't.*

As we ghosted past Plymouth's breakwater, Dave at last slammed shut – rather too theatrically I thought – Peter Bruce's seminal *Heavy Weather Sailing*, glad, I suspect, that we had followed, or had tried to follow, most of the advice contained between its covers (although I've never actually read it for I know it to be much too frightening). We had been, in his words, toughened by our mutual experience, as had, by proxy, the more-than-anxious 'Home Secretary' who seemed pleased to see me even if it was less than a week before the wedding.

So ended a cruise of over 3,500 miles and 67 days that had satisfied climbers, yachtsmen, explorers, filmmakers, gourmets, sun-seekers, bad-weather freaks, and one in which the very meanderings had had a real meaning and become part of the purpose.

Chapter 23

Cool Bananas Among The Penguins

First published in the Royal Cruising Club's journal *Roving Commissions*, 2003

I've only been to two pole-dancing clubs in my life: one was in Barcelona and the other on board a yacht in Stanley.

Skip Novak's then new, South African-built, sailing vessel, *Pelagic Australis*, was quite something. So here are some facts before we chart her 633-mile, 14-day, maiden adventure through the Falklands archipelago in December 2003.

Sloop-rigged with an overall length of 75 feet 6 inches and a beam of 19 feet 7 inches, she displaces 60 tons. The lifting keel takes up twelve of these, while three tons of fresh water and seven and a half of diesel absorb some of the rest. Constructed of aluminium and powered by a 255hp diesel, she is, very definitely, a heavy weather ship (she's pretty good in calm weather too).

With the keel lowered she draws just over 13 feet, but with it and the rudder up this figure reduces to a handy 4 feet 6 inches - vital for exploring those blank bits on the chart or anchoring where rogue 'bergs' cannot reach. The truck of the mast is 92 feet above the waterline, the mains'l is fully battened, while three headsails, each on its own roller-reefing system, add to the simplicity. Twelve bunks in six cabins suggest the designed sleeping arrangements but as each cabin has a double and a single bunk, the more adventurous crew members might find room for amusing mischief.

For her inaugural cruise *Pelagic Australis* was skippered by Stephen Wilkins, a Tasmanian who came with a selection of amusing Aussie aphorisms to reinforce his views on life. Inevitably, only 'cool bananas' is repeatable here. He was (and remains) an experienced yachtsman, with then, one round-the-world race and thousands of high-latitude miles under his safety harness. Stephen was aided by Nico Pichelin, a young and tall, humorous Frenchman, and ex-member of *Mari Cha's* record-breaking, trans-Atlantic crew, and a master of most nautical trades - including that of making poker dice from a calf's shinbone.

Six 'passengers' had signed-up to cruise to as many war and wildlife sites as could be achieved in the fourteen days, and although not required to work the ship, they split themselves, unevenly into two watches and volunteered for the various domestic duties on offer. It was quickly established that all on board possessed a remarkable capacity for laughter and by the second evening each had slipped with good humour into his or her self-appointed duty. Late nights, early starts and strong winds might spell trouble elsewhere, but under no pressure to compete amongst ourselves or with other yachts, these ingredients for discord were ignored.

In the starboard watch were Peter Cope, ex-Royal Navy submariner, Hampshire publican and yacht owner (volunteer dinner cook), and Sir Victor Walker, ex-Grenadier Guards, yacht owner and bon vivant (potato peeler). Port watch included Julia Ray, management consultant with a round-the-world race and cruise to Spitzbergen behind her (sous-chef and pudding expert); Jill Franks, environmentalist and round-the-world race crew (sail trimmer); Michael Davies, chartered surveyor and yacht owner (breakfast cook), and last, but because of his trade, by no means least among equals, was Bo Eriksson, Swede, whisky connoisseur, yacht owner and chocolate manufacturer (after-dinner purveyor of sublime luxuries). The ninth soul on board was myself, retired Royal Marine, yacht owner and lover of the Falkland Islands. I was, *de facto*, the 'unpaid, paid hand' for I was neither paying nor being paid, tour guide, navigator and an ex-officio member of the starboard, Saga or military watch (186 years between the three of us) to make up their numbers.

At Mount Pleasant Airport on 6 December we squeezed into two Land Rovers for the cross-country journey to *Pelagic Australis* lying off San Carlos settlement. I had suggested that we start from the spot where 2nd Battalion, Parachute Regiment, had landed before dawn on 21 May 1982, and so it was, on this significant beach that we met Stephen and Nico, then after a visit to the cemetery, we were soon settled into the ship's saloon with a glass of South African wine.

My task each evening, as in 1982, was to lay before the skipper and passengers a matrix of destinations and routes for the subsequent twenty-four hours and, apart from permanently trying to remember when our aeroplane left for Chile, we seldom planned further in advance.

For the first full day, a 60-mile sail to Pebble Island was agreed, as this settlement's grass airstrip had been the target of a classic, special forces raid against eleven parked aircraft, while more peacefully, the island is also renowned for its translucent pebbles which, when polished, are a distinctive feature of Falkland's jewellery. We weighed at 0630 and after pouring a libation over the resting place of HMS *Antelope*, sunk on 23 May 1982 with the loss of two lives, settled down for a cracking close-reach westwards.

Ignoring the shorter route through the Tamar Pass – it was, vitally, not slack water – we pushed on to Kepple Sound's north-western entrance, thence a transit of the narrow Northwest Passage before anchoring in a strong onshore wind off Pebble Island's jetty where the holding ground, away from the kelp is good.

True to my training (and as a guide with a politically correct 'duty of care' attitude to his 'punters') I suffered a wet landing while tugging the laden dinghy inshore, before the unimpressed cox'n, Nico, returned with his empty vessel to the jetty's ladder that I had said did not exist. Raymond Evans, the settlement owner, gave us permission to visit the remains of the last Pucara ground-attack aircraft yet to be removed, and then insisted we take 'smoko' with his family where the crew tasted (and drank) true settlement hospitality. This set the standard for every subsequent landing except one. I, amid some amusement, took off my trousers and boots to dry them by the peat fire.

A peaceful, if windy, evening followed, during which Peter, once he had seen the array of freshly dead and newly dug goodies hanging in the fore-peak, offered to cook every night – his original bid having been conditional. This unselfish (but ulterior) decision was much to the ship's company's mutual benefit – although it meant that the grenadier and I, with no culinary expertise to offer, were relegated to permanent potato-peeling duties. Among his other epicurean adventures, Peter had owned the Cornucopia Hotel on Gozo that, under his patronage, had been famed throughout the naval service for its exotic food, late and wild nights. Naturally, each evening's spud bashing was turned into a cockpit-party when, until prevented by the submariner, Victor would cut his spuds into regulation, army cubes. Having tried to boil a lettuce in mistake for a cabbage, I was regarded with similar contempt. Consequently, neither of us was to be promoted in the galley department – but we did wash-up a great deal.

The second evening's conference suggested a 45-mile leg to Carcass Island via the original Royal Navy settlement at Saunders Island where, after a wet motor into a good Force 5, we were greeted by the entire Pole-Evans family on their newly built concrete slipway. Following a briefing on the changes since my previous visit, a brisk walk brought us to the substantial stone walls and small boat jetty that had served the British so well in the 1770s, as the result of Commodore Byron's even earlier view that 'the whole navy of England might ride in perfect security from the winds in Port Egmont'.

The three graves from that era had been tidied up since my last visit in 1982, and were now enclosed by a white-painted, wooden fence. Nearby, a union flag flies permanently. It is a moving place where it is easy to sit in the diddle-dee (a low shrub with bright red berries), imagining ships at anchor in the roads, drying their canvas as marines ashore tended their vegetable gardens, through which still flows wonderfully fresh water. The view is unchanged since the barracks was last inhabited in 1778.

Satiated with naval history and heeding earlier advice we weighed anchor - and fathoms of heavy kelp - to call at 'The Neck', towards the north-west of Saunders, for here the penguins were in full breeding cycle. Although the swell prevented a landing, we were rewarded with our first glimpse of rockhoppers perched precariously on their steep-to cliffs above the gentoo on the gently shelving sand. On then to Carcass - a prime wildlife island and a proposed Harrier base in 1982 - for a drink with the owner Rob McGill. Rob helped us plan the next day's walk to his west coast, where we hoped to revel in the finest views of the Jason Islands from among the dozens of seals along the foreshore.

Come the morrow, the Jasons were hidden by low cloud, although the occasional, tantalising glimpse suggested what the scene should have been. Neither were the mammals - represented by just one female elephant seal - in evidence. So after a brief picnic in the tussock bogs and an unsuccessful attempt to catch a rock shag using a bolas, we called it a day. Rock shags' breasts make good eating, but clearly believing themselves to be in the presence of lunatics, the birds simply flip-flopped contemptuously and lazily across the rocks, out of harm's way. Thus, without locally snared supper and with the deteriorating weather preventing further exploring, it was time to head for a serious lamb curry on board, with Rob as our guest.

The following morning *Pelagic Australis* beat across to Westpoint Island where her crew were humbled by the splendour of the black-browed albatross colony perched among the majestic sea cliffs. This was a wonderful visit to these un-phased birds that ended with a brace of Roddy Napier's notorious gin and tonics (mixed, as I knew they would be, in reverse ratio), before we slipped from the luxury of a mooring buoy (no kelp fouling the anchor) to catch the tide for the short run through the Woolly Gut. An inspection of Stevelly Bay was anticipated, to see what nautical rubbish might have been washed ashore, for an eddy here tends to deposit all manner of international flotsam and jetsam on the beach.

This blustery, windward anchorage was alive with puffing pigs, the stocky, white-flanked Commerson's Dolphin which are as playful as kittens; it is even possible to stroke them from the dinghy, and (pre-digital) expensive to photograph. However, the idyll was shattered as we disembarked from the dinghy by a woman dismounting from her quad bike, already quaking with rage. This harridan confronted us crew with ninety seconds of unstoppable invective while for my part, this was the first time in twenty-seven years, I encountered personal abuse from an Islander.

'We had no permission to land on the beach' - which was true, but it is equally true, that among the Islands, as in the United Kingdom, it is Crown property below the high-water mark. Nevertheless, we decided that we were there for the pursuit of happiness and as that ideal was not to be found in her company, we renamed the place (Falkland Islanders, please forgive me) 'Bitch Bay' and turned for the south. I was more puzzled than angry, yet only just managed to prevent myself from commenting that 'while we might have expected opposed landings in 1982....'

The story of this encounter was to reach Stanley before we did, and almost immediately upon arrival we would be offered apologies on behalf of the community as a whole that were every bit as sincere as the original tirade had been unpleasant. We'll land again. Next time we will be fully prepared and with the knowledge that we have widespread support and sympathy.

Weddell Island had, temporally I trusted, been abandoned to the foxes and rats but as Gull Harbour is still a good - but sandy - anchorage, we headed for this settlement, enjoying a wonderful, close-reach via East Passage with one reef in the main, plus full jib and stays'l.

With the undoubted benefit of service drinking habits, starboard watch was responsible for this leg while everyone else slept off Roddy's gins - everyone that is except Nico who announced that he was busy on a 'secret project'. No better time could have been spent off watch for at the 'yard arm hour' and with a Gallic flourish, he produced five magnificent poker 'dices' fashioned from a Westpoint Island bone with each of their six sides neatly scrimshawed with Aces, Kings, Queens and so on. During the previous days he had listened, puzzled, to the naval members of the crew bewailing the absence of these vital artefacts for their evening, on-board entertainment. He had never seen such 'dices' before and had known nothing of their use but was quick to learn and became financially better-off for his 'beginners' luck'.

Weddell settlement was deserted, yet with places laid for meals and magazines open on tables in the guest houses. Nevertheless, Peter had brought ashore eighteen hogget chops, which, when barbecued, were as tender as any lamb. And so, with our legs well-exercised and our tummies well-filled, we sailed for Fegen Inlet - once the grenadier had been rescued from an involuntary and total immersion 'twixt dinghy and ship. In the near gale, finding a sheltered spot was impossible as the surrounding land is low lying and humped, accelerating the wind, much as happens above an aircraft's wing, but in compensation, the bottom provided excellent holding ground.

The next day, a cruise highlight was a visit to the wrongly named Horse Block Rock, Scottie Dog Rock would have been more appropriate, but it is still an impressive structure, 220 feet high. Sadly, physical contact was out of the question as we circumnavigated the 'animal' before turning towards the south-east under one reef and the stays'l, but it had been a magical moment.

Cape Meredith is notorious in heavy weather, yet we rounded in fine order and with a good offing before bearing away for Albemarle Harbour and a plan to motor through the inland waterways that make up this fascinating stretch of Falklands coastline. Replant the gently sloping, diddle-dee banks with trees and we could have been up the Fal or Tamar estuaries. The aim was to make what I was sure would be the first transit of Chaffers Gullet by a yacht.

Peter and I took over this fascinating piece of pilotage while Stephen affected a nonchalant, but widely alert, pose on the quarterdeck, having hauled the keel to its halfway position. We motored cautiously up the narrow, twisting gullet without the ubiquitous puffing pigs. It was too shallow for them and for a moment or two we thought it might have been too narrow for us. We were in no danger of course; if the keel had touched we would simply have hoisted it further or backed out.

Then – after the last tight bend – we were into a broad expanse of dark-brown, land-locked water surrounded by sun-dappled, dragon-backed hills with not a hint of man and his 'civilisation'. It was perfection as beyond a kelp-marked, shallow, underwater ridge and well into the upper-most reaches, the anchor was lowered into the peaty waters – the first of the evening's gins were poured and Mike took a swim.

The next morning, while others stretched their legs, Nico and I sounded for a deeper passage across the reef to our inner haven and were rewarded by a narrow gap with at least a depth of 20 feet, and conveniently, in transit with the entrance and a far hill. Once the shore party had returned from the dominating Gibraltar Rocks, we were off for a look at Port Edgar and a night at Fox Bay East. Here Ken Halliday, the local government representative, a number of children and a ginger cat, swarmed aboard while we replenished the stocks of gin and eggs.

It was also 'club night' – and what a party! In addition to Islanders and ourselves there were servicewomen from Mount Pleasant, all helping to ensure that the club's coffers remained topped up for the foreseeable future. By the time we resurfaced the next morning Mike's reputation as a breakfast cook – and Bo's as a source of exotic chocolate – had spread to the settlement's younger element and the ginger cat, yet we still managed to sail at 0900 for Goose Green.

Blowing hard and cold from ahead, the wind had other ideas so *Pelagic Australis* forged eastwards under motor, while a pod of pilot whales took station off the port quarter. I had first suggested Bull Cove as an interim anchorage but Blake Inlet was better in the conditions, and so it was there that we spent another not-so-quiet night of dinner and dice between vast banks of protecting kelp.

15 December brought a wind veer, a close reach in sunshine and a wind chill of -2°C, all of which allowed Jill and Julia to enter their respective 'round-the-world-race' heavens, as they grinned and trimmed the full main, stays'l and genoa. There was even talk of 'flying a geneker' (?) at which I slipped below to pour noon-time sustenance and thus escape any involvement in what sounded to me ominously like a non-cruising evolution. Luckily, by the time I returned, sense had prevailed and we were heading north-west towards Goose Green, where in driving rain, we moored to the jetty which lies alongside the hulk of the three-masted barque *Vicar of Bray*. This brave little ship is the sole survivor of the 1849 gold-rush to San Francisco and was wrecked in 1880 during her twentieth (or thereabouts) such round journey.

At dusk the wind veered further to the north and dropped, bringing with it one of those stunningly clear, multi-coloured sunsets so unique to the Falkland's unadulterated atmosphere. Then, once the brilliance had faded, we revelled in the last of the hogget and a ferocious game of 'Beat That You Bastard' with Nico's 'dices'.

A drizzly, windy morning greeted us for the walk past extensive, well-marked, minefields to one of the many memorials that stand sentinel over the events of 1982. Here we polished the brass plaque and stood in silence, shuddering not just at the cold wind but, more significantly, at the barrenness across which the Parachute Regiment had been obliged to fight.

There was yet another melancholy duty to perform, this time in Choiseul Sound and one closer to my own memories. After slipping from Goose Green's hospitable clutches at 1300 we hove-to one-mile due south of Johnson's Island where, on the evening of 8 June 1982 my Royal Marines landing craft, *Foxtrot Four*, had been hit by a bomb. For the first time since that dreadful day I was able to read the citation for Colour Sergeant Brian Johnston's posthumous award of the Queen's Gallantry Medal, and the names of his five crew, at the precise spot where they died. As Binyon's exhortation 'They shall grow not old…' ended the short memorial, Julia sprinkled the Sound's surface with flowers picked earlier from the Goose Green battlefield, while the submariner and grenadier poured nine tots of whisky - one for each of my marines plus three for the three islanders to have been killed in the conflict.

The anchorage off Fitzroy was exposed and tricky but the Felton family, with whom it would have been pointless to argue, was expecting us. Eighteen hours later, and the better for having visited Sonia's beautiful gardens; admired her wildlife paintings; bought two Chilean chickens, two bottles of gin and picked a bucket of mussels, it was time to leave. So, with the barometer dropping vertically past 992 millibars, we headed for Johnston's Harbour in preparation for the morrow's visit to the king penguins at Volunteer Point.

These penguins were another cruise highlight and especially so as all seemed well with the 470 inhabitants; a number that was expected to rise to 700 once the eggs hatched. After an exhilarating struggle through their wind-scoured dunes, we made it back to *Pelagic Australis* without too much of a ducking from the pounding surf.

Too soon, we were alongside in Stanley. The mandatory meal in the Upland Goose Hotel; a day of Christmas shopping; visits by the Commander Falkland Islands Forces, and one from the Governor (cancelled at the last moment due to 'trouble with the neighbours') and a final dinner in the Brassiere - at which we entertained Nico and Stephen - filled our time until our reluctant departure by air on 20 December.

And the pole dancing? You will have to ask Julia. But it is recorded on a very shaky video (the laughing was too much for the cameraman) and was as unexpected a sight as it was convincing, making us suspicious of her claim to be a modest business consultant. Of course we had never enquired the nature of her business but we do know that she was as surprised as the rest of us with the video replay the next morning. All that can be revealed through the written word is that this dance - this final cruise highlight - involved the two stainless steel stanchions that keep *Pelagic Australis*'s 'quarterdeck' from collapsing into the saloon below.

The 'cool bananas' are more easily explained. Apparently this is an Australian expression that suggests total happiness and was often uttered by Stephen before being adopted by his equally content passengers and crew.

Chapter 24

The Day I Nearly Lost *Black Velvet*, 2007

While motoring round from Queen Anne's Battery Marina (QAB) to my peaceful and secluded, swinging mooring in the upper reaches of the Yealm river (a two-hour journey at the very most), I slowly became aware that something was not quite right. *Black Velvet*, my 12-ton gaff-rigged Tradewind 35 was becoming sluggish, difficult to steer, clearly down by the head and was not coming straight upright after each roll. The companion hatch had been shut to prevent the short, steep, occasionally breaking seas from going below, so I reluctantly left the helm and slid it back. I was not amused by what I saw. Seawater, at least two inches above the cabin sole, was slopping from side to side, forrard to aft and clearly rising - fast. Decisions had to be made quickly - very quickly indeed.

I could not leave the helm to investigate the source as it was Force 6 with a heavy (for a twelve tonner) quartering and breaking sea. I couldn't turn back to head into the wind and sea off the Mewstone and thence to Plymouth, as that meant much longer at sea heading back to QAB. Then to where, as it was an ebbing tide and the marina wall would already be out of the question? Although not knowing the cause I knew that I didn't have long.

My first reaction was to beach her in Wembury Bay to port (lee shore and rocks - I would have lost the boat but saved myself), yet as we got closer and into marginally calmer water in the Mewstone's lee, I decided to take the risk of getting her to her buoy, at least another half an hour away up the river. The diesel engine, now half submerged, was beginning to hiccup. Setting a sail while trying to bale by hand (the big cockpit bilge pump was clogged with God knows what) was out of the question, as she was by now difficult to control under power let alone, had I had time to hoist it, a heads'l.

Thinking rationally, I reckoned I had less than an hour before she went under. She was almost unmanoeuvrable. As she rolled to at least 60 degrees to port (staying there for some minutes each time) and about 40 degrees back to starboard, the situation was becoming dangerous as the free-surface water slopped over the bunks and up the insides of the saloon. This put the freshwater pump, the grey water pump and the 240-volt charging box and 12-volt batteries

Christening. 1st March 1942, Stobs Camp, Hawick. Seated left; June Tailyour with SEST, back row centre Norman Tailyour, right, Pat Phibbs (Photograph taken by Evelyn Waugh with June's camera.)

Sea Vixen off Start Point, circa 1936

Olga in the Bay of Biscay, circa 1947

Aged four rowing *EM*'s pram dinghy at Newton Ferrers. No life-jacket!

Aged five at *Olga*'s wheel

The first *Black Velvet*

The second *Black Velvet* (Graham Adam)

Patricia and Hermione at the third *Black Velvet*'s launch before Hermione poured Guinness and champagne over her bows. Lymington, 1993

The third *Black Velvet*, skippered by Hamish with Steve Sleight, Winner of *Yachting Monthly*'s Hell and High Water Trophy, 1993 (Yachting Monthly)

The fourth *Black Velvet*. Skippered by Hamish in the Jester Baltimore Challenge, 2015

Hamish, Heather, Jacob and Oliver pouring Guinness and champagne over the fourth *Black Velvet*'s bows. Pentillie Castle, 2011

Esso Norway down by the stern

HMS *Anzio* (MoD Navy)

LCA (later LCVP) similar to those carried in HMS *Anzio* (MoD Navy)

Speedwell during the 1970 two-handed round–Britain and Ireland race

The fate of the *Bonnehomme Richard*

Remains of the Royal
Marines camp at
Settlement Cove,
Saunders Island

Hoisting Hermione in a mail bag onto the deck of the *Lady Elizabeth*

Navigating *Capricornus* up Choiseul Sound to Goose Green, 1978 (Painting by David Cobb, ROI, PRSMA)

The Governor did not approve of my work and once sent the Beaver float plane to 'drag' me back to Stanley from Goose Green

Horse Block Rock

Hermione, *Shutlinsloe* and a lock

Larusanne en route for the Arctic in one of my landing craft, 1988

The Lofoton Islands in early spring and the arctic-wolf fur hat

Karen Plaza beach

I was sad not to have known *Eloise* better!

Spreading the chum

Rockall – too rough to climb

Black Velvet – under full sail – entering Iceland's last un-surveyed fjords

Storis. Fifty miles of this was not a good idea

Hamish standing on a previously un-charted *eyri* – a thin, vertical wall! A very cold duty

Stapafell – a foreboding sight!

The third *Black Velvet* in the Somme's canals – a comforting sight! (Until she was burgled.)

The annual booze cruise crew. Mike Groom, Mike Shuttleworth, ES-T, Peter Cameron

Pelagic Australis off Volunteer Beach with Gentoo penguins

Black Velvet towing *Jester* to the start of the inaugural Jester Challenge, 2006

Firing the starting 'cannon', a 12-bore shotgun full of Johnson's Baby Powder

The fourth *Black Velvet* with the author (left) alongside the third *Black Velvet* and Mark Litchfield

Maria Asumpta outward bound (Mark Litchfield)

ML 286. *Naughty Princess*. Millbay Docks, Plymouth, 1946

Racing a Firefly on the
Thames at Pangbourne,
1959

Sailing a *Star* on Lake Garda, 1957

Sailing a dhow in Aden Harbour, 1961

Sailing master of *Sea Soldier* 1964 – 1968

Sunset and time to pour that tot in celebration of the Glory of the Ride! (Hamish Southby-Tailyour)

The final toast

Perfection on board the fourth – and final – *Black Velvet*

underwater, and of course, all the electrical fittings at the heel of the mast were flooded – masthead lights, steaming lights, VHF and radar.

If I had been about 20 miles offshore, I would definitely have lost her, as the lifeboat would have taken precious time to reach me, the seas were too heavy to get a pump on board, and she would have sunk under tow.

When the engine started its hiccupping I waded below – up to my thighs at one point – to grab the handheld VHF, flares and a lifejacket. I had no life raft at that stage of the season while the rubber dinghy lay deflated in the fore-cabin. It was, supposedly, a standard trip from Plymouth to the moorings, undertaken many dozens of times, in both good and bad weather.

Once committed to the river entrance I had few options: get to the mooring, bail as fast as I was able, to find the source of the leak, or, if she was in imminent danger of foundering, slam her on to the muddy riverbank before the engine failed completely. Anchoring was certainly another option, but I was not keen to do so while there was still hope of making the river, anyway, once inside the entrance, the only spare anchoring space was twixt the upper and lower reaches – and by then my mooring buoy would be in sight.

At one point the River Yealm harbourmaster was motoring towards me, back from his evening inspection of the upper reaches of his bailiwick. Desperate for help I bellowed across to ask if he had a pump. He must have misinterpreted my question and shouted back, pointing to the darkening sky: 'Yes, isn't this rain terrible,' then shot past and out of earshot.

By some miracle, not helped by the ebbing tide and hindered by *Black Velvet*'s near inability to steer a straight course, I was able to reach the mooring. Once moored in double-quick time, I took a few precious minutes to telephone home, for by now the harbour office would have shut. Amazingly, for reception between the high, steep, wooded riverbanks seldom worked, I spoke to Patricia. She in turn telephoned Mervyn Wheatley (he of the *Queen Mary 2* rescue fame from his own sinking vessel in mid-Atlantic), who knew the mooring master's private number. Meanwhile I returned to frantic bailing. Unable to keep up with the rate of rising water in the saloon with the one canvas bucket, I decided to slip the buoy and put *Black Velvet* on the mud – providing the now three-quarters-submerged engine started.

Suddenly, out of the darkening gloom came the more than welcome noise of a diesel engine. Soon Mark Wilson, the River Yealm moorings master (a professional seaman and not to be confused with a marina mooring master) appeared, and so began a two-bucket bailing operation. It was only after two hours of back-breaking lifting (for the first hour all we seemed to do was to keep pace with the incoming water) we felt that we might have been winning as the level noticeably began to drop. Eventually we found the cause and - hurrah - could actually fix it. Water was not just squirting in from around the propeller shaft and stuffing box, but pouring through as though from a hosepipe for the whole fitting had somehow come lose and had slid six inches up the shaft. We simply pushed it back. Actually it needed some simple engineering - involving no more than four screws and a screwdriver - to make it secure. Later it was professionally secured.

The collateral damage though was rather more substantial. All electrical plugs, leads, sockets, batteries and switches had to be replaced and the engine taken out and stripped down. Meanwhile I had a massive cleaning task ahead of me, but at least I still had *Black Velvet*. For that I was grateful, although immediate sailing plans were on hold until much later in the season.

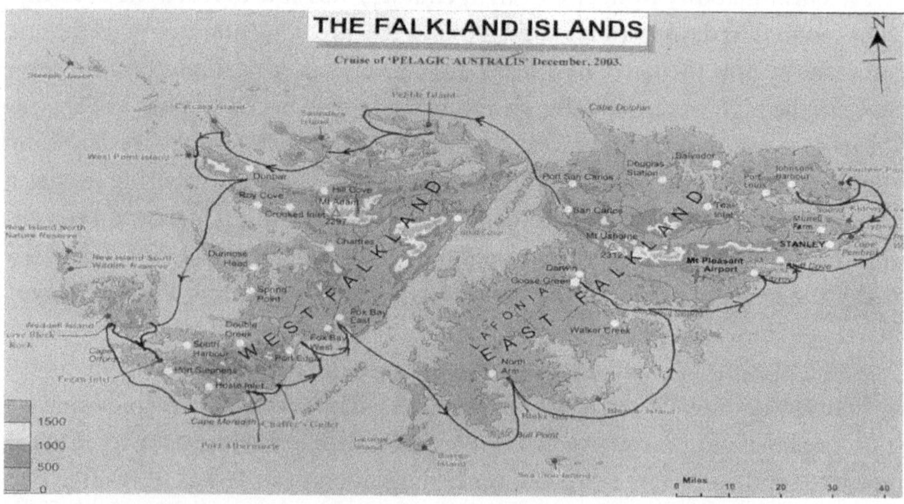

Pelagic Australis's 2003 route from San Carlos to Stanley (Sir Victor Walker)

Chapter 25

New EU-generated Rules, 2009

Continuing on its path towards criminalising as many of us as quickly as possible, our urban-centric government has once again acted without serious thought to the practicalities of life at sea in a yacht.

Apparently, I am shortly to be obliged to notify, twenty-four hours in advance (I have seen forty-eight hours quoted elsewhere) and by email, any foreign-going journey I intend making in my yacht, or face a £5,000 fine.

What on earth is going on here? I and my friends go to sea to escape such tyranny. When we leave our moorings in south Devon we have no idea of our destination. That will depend on the actual weather conditions as soon as we clear the river's mouth and not the predictions of the seldom precisely accurate shipping forecasts that only cover the subsequent six hours - not twenty-four. The state of my crews' stomachs, once we have 'slipped the surly bonds of earth' will then be added to the equation. Even so, our destination - that almost certainly will not be a formal port, or even, heaven forbid, a marina - may alter frequently during the course of the voyage. Decisions will be continually made, reassessed and changed, depending on the many variables and imponderables associated with the sea, wind and tides. This is the freedom and the joy of small-boat cruising.

Putting to sea from Newton Ferrers my vessel is able to cope with any destination which in an ordinary summer could, on a whim, be as far afield as Iceland or as close as Looe. If, say, we head for the Isles of Scilly and the weather turns bad from the north we could be forced, with no way of informing Westminster, to run downwind to a safe and secluded anchorage on the Biscay coast of France. Or we could slug it out to an equally isolated refuge on the south coast of Ireland, bypassing that beautiful and rock-strewn archipelago off Land's End. Who knows where we shall end up - until we get there!

Two other practical considerations loom: access to the internet, and being erroneously reported as overdue. The government presumes that small vessels have an internet connection for 24 hours a day but few have such devices and those that do find a 24-hour connection unusual. It is, I believe, also very expensive. Without internet (and since the lamentable removal of the coast radio stations, with their range far in excess of a mobile telephone - which not all of us take to sea either I am glad to say), we shall have to break our otherwise leisurely progress and make for the expense of a marina berth and an internet café in order to report our new, but not necessarily certain, foreign destination to the totalitarians who now wish to govern our every move, even when at sea. The unseamanlike requirement to declare, firmly and officially, our destination 24 hours before we even begin to face the elements will lead to a rise in overdue reports, increasing worry to families, and unnecessary expenses to the safety services.

Let us continue to do what we have done all our lives: report our safe arrival to our next of kin and the appropriate coastguard authorities - a government agency. This is unambiguous, factual and fool proof. We all make a very rough plan for our families' peace of mind (and many, prior to sailing, report their proposed passage - whether to a home or foreign destination - to the relevant coastguard station) but for a small sailing vessel to involve central government with its threat of fines to satisfy, it would appear, the far-from-proven argument that it is vital to our country's security, is really not on for British yachtsmen.

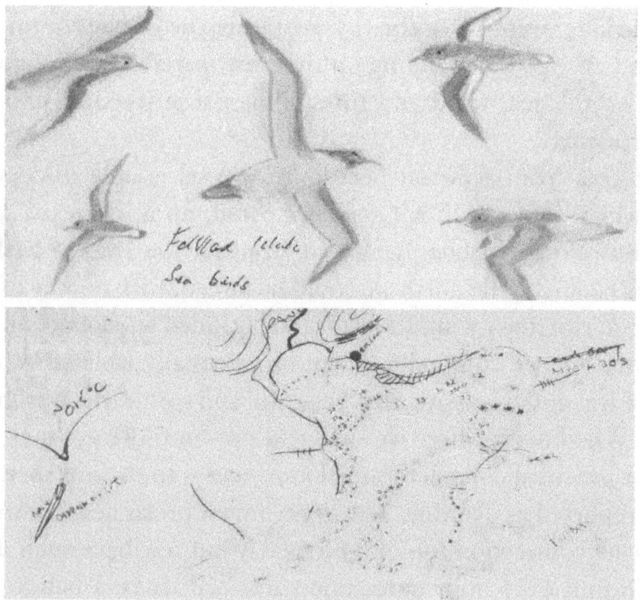

Sample of an original soundings chart.

Chapter 26

OSTAR at 60, 2020

No one, probably not even 'Blondie', could have guessed that 'Hasler's wonderful idea', conceived in 1956, would still be going strong in 2020, sixty years since the first event and sixty-four years since the notion first took shape. During the intervening years the Observer Single-handed Transatlantic Race (OSTAR) has been through a number of iterations and titles plus a few ups and downs, yet it is still flourishing.

In 1951 Blondie Hasler developed an 'intensifying' desire to design a 'radical cruising boat' that would in his own words 'be my servant and not my master'. Eventually the junk-rigged *Jester* – 'because she is such a bloody joke' with her self-steering gear and central, enclosed steering position to which all lines led, and from which the skipper need not move – was built to ride out a storm, if not in comfort then at least in safety. A serious consideration was that 'she would need to keep a girlfriend keen in the early, impressionable stages of a romance, by not having to fight sodden canvas at forty degrees angle of heel in seven-eighths of a gale'.

In September 1957, the second of Hasler's inventions that was to change the face of short-handed ocean sailing was also taking shape. The trim tab fitted to the trailing edge of rudders was not new, but he had to start somewhere in his quest to transfer power from the water flow to the tiller – and so was born the Hasler Pendulum-Servo Vane Gear.

To understand the gestation of the event that transformed many of the world's offshore racing calendars, it is necessary to return to 25 November 1956 when Hasler's eye was caught by an article in *The Observer* describing how two retired Royal Navy officers had recently crossed the Atlantic single-handed.

Hasler knew that there had been a single-handed transatlantic race in 1891, albeit from west to east, but these latest crossings sparked an idea. So, on 11 January 1957, anxious to prove and advertise his two 'inventions' in a contest, Hasler wrote to his friend David Astor of *The Observer* newspaper: 'I have been brooding for some time on ...organising a transatlantic race for single-handed sailing boats...Is there any hope that *The Observer* would like to sponsor it?'

Astor's reply was not encouraging, 'I rather think that my managing director will be against it.'

Undaunted, Hasler turned to New York's Slocum Society: 'By all means send us the proposed organisation of the race...the prospect is most exciting'.

Thus began an exchange of conflicting ideas between Hasler and the Slocum Society, who wanted for instance, the use of radio transmitters and engines with the race staging via a compulsory stop in the Azores. In Hasler's response, engines 'seem to be almost mandatory'. Referring to the radios, he commented: 'I would be happy to drown with dignity for I dread the idea of ships having to conduct rescue operations.'

Meanwhile a new team was gathering in *The Observer* led by its sports editor Christopher Brasher who held the same opinion as Hasler concerning 'nautical nannies'. With Brasher's persuasion the managing director now agreed to 'help' but, anxious not to have the Observer's name associated with the race for fear of ridicule, he decided to call it the Atlantic single-handed yacht race. Later, following the early successes, he agreed to sponsor it while changing its name to the Observer Single-handed Transatlantic Race or OSTAR. The paper's involvement would last until 1986.

David Lewis and Val Howells, having heard of Hasler's 'amazing idea', expressed firm intentions, so without yet a sponsor, the three determined to start themselves and take their own finishing times. Who needed a sponsor or yacht club? The myth of them each putting a half crown into a 'purse' is just that – a myth generated, post facto, by Francis Chichester.

Chichester had by now declared an interest and, fortuitously, took on much of the correspondence from his London office. Finally, Jean Lacombe made up the fifth of the original starters. Further good news came with the Royal Western Yacht Club's agreement to handle the start, under the leadership of their Rear Commodore, Jack Odling-Smee, who too, shared a similar outlook on life and the 'nannies of the cotton wool society that try to dominate it'. Having been beaten, the Slocum Society now offered to oversee arrangements at New York.

The first four yachts started from Plymouth on 11 June 1960 with Lacombe following three days later. All five yachts (four of whom were 25 feet or under) reached New York in good order – a 100 per cent record that still stands. Just as interesting is that among the fifteen starters in the 1964 OSTAR all five 'originals' again finished – this time at Newport Rhode Island. Hasler was to predict that a higher percentage of under 30-footers would always finish, compared to a similar percentage of larger vessels.

Although multi-hulls had been accepted by Hasler for the first race, none took part, but during the second OSTAR multi-hulls successfully completed the course - two catamarans and one trimaran.

With success guaranteed, the OSTAR now attracted big money, big names, and inevitably, big egos. Indeed, so popular was it, that by 1968, Hasler worried that the race's success 'contained the seeds of its own death with excessive competitiveness being one of the reasons'. Yachts of 128 feet in 1972 and 236 feet in 1976 (with a 125-entry list) did not help the image. Fearing demise, he planned a scaled down Series Two race that if necessary, would begin in 1980.

By the 1970s, it was also feared that the French, upset at the fluctuating length and number of restrictions, would take over the OSTAR. They didn't but instead introduced their own *Route de Rhum* in 1978.

There is no doubt, that following Éric Tabarly's popular win in 1964 (no one was more pleased than Hasler), France had found a new national sport and hence, new heroes. With this French interest came a proliferation of single-handed trans-oceanic contests that continue to this day. The OSTAR also gave Chichester the impetus to circumnavigate the globe single-handed in 1966, and that too led to yet more global races.

The Royal Western Yacht Club, equally concerned that the OSTAR was unmanageable, swamped by professional organisations, wisely hived off this element to Offshore Challenges in 2005, then reverted to running a Corinthian event with an upper size limit at 60 feet and a lower limit of 27 feet. This was primarily because of evolving international stability requirements which made compliance for smaller vessels difficult. Thus perfectly seaworthy yachts became excluded from a race that has at its very heart the 25-feet *Jester* herself. Perhaps though, owners of these vessels are not so troubled at being forced out, when they know that a staggering £1,800 is required just to enter - over double what *Jester* herself cost.

This nautical nannying (emphatically not of the Royal Western Yacht Club's making) is a nonsense, and surprises owners of, for example, Twisters, Contessa 26s and even the diminutive Corribee 21s, who were quite suddenly, disenfranchised. Experienced yachtsmen know that safety at sea is a complicated matrix of human and physical facts, rather than just size. 'The only arbiter of safety at sea is the sea itself', wrote Hasler, and not a health and safety-orientated committee of nannies with slide rules and copious regulations.

Although the familiar - iconic - acronym OSTAR remains, the same full title has been subtly altered by replacing 'Observer' with 'Original'. Nevertheless, the new OSTAR enjoys well-deserved and continued success, and for that Hasler would surely be relieved. But, and a significant 'but' – he would not have approved of the word 'original' to describe 'his' trans-Atlantic race that bars four out of the five 'originals' from taking part. Happily, the Half-Crown Club also flourishes - despite having been founded on a Chichester-generated myth.

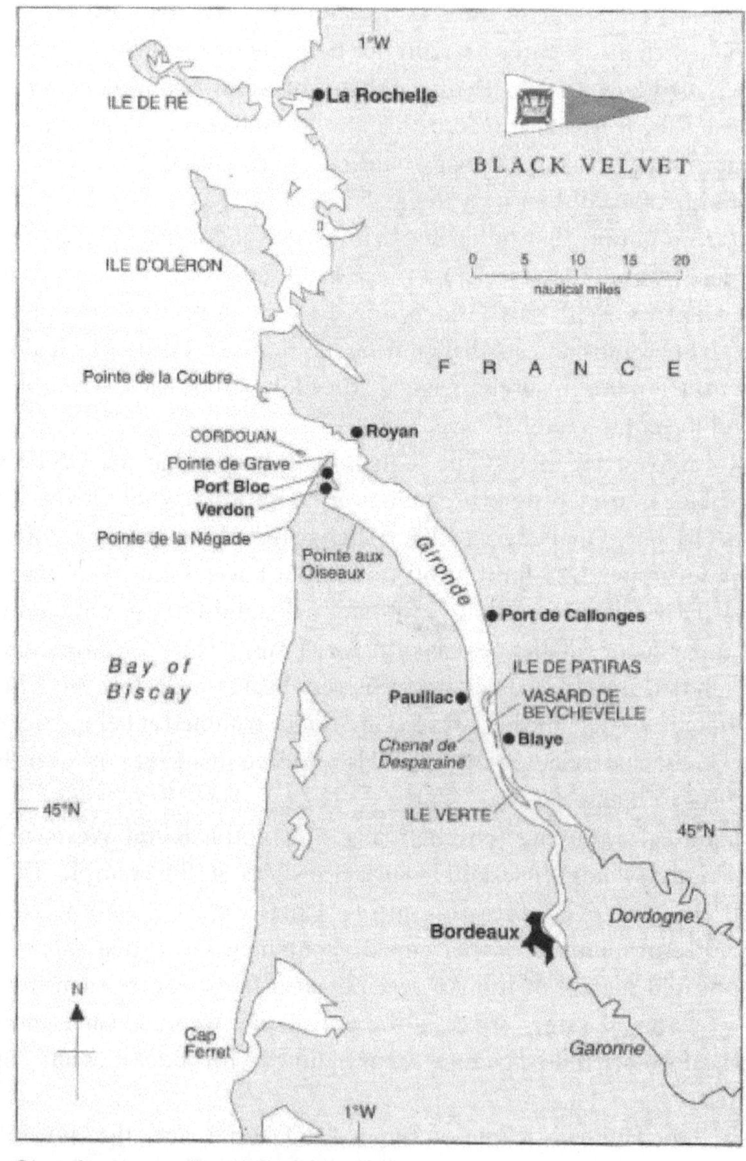

Gironde estuary. (Royal Cruising Club)

Chapter 27

The Golden Age

The Royal Marines' participation in single-handed and short-handed oceanic races, 1960 to 2019

On 28 October 2014, a number of retired Royal Marines, of all ranks, dined at the Royal Western Yacht Club (RWYC) in Plymouth for the 350th birthday party of their Corps. The president for the evening was the Club's Commodore, Major John Lewis, Royal Marines. During his welcoming speech the Commodore reminded us that the Corps has a long tradition of involvement with his Club's races. In earlier days, members of the Royal Naval Sailing Association (RNSA) and thus members of the affiliated Royal Marines Sailing Club (RMSC), were honorary members of the RWYC, as were members of Stonehouse and Bickleigh Officers' Messes. Many Royal Marines cut their teeth with the Royal Ocean Racing Club's (RORC) Fastnet races from Cowes that ended in the Royal Western's supremely hospitable clubhouse at the western end of Plymouth Hoe, and now, equally hospitably, at Queen Anne's Battery Marina. Aficionados for these and other fully crewed RORC offshore races included highly successful skippers such as Majors Hugh Bruce and David Tweed, Captains George Wheatley and Jim Burton, and Colour Sergeants Graham Tongue and Geoff Daulman.

However the Royal Western's most enduring relationship with the Corps began in 1960 with Lieutenant Colonel 'Blondie' Hasler's 'amazing idea' for the Observer Single-handed Transatlantic Race (OSTAR), followed in 1964, by his equally challenging two-handed Round Britain and Ireland race (RB&I). These then followed each other through a four-year cycle, two years apart and that, by and large, continue to this day. The OSTAR, from Plymouth to New York for the first race, and from then onwards to Newport, Rhode Island, is roughly 3,000 miles of (mostly) windward sailing, unless the southern, and far longer, 'Azores route' is chosen. The RB&I from Plymouth to Plymouth clockwise, around the British Isles is about 2,000 miles of tricky coastal and tidal navigation, with four compulsory, 48-hour stops at Crosshaven (later Kinsale), Barra, Lerwick and Lowestoft. Views differ as to which is the more challenging as both, in their different ways, are considered a tough test' of seamanship, stamina, determination, navigation and in the case of the latter, compatibility.

This essay is not a history of Blondie's races but a salute to the Royal Marines who took up his challenges. Adding up all the Royal Marines competitors that stretch back for fifty years, it is certain that no other military service has been so involved with the RWYC's races, while some of these competitors were to go on to even greater achievements. Names such as 'Blondie' Hasler, of course, are to the fore in this category but so also are those of the much-lamented Mike McMullen, the equally doughty and determined Richard Clifford (sadly also no longer with us) Mervyn Wheatley, Pete Goss and Andy Lane. There are other Royal Marines whose names are also linked to tales of fine seamanship, sheer doggedness, some errors, riotous runs ashore and tragically, one missing at sea.

Following Blondie Hasler's OSTAR entries in 1960 and 1964 in his revolutionary, junk-rigged, 25-feet *Jester* ('because she is such a bloody joke' as Hasler himself described her) he then instigated the RB&I in 1966. For this event he was partnered by his wife Bridget in the equally extraordinary forty-five-and-a-half-feet sloop *Sumner*. The die was cast.

From the second RB&I in 1970 onwards, over twenty Royal Marines would follow in Blondie's footsteps, covering in excess of fifty separate entries. To begin this saga, in 1966 the RMSC's wooden sloop *Sarie Marais* had been entered for the first RB&I, but the skipper, Lieutenant Ewen Tailyour, was forced to withdraw on his appointment to the Sultan of Muscat's Armed Forces. His crew would have been the late Captain Johnny Ackroyd-Hunt.

Then, in 1970, the RB&I opened a small floodgate of Corps entries, when no less than five Royal Marines took part that year in three yachts out of twenty-five. Leading this mini-charge was Lieutenant Mike Shuttleworth as co-skipper in the 42-feet trimaran *Gancia Girl* which, as *Toria*, had won the first of these two-handed races in 1966. *Gancia Girl* forfeited any chance of repeating her earlier win when she all but lost her rudder off Barra Head in a Force 9 and thick fog. Superlative seamanship brought her into Barra for repairs from whence she continued to come a very respectable eighth overall. Since her previous success she had had a cockpit added, so now with other comforts, was 30 per cent heavier.

Next into Plymouth were Ewen Tailyour with Lieutenant Roger Dillon, whose tale of his encounter (naked) with a pigeon (clothed) on the first leg to Crosshaven caused much amusement across the fleet - and in the press. They were sailing the heavy, wooden-hulled, 49-feet yawl *Speedwell of Cremyll* and were followed in thirteen hours later by Lieutenants Mike McMullen and Martin Read in the twenty-five-and-a-half-feet sloop *Binkie*. By rowing, quite legally, from Salcombe to the finish line off the RWYC, McMullen and Read won the race on handicap. Because of the disparity in size *Speedwell* had carried all *Binkie*'s food, beer and gas cylinders for dropping off at the various compulsory stops, so it had been vital that this 'RFA' remained ahead. Not always an easy task when faced with the determination of McMullen and Read.

We first see serving Royal Marines in the OSTAR in 1972, when Mike McMullen, sailing the 32-feet *Binkie II*, was joined by Lieutenant Richard Clifford in his twenty-five-and-a-half-feet *Shamaal*. They both reached Newport in impressive times for their sizes – thirteenth and twenty-fourth out of fifty-five starters.

By now Blondie was keeping a fatherly eye on the rising stars of Royal Marines yachtsmen, as evidenced by this extract from a letter he wrote in 1972 to the then commandant general:

> *You have some fine seaman among your serving officers these days and chaps like Mike McMullen and Richard Clifford earn of lot of respect for the Royal Marines among sailing people...We are hoping to send off some hot Royal Marines entries from Plymouth on the Round Britain race in 1974.*

Colonel Hasler was quite correct for in the 1974 RB&I; there were eight Royal Marines out of 122 contestants. Mike McMullen had now acquired the highly competitive, 46-feet trimaran *Three Cheers* after she had come fifth in the 1972 OSTAR. In this 1974 race around the British Isles, McMullen was again co-skippered by Read. Not only did they come second to the huge 70-feet catamaran *British Oxygen* but Read had managed to save McMullen's life through clever and swift ship-handling after he had been knocked overboard in the North Sea. Another Royal Marine in this event was Richard Clifford in *Shamaal II*, who was awarded the RNSA's Round Britain Sailing Trophy as well as the Contessa Association's Nielson Trophy. Captain Mervyn Wheatley, co-skipper of the most uncompetitive, wooden ketch *Eclipse of Mylor* came in last of the thirty-nine finishers out of sixty-one starters, while Ewen Southby-Tailyour, was crewed by Corporal Steve Cook (name changed to save his blushes) in the first of his four *Black Velvet*s – a 24-feet sloop. Unfortunately Cook was taken ill during the approach to Barra so they returned non-stop to Plymouth from where Southby-Tailyour sailed with Captains John Chester and Roger Dillon to Lowestoft to meet his fellow competitors coming south from Muckle Flugga. He then sailed, mostly single-handed – Dillon helped as far as Newhaven – back to Plymouth. That Clare Francis had poured a substantial amount of draught Guinness into *Black Velvet*'s only fresh water tank may have had a bearing on Steve Cook's collapse.

This, in 1974, was the first of the Blondie/RWYC races that involved, at last, Royal Marines who were not commissioned. Originally, Sergeant Jerry Norman was to have co-skippered with Southby-Tailyour, but a month before the start Tankard Yachts offered the Royal Marines a 24-feet sloop. This was accepted with alacrity, but on the condition that she was not to be sailed by officers. Consequently Colour Sergeant Graham Tongue of the Royal Marines camber at Stonehouse chose Sergeant Jerry Norman, already a qualified skipper, and appointed Marine John Reynolds as his crew. Two superb choices. Cook then took Norman's place in *Black Velvet*. Reynolds's standard sailing gear, regardless of weather, were service denims and a pair of 'pussers' gym shoes, although this did them no harm for they completed the circumnavigation in good order, albeit outside the time limit.

The 1976 OSTAR saw two Royal Marine entries out of a total of a hundred and twenty-five. McMullen, an experienced member of the Mountain and Arctic Warfare Cadre, was sailing his *Three Cheers* in a realistic bid for line honours, while Clifford, an SBS officer, in *Shamaal II* – was hoping to better his earlier position of twenty-fifth. He was to reach Newport thirtieth overall but a notable third on handicap. This was an especially outstanding performance as his journey had included two serious knockdowns and the loss of his steering compass. For this notable display of navigation and determination Clifford was awarded the Royal Cruising Club's Seamanship Medal and the RNSA's Alec Rose Trophy as well as becoming the first recipient of the RMSC's McMullen Trophy. He was later awarded the RNSA's Tim Sex trophy for his single-handed achievements. Ewen Southby-Tailyour had been (unusually) given special dispensation by the RWYC to enter the very small sloop *Black Velvet* but (thankfully) he did not start due to service requirements.

The tragedy of this OSTAR was the loss of McMullen and *Three Cheers*. Four days before the start Lizzie, Mike's wife, was killed while polishing *Three Cheers*' hulls; she dropped the electric polisher into a puddle and bent to pick it up. Fellow competitors and friends created the Lizzie McMullen Trophy for the first multi-hull to reach Newport – an award that McMullen was determined to win, but a day after the start *Three Cheers* was sighted off Galley Head and never seen again. Wreckage was eventually trawled up after four years from the seabed south-west of Iceland.

Two years later three yachts crewed by Royal Marines, out of seventy-four starters, took part in the 1978 RB&I. Martin Read and Philip Grieg in the 35-feet trimaran *RFD* came home ninth overall. Richard Clifford in the thirty-seven and a half feet *Robertson's Golly* was thirty-first overall. while Mervyn Wheatley in *Slightly* was thirty-seventh, a creditable place for a 36-footer. Ewen Southby-Tailyour, again in his first *Black Velvet*, was obliged to withdraw before the start because of a posting to the Falkland Islands.

Clifford was the only Royal Marine competitor in the 1980 OSTAR sailing his immaculate 38-feet home-built sloop *Warrior Shamaal* into twenty-second place in his class.

Up to 1982 the RB&I had been known simply as the two-handed round-Britain Race, until the Irish, with unarguable logic, pointed out that not only was the first stop in Eire but the yachts also had to sail west of their island.

Although three Royal Marines (Clifford in *Warrior Shamaal*, Dillon and Southby-Tailyour in *Caressa*) had entered the 1982 RB&I, events in the South Atlantic took priority, so it was not until 1985 that Southby-Tailyour and Marine Chris Johnson were able to enter the RMSC's new, 34-feet sloop *Sarie Marais*. Unfortunately Tailyour was taken ill at Barra leaving Johnson to make his way homeward with various Royal Marines friends.

In 1986 the RWYC ran the second two-handed trans-Atlantic race with Marines Chris Johnson and Pete Goss competing in *Sarie Marais*. They were fast enough in a far from fit vessel (the keel bolts were working well loose as they limped into Newport) to achieve third place on handicap.

The 1988 OSTAR saw two Royal Marines out of ninety-five starters. Pete Goss in the diminutive 26-feet catamaran *Cornish Meadow* and Captain Jerry Heal in the competitive 30-feet sloop *Alice's Mirror* respectively coming second and third in the same class.

In the 1989 RB&I, Pete Goss returned to the fray in the 35-feet *Beneteau Marines*, this time with Captain James Getgood as his crew, while Southby-Tailyour co-skippered the 27-feet sloop *Fidget*. The former were first in their class, while the latter was disqualified for missing out the compulsory stop at Lowestoft, considering Brighton to be a better run ashore!

For the 1993 RB&I Mervyn Wheatley sailed *Independent Freedom*, a thirty-nine-foot Freedom class sloop and Southby-Tailyour, with his son Hamish (Royal Marines CCF - retired!) took part in the third *Black Velvet* - a solidly built, 35-feet gaff-rigged cutter. Although the latter were the last to finish they still came thirty-second out of fifty-two starters. *Independent Freedom's* finishing place is not recorded but just before the finish line in Plymouth Sound, Wheatley and his co-skipper rescued three actresses who had capsized their Wayfarer dinghy – so the result did not matter too much!

The 1996 OSTAR saw the now rising star, Pete Goss in *Aqua Quorum*, come second in class and ninth overall. Later the next year (the race had started in late 1996) he came fifth in the *Vendèe Globe* single-handed race. This fine result was achieved despite rescuing Frenchman Raphaël Dinelli from his sinking yacht, for which Goss was appointed MBE and investiture into the *Legion d'Honneur*.

In 1997 the RWYC expanded its horizons and ran a two-handed race to Reykjavik in Iceland, in which the sole Royal Marines entry was *Black Velvet* sailed again by Southby-Tailyour and Hamish. They came in well last against a fleet of racers – their excuse being that they were overladen with skis, pulks, three months of food and duty free for a four-man climbing expedition in Greenland!

Also in 1997 Pete Goss competed in that year's two-handed *Transat Jaques Vabre* from Le Havre to Salvador de Bahia in Brazil with Raphaël Dinelli as his crew in *Aqua Quorum* and came first in their class.

The 1998 RB&I saw Mervyn Wheatley sailing his own 42-feet Formosa sloop *Tamarind* with Southby-Tailyour in *Black Velvet*, and while the former retired with a broken boom off Barra Head, the latter was disqualified when he put into Brest.

In 2002 Mervyn Wheatley won his class in that year's RB&I in *Tamarind* but this time he was co-skippered by his son Marine Richard Wheatley, the only serving serviceman in that year's race.

By 2005 Wheatley was establishing himself as a formidable, single-handed trans-oceanic skipper. In the OSTARs of 2000, 2005, 2009 and 2013 it was left to him to represent the Royal Marines. These were all noteworthy performances that led him to be twice (2000 and 2005) sixth in class, voted the RWYC's Yachtsman of the Year, followed by being awarded the Jester Medal from the Ocean Cruising Club in 2010, and the RNSA's Alec Rose trophy in 2013. In the 2017 OSTAR *Tamarind* was hit by a hurricane and inverted. Although she righted herself the damage was so extensive that Wheatley had to be rescued by the RMS *Queen Mary 2*, having first prepared his vessel for scuttling.

In 2010 Pete Goss entered the single-handed *Route du Rhum* between St Malo and Guadeloupe sailing the monohull sloop *DMS*.

Just for good measure, in 1973 Ewen Southby-Tailyour had taken part in the one-off, single-handed Round Majorca Race from Leucate in the south of

France, although he had to beach his loaned, 21-feet, sloop *Pandora* to prevent her foundering, having been swamped in a heavy sea. Meanwhile Mervyn Wheatley entered the Azores and Back single-handed races (AZAB) in 1975, 1995 (second in Class 1) 1999, 2003, (third in Class 2, and winner of the John and Sally May Trophy), 2011 (second in Class 2), 2015 and 2019.

When, in recent years, the RWYC was forced to increase the lower size limit for yachts taking part in the OSTAR, a series of 'no–rules', single-handed Jester Challenges (in turn to Newport, Rhode Island, Praia de Vitoria at Terceira in the Azores, and Baltimore in Eire) was instituted by Ewen Southby-Tailyour. This was to cater for boats the size of Blondie's original *Jester* (up to 30 feet overall) which were now effectively disenfranchised from the more formal, oceanic races. The only Royal Marine in this offshoot of the OSTAR was Captain Andy Lane who, not put off by losing his mast (and subsequently his vessel) in mid-Atlantic in 2010, continued to take part. If one counts retired membership of the Royal Marines CCF then Hamish Southby-Tailyour entered the fourth *Black Velvet* (a 30–feet gaff cutter) in the 2015 Jester Baltimore Challenge but there have been no Royal Marines entries since.

So why is it that the OSTAR, the RB&I, the Jester Challenge and, briefly the *Vendèe Globe* and others were more popular with Royal Marines than with any other branch of the armed services? The answer is, I believe, simple. These races demand every one of the values required by the 'commando spirit' and particularly that most vital tenet of all, 'remaining cheerful in the face of adversity'.

The golden age of Royal Marines participation in trans-oceanic, single- and short-handed racing between the years 1960 to 2019 seems to be over and, from a current perspective, is unlikely to be revived although I sincerely hope that I will be proved wrong. Thus it would have been nice to end this essay with the comment that 'long may all these events continue to take place and long may Royal Marines continue to take part in them'. At the present while the races do continue to be run, Royal Marines entries have ceased to appear since 2019, so let Mervyn Wheatley have the penultimate word: '*The races are now an historical episode in Royal Marines sailing. In the modern Corps people simply don't get the time to take part in such events.*'

Added to this is the enviable fact that in the early days serving Royal Marines were considered to be 'on duty' while I suspect that this is no longer the case. Another factor is the proliferation of largely unnecessary rules and unrealistic regulations that often negate those essential components of 'personal responsibility' and 'self-reliance.' These often-superfluous constraints tend to exempt, or certainly put off, the true Corinthian while the vast entry fees, well beyond a serving Royal Marines' budget, do not help. Sponsorship is one answer but apart from this being the very antipathy of the Corinthian spirit, it also brings impractical expectations of success that often engender poor seamanship. Thus, it is hardly surprising that enthusiasm has dampened.

On a final and personal note much of the navigational challenges, fun and excitement disappeared with the arrival of GPS and sophisticated, global communications.

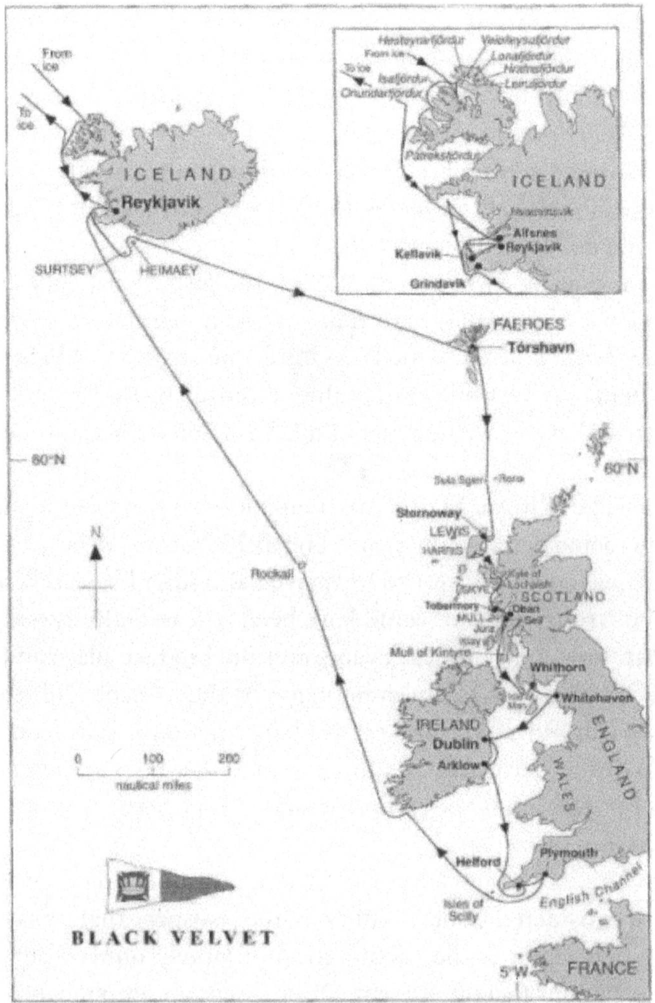

The third *Black Velvet's* 1997 voyage (Royal Cruising Club)

Chapter 28

Black Velvet of Tamar, 1993–2011

Tradewind 35ft, 12-ton gaff-rigged cutter
Lloyds ON: 727141. RT: 11.79. C/S: MRCW5

The idea

I retired from the Royal Marines in January 1992 when, following thirty-two very happy gap-years, a grateful government gave me a handsome gratuity. By then my family had owned yachts and motor vessels of various rigs and sizes since the early 1930s and, in recent years, I had owned two 24-footers: one gaff-rigged and one a Bermudian sloop. Since joining the service in 1960 I also had the use of the service's sailing vessels and had been the sailing master of a 50-square-metre, ex-German, 'windfall' sloop. Now that I was 'free', what next?

During my career I had spent thirteen winters in the Norwegian Arctic operating small, fast, open-landing and raiding craft and had quickly become captivated by the challenges of 'boating' in such conditions as well as the beauty of the islands and fjords. High latitudes, I decided, were the place to sail, an idea that appealed not only to my aspiration to explore under sail but to do so where there are few, if any, other yachts. Twelve years earlier I had honed this ambition by exploring much of the uninhabited and uncharted coasts of the Falkland Islands. I needed a suitable vessel and, for once, had the money to help realise this ambition - but what vessel was suitable within that budget?

The concept

The basic concept was to explore and cruise in the northern high latitudes, coupled with commercially chartering the vessel to for instance, 'ographers, 'ologists, 'oligers, mountaineers or any such professional body. When not otherwise employed she would also be used in more local waters by my friends and young and growing family.

Desired specifications

To meet the concept, and before my search began, I listed my desired specifications in no specific order:

She had to be sailed single-handed when necessary.

She had to be gaff rigged – a personal love.

She had to be strengthened for ice around the waterline. Not to break ice but to be able to manoeuvre among small floes and brash ice with impunity. Likewise the rudder had to be solid and not hollow.

She had to carry up to two-and-a-half tons of food, water, fuel and climbing stores. Up to three months of self-sufficiency away from civilisation was the aim.

She had to cross a squares'l yard for ease and comfort when downwind sailing.

She had to have a black hull for a cold-weather climate.

She was to be fitted with a police-approved gun-safe sized for one rifle and one 12-bore shot gun with space for the appropriate ammunition, including 'polar bear' shot.

She was to be fitted with a safe large enough for the ship's papers plus the crew's passports, money and valuables.

She was to be fitted with a radar and the aerial as high up the mast as was practicable. VHF of course. Wireless/CD/cassette player with repeat, waterproof speakers in the cockpit. GPS was to be an afterthought as I had three sextants. Plenty of paper-chart stowage would be needed.

Six bunks were the minimum preferred number, each with plenty of individual locker space and individual reading lights.

A self-draining wet locker/compartment adjacent to the companion ladder was necessary.

The galley to be equipped with a two-hob stove, grill and oven. A large tub-style fridge.

Saltwater hand pump, in addition to the usual hot and cold freshwater pressure taps.

Warm air heating throughout.

Navigation port and starboard sidelights to be in the shrouds and not at the truck of the mast.

Underwater hull fittings to be kept to a minimum.

Heads with shower, basin, hot and cold fresh water taps with plenty of locker space for personal equipment.

Copious bookshelf(s) in the saloon and above the chart table which, at its smallest, had to fit a once-folded Admiralty chart.

Construction in order of preference: wood, steel, aluminium, cement, grp.

Hull to be 'copperbot' coated or similar.

She was to be fitted with a 'bonded stores' locker that could be sealed by the customs.

Three anchors, one to be Admiralty Pattern for anchoring in kelp.

She was to have a long keel with a keel-hung rudder.

The search

Having listed the ideals I knew that I would almost certainly not be able to meet all the desired criteria in a second-hand vessel but also knew that I would not be able to afford a new build. As a compromise was inevitable, I set about studying the second-hand market for a suitable size and style of hull that most closely fitted the ideal and that could be, vitally, converted to gaff-rig.

Being a traditionalist I was not familiar with modern yacht designs and so, after little more than a cursory study, I realised that I was going to have to look towards more elderly vessels, reduce my aspirations or, a last-ditch solution as I prefer to be on my own, look for sponsorship.

I took many modernish Bermudian designs (there were no modern gaff-rigged vessels that made sense and no wooden, second-hand vessel came close) of roughly the desired size and hull shape and drew gaff-rigs on them, while trying to find a balance. I knew that with most moulded hulls the position of the Bermudian mast is fixed and I did not want to alter the fore and aft centre of effort on a proven hull by fitting a gaff rig and substantial bowsprit. I was prepared to lower the centre of effort to make the hull stiffer - indeed this would be beneficial. In the end two candidates stood out: one was a West Country design by the well-established company, Skentlebury who built beautiful double-enders and the other was a Tradewind 35 - both hulls were rigged as Bermudian cutters but both were suitable for conversion.

The Tradewind was built by, among other boat builders, Blondecell of Lymington so I approached them to ask if they had any second-hand Tradewind 35s on their books and explained what I wanted to do with one. They did not have any but a day or two later telephoned to ask if I would like to meet them to discuss the outline of a project they had in mind. In the meantime,

Skentleburys, with whom I had discussed my ideas and who had been more than interested had no second-hand vessels on their books and, sadly in the end, were not sure my plan was feasible with their hull.

I drove to a pub in the country outside Lymington for the first of many meetings with Blondecell. Their offer was generous: they needed the publicity and suggested they built the vessel as close to as many of my specifications as possible and I would pay a minimum price for the vessel on the understanding that she would attract £100,000 worth of publicity in her first year. Sponsorship of a type but – agreed! Building began in Blondecell's factory at Sway, happily incorporating all my specifications.

Build

I am not sure when building actually started but it must have been very early in 1993. The 'copperbot' was moulded into the hull and did not need replacing for at least seven years. The hull was thickened/strengthened for ice around the water line and the interior was as already designed.

Six berths was the standard Tradewind 35 layout in two cabins but the pilot berth on the port side of the saloon, the deep quarter berth on the starboard side abaft the chart table and one half of the double bunk in the fo'c'stle could be sacrificed for stores in addition to the normal storage spaces. In full expedition mode 'hot bunking' would be the norm.

Rig

The rig I wanted – and got – is best shown in photographs. In the end my centre of effort (bearing in mind we could not alter the position of the mast) was two feet lower (good), than the Bermudian version, and if I remember correctly, just six inches further forward (acceptable).

Trials in the Solent

Trials took place immediately after the naming and launching and were conducted by me and a member of the Blondecell team. They were witnessed by the yachting press, including particularly *The Times* and *The Daily Telegraph* over a two-day period.

Following the trials, Hamish S-T and I sailed her to Plymouth, anchoring in Studland Bay to alter the fall of the running rigging to the belaying pins as the Blondecell riggers (unused to gaff rig) had not much idea.

The commissioning party and blessing was conducted by the Reverend Albert Hempenstall, RN, at the Royal Marines' small-boat camber, Plymouth, on 17 June 1993, with about fifty friends present.

Publicity

The publicity was far more than we had hoped for as the buzz had got about across the yachting press. Front cover of *Yachting Monthly* was a real bonus for the boatyard but who then complained that I had not met my side of the contract as we had all the publicity in one week and not spread, as agreed in the contract, over one year!

Two-handed Round Britain and Ireland Race (RB&I), 1993

In June 1993, *Black Velvet* was entered for the two-handed Round Britain and Ireland (RB&I) race with my son Hamish as the co-skipper - at nineteen the youngest ever to take part. I think there were fifty-seven starters and we came last out of twentyish finishers. As she was not built for speed and I am not a competitive person, we were delighted with the result and, by staying around the middle of the fleet, we had been able to join most of the parties.

Exhibit at the 1993 Southampton Boat Show and lay up.

Black Velvet was exhibited at the 1993 Southampton Boat Show and attracted much interest and very many visitors. Following this she was returned to Blondecell for after-sale defects and rectifications covered by the initial warranty. She was then laid-up at the boatyard while I was employed for six months in the Former Republic of Yugoslavia by the Foreign Office. During this time, thus in my absence, Blondecell tried to sell her as, according to them, I had not completed my side of the contract. In fact, I had been too successful! Luckily, I was warned of this move by *Yachting Monthly* so immediately had a writ placed on her mast.

On my return from Croatia in mid-1994 I had a high court hearing that found in my favour but as a goodwill gesture, I paid an extra sum of money to Blondecell and then, thankfully, had no more dealings with the company. Except that is for two visits from the VAT office as Blondecell's CEO and finance director were being accused of allegedly fiddling their VAT returns. Whether they were or not I never knew.

Certificated as a commercial sailing vessel

I already held an ocean skipper's ticket and was an ocean examiner with a commercial skippers' endorsement so now it was time that *Black Velvet* earned her keep. She was inspected and granted a commercial sailing vessel certificate. When it ran out I did not renew it for some of the safety requirements were ludicrous.

On 24 August 1995, the Devon Wildlife Trust (DWT) hired *Black Velvet* for the first of many trips taking ornithologists deep into the Western Approaches looking for the Wilson's petrel; known by the Trust as 'willy-watching patrols'. For these expeditions two qualified skippers were required. Four 'passengers' were embarked for each trip, although they did not take part in any chores such as cooking and washing up. After some years - and occasionally more than one trip a year - we stopped when vegans began to appear!

Up to 1995 I only used traditional navigation equipment but was forced to fit a GPS by the DWT, as the birders were not convinced that I knew where we were.

Iceland

In 1997 I entered *Black Velvet* in the first two-handed Iceland race, with Hamish again as co-skipper. There was a reason for this as four climbers wanted to attempt a number of virgin peaks in south-east Greenland. On our way we called in on Rockall with the idea of landing, had the sea state allowed. It didn't, but we had the pleasure of speaking to a two-man and one-woman team who were camping there to protest about whaling.

Unsurprisingly, we were well last into Reykjavík where we were joined by the four climbers. The sea ice was too bad for us to reach Greenland, so the climbers flew there, while Hamish and I spent three weeks charting the remaining four uncharted fjords of north-west Iceland. At the end I flew home, allowing Hamish to bring *Black Velvet* back via the Faeroes. Steve Sleight was again a member of the crew, along with Sammy Coryton.

As a matter of record Hamish was awarded the Royal Cruising Club's Sea Laughter Trophy.

RB&I 1998

Black Velvet was entered for the 1998 Round Britain and Ireland Yacht Race but retired at Falmouth for personal reasons and so headed south where she was the only British vessel (out of about 500) to attend the afloat memorial service for the late Éric Tabarley.

Iceland 2000

The 2000 attempt to reach east Greenland was thwarted by atrocious weather in the Denmark Strait. After three weeks of beating to windward *Black Velvet* cruised the west coast of Ireland.

Iceland 2002

A third attempt to reach Greenland was made two years later with the climbing team (led by my son-in-law with all their kit) embarked from Plymouth. Beaten back to Newlyn by a ferocious northerly gale off the Isles of Scilly, we eventually reached Reykjavik in good order. On the way we had stopped at Rockall but, again, the sea state prevented a landing. The east Greenland sea ice or storis was too thick and extensive so the climbers flew to Scoresby Sound and successfully climbed a number of virgin peaks.

While the climbers were climbing, Mark Litchfield flew from the UK and spent three weeks helping me explore the north-western fjords and especially Hvalfjorder where the Arctic convoys had formed up during the Second World War. On the climbers' return they and Mark flew to the UK leaving one climber to help me sail *Black Velvet* back to Plymouth.

One hundred miles south of Iceland we encountered a southerly Force 11. How we survived this fast-reducing lee shore is best told in a chapter in Adlard Coles' and Peter Bruce's textbook *Heavy Weather Sailing* under the heading *Black Velvet's Bothersome Return from Iceland*.

French canals 2003-2004

In 2003, it was decided to cruise the French canals and so, stripped of her spars, we motored to the Somme and spent a year slowly meandering south in snatches of a week at a time. After exactly one year, *Black Velvet* was burgled in Creil, an immigrant town 70 miles north-east of Paris. Not only did *les voleurs* take everything but they also damaged the gearbox and so she was obliged to return to Plymouth on a lorry. The thieves did though, have a sense of humour for they left an unopened bottle of cheap, Tesco cooking brandy on the centre of the saloon table with the label facing the companion hatch – obviously not good enough even for an Algerian!

Cruising and moorings

Throughout my ownership, *Black Velvet* (while not employed by climbers or bird watchers) cruised extensively among the Channel Islands and the north Brittany coast but mostly along the Biscay coast for usually two or three voyages each summer, often skippered by Hamish.

In the early years she was berthed in the Queen Anne's Battery Marina, but latterly, and more happily, she was on a swinging mooring off Steer Point on the River Yealm. Throughout these years she sailed under either the White Ensign of the Royal Yacht Squadron or the Blue Ensign of the Royal Cruising Club.

Sold

On 22 October 2011 *Black Velvet* was sold to Mark Litchfield. Why the name? In the early 1970s I had a 73-feet, three-masted schooner designed by Angus Primrose and 'Blondie' Hasler, for a single-handed round the world race. As she was sponsored by Blue Circle Cement we all agreed she should be called '*Black Velvet*' as a mixture of the rough (cement build/Guinness) and the smooth (champagne/a beautiful design). I also happen to like Guinness!

Chapter 29

The Jester Challenge – Seamanship
without Showmanship

Newport, Rhode Island – Praia de Vitoria, Terceira, Azores – Baltimore, Ireland
Written in 2022.

Saturday 3 June 2006

At 1150 a huge white cloud of Johnson's baby powder was shot into the air one mile due west of Plymouth's breakwater lighthouse. The same happened again at 1155.

Then precisely at twelve noon BST an even larger puff of baby powder was exploded across the Sound, as both barrels of a 12 bore shotgun signalled the start of the inaugural Jester Challenge to Newport, Rhode Island. Any competitor too close to the committee yacht, a 12-ton gaff cutter, at the gun would smell sweetly, way out into the Atlantic.

There was nearly a delay for the skippers of that first Challenge in 2006 refused to sail if *Jester* herself, Blondie Hasler's iconic 25-feet, junk-rigged vessel, was not with them. Yet *Jester* was, that morning, still ashore at Alec Blagdon's boatyard. Almost at the last minute she was lowered into the water and swiftly taken in tow towards Cawsand Bay by *Black Velvet* – the 'non-committee' boat – while her new owner, Trevor Leek, and recent owner, Mike Richey, hastily bent on the 'Chinese' mains'l. It was, as they say, a 'damned close run thing'. But to the delight and relief of the eleven other entries, every one under 30 feet in length and being sailed single-handedly, the cause of all the fuss was at last present on the start line.

Since that day the Jester Challenge has increased in scope and is now held on a yearly basis, with the destinations being Newport every four years (JC), the Azores every other four years (JAC) and in between during the odd years, Baltimore in the Republic of Ireland (JBC). But what forced this event to take place and why has it become so popular?

To understand that we must go back to the summer of 1960 when Blondie Hasler's 'amazing idea' for a single-handed race across the Atlantic was first sailed by five yachts, four of whom were under 25 feet in overall length. Navigation was traditional and self-steering experimental yet all reached Newport in good order. The first and, interestingly, the last time this was ever to happen. However, so popular was the Observer Single-handed Transatlantic Race, or OSTAR as it became known, that by 1968 Hasler was worried that the race's success 'contained the seeds of its own death' with excessive competitiveness one of the reasons cited. Yachts of 128 feet and 236 feet overall in 1976 did not help the image. Fearing a demise he planned a considerably scaled down Series Two single-handed transatlantic race that, if necessary, would begin in 1980.

Hasler's Series Two never occurred because the Royal Western Yacht Club (RWYC) equally concerned that the OSTAR was becoming unmanageable, through being swamped by professional organisations and exciting if unrealistic designs, wisely hived off this professional element to Offshore Challenges and reverted to running a Corinthian event while increasing the lower limit up to 27 feet. A size restriction of 30 feet had been introduced earlier, partly for administrative reasons but primarily because of evolving international stability requirements which, although not banning the smaller vessels, made compliance difficult in formal events. The result, intended or not, excluded seaworthy yachts from a race that had at its very heart the 25 feet *Jester* herself.

This nautical nannying (emphatically not of the Royal Western Yacht Club's making) was and remains a nonsense and surprised owners of, for example, Twisters, Folkboats, Contessa 26s and even the diminutive Corribee 21s who were, quite suddenly, disenfranchised from most recognised trans-oceanic races. Experienced yachtsmen know that there is more to safety at sea than size and the righting moment of a displacement hull, for it is also a complicated matrix of human and physical factors. '*The only arbiter of safety at sea is the sea itself*', wrote Hasler, and not a health and safety-orientated committee with slide-rules and copious regulations. At that time Hasler believed, rightly as it turned out, that a higher percentage of under 30-footers would reach Newport compared to a similar number of larger vessels. Thus it is also interesting to note that the only class in the OSTAR 2005 with no retirements was the Eira class of the smallest vessels.

Another aspect of concern to the owners of under 30-footers was the entrance fee which, for the OSTAR 2020, stood at a colossal £1,800 pounds: most Jester Challenge yachts are hardly worth that price. And their skippers would rather spend that sum on their vessels and not into a communal pot which would, in practical and seamanlike terms, not benefit them one jot.

If size had not been a limiting factor the entrance fee most certainly was, along with some safety regulations that were quite impractical to implement in such small vessels. The time limit, to be an official finisher, currently at forty days was, too, unrealistic for those of *Jester*'s dimensions.

Thus we see the antecedents that necessitated the inventing of a quirky, eccentric, rather British solution that would allow yachts under 30 feet to compete on friendly terms with no entry fees, no time limit, no inspections and with negligible fuss - just a few guidelines - and minimal interference. So was born a nautical challenge like no other; a contest that has at its heart what the Jester Challenge skippers have nick-named a collection of 'non-rules', yet a challenge that requires plenty of seamanlike decisions from a growing family of participants. In establishing the Jester Challenge I believed that the skippers alone, and not sponsors or nautical nannies, should bear the responsibility for what vessels they sail and what equipment they carry, indeed, whether to sail or not.

But why Jester? Following the loss at sea of the original *Jester* during the 1988 OSTAR a collection of friends formed the Jester Trust, of which I was a member, to build - at our own expense - a facsimile of *Jester*. This would allow Michael Richey, her then owner who had bought the vessel off Hasler, to continue taking part in the OSTARs. However in 1997 while returning from the previous year's contest, Richey celebrated his 80th birthday at sea and on arrival in the United Kingdom grudgingly conceded that he was now too old for further trans-Atlantic voyages. We put *Jester* on the market. I knew Trevor Leek from the two-handed round Britain and Ireland races and I knew too, that he had participated in at least one OSTAR. So with relief that we had found a suitable purchaser, I recommended him to the Jester Trust as the best option, a view reinforced by his declaration that he had no intention of modernising *Jester* and would leave her precisely as designed by Hasler.

Once Trevor had taken possession it was only right that we should plan a public future for a vessel that had been described by the yacht designer, Angus Primrose, as 'the only radical advance in yacht design this century'. Then, suddenly, the solution was staring Trevor and myself in the face: reinstate Hasler's Series Two and let *Jester* herself lay down a challenge to cross the Atlantic. And so the Jester Challenge to Newport was born. It was, unequivocally, not a race (for therein lay legal responsibilities for the 'non-organiser' - me) but a simple challenge between amateur skippers in similarly sized vessels. It would not be a tournament between professional foes but a contest (if one must use this description) between 'family' members.

Having decided to lay down the Jester Challenge to all comers I thought it sensible to study and amend Blondie Hasler's original 'non-rules' which, in part, were:

'The race will have no sponsor, no organising clubs, no rules, no official acceptance, no prearranged facilities of festivities at either end' (I partially ignored that), 'no entrance fee, no handicaps, no disqualifications, no race numbers, no official finishing order, no prizes and no official dinner… (I ignored that too, on the understanding that such social occasions would help bring together what I hoped would become a growing Jester family).

'Each skipper takes part in the race on his own responsibility as an ordinary seaman making an independent and legal passage. The design, condition, equipment and handling of the boat being entirely his own affair.'

'No search and rescue operation will be mounted. Any skipper who is unable to remain alive by his own efforts is expected to die with dignity.'

And so there we had Hasler's reconstructed prototype although from the beginning I felt the need for informal festivities at both ends were fitting. They were bound to happen anyway so why not make them part of the fun that would also help bond a growing collection of international skippers with small vessels and little money.

I felt that to achieve this simplest of aims we did not need committees flying to the destinations. Nor did we need lavish parties and receptions and we certainly did not need silverware as prizes. In effect, Jester Challenge skippers compete against themselves and the ocean with all arrivals at a safe haven - even if it is not the official destination - being regarded as a success. And so that is what the skippers do and they do it without having the pressure of sponsorship, nor the need to massage images and reputations of either themselves or their backers. With no public glory - and no sponsor - waiting at the finish the highest standards of care and seamanship tend to be exercised.

To start with I issued the first and last press release in order to get a quorum of people interested. After that I hoped any publicity would become self-generating through reputation and word of mouth.

The Jester Challenge was, inevitably, not without its critics with accusations in advance, as it were, of needlessly calling on the emergency services. Now, after fourteen years, a lifeboat has only once been called out and that not by the skipper but by a third party who had no idea what was going on, while the skipper herself was making her way to her chosen destination in perfect safety. One yacht has foundered following a dismasting, with the skipper taken off by a passing merchant ship in a textbook evolution. There are, sadly, bound to be further incidents, but so far, common sense and good seamanship have held the day. Compared to other events where keels fall off, crew fall overboard, vessels run onto reefs despite the most modern of navigational systems, we consider our record to be pretty enviable. [Sadly, since writing this there has been one unexplained fatality.]

Although, like Hasler, we are not against sponsorship per se – one case of Plymouth gin is our tally so far – but with sponsorship comes pressure to succeed and with that pressure can come poor seamanship, which is why my unofficial tag line for the Jester Challenge is 'Seamanship without Showmanship'. Additionally, Jester Challenge skippers are likely to own their own vessels and thus will have invested significant, personal savings in them (for some they are also a home), ensuring that unlike sponsored, almost expendable, professional ocean racing vessels, these yachts – precious personal possessions – are cosseted and nurtured.

The Jester Challenge fills a gap and satisfies a desire. The 'non-committee' overseeing the very few 'non-rules' is just one 'non-organiser' – me! No one has a duty of care to the competitors other than the skippers to themselves, their dependents ashore and their fellow seafarers. As the mandatory 'blood chit' I ask all to sign (the only piece of formality before the start) states:

The decision to accept the Jester Challenge is mine alone.

The safety of my yacht and her entire management including design, construction, rigging, sails, gear, engines, rudder and steering gear, insurance, navigation, safety equipment and suitable experience shall be my sole responsibility. I will also ensure that both myself and my vessel are adequately equipped and prepared to face any conditions that may arise in the course of the Jester Challenge.

Neither I nor my dependants will hold the Jester Challenge co-ordinator or any person associated with The Jester Challenge responsible for any loss,

> *damage, death, personal injury or structural damage howsoever caused to me*
> *or by me as a result of my taking part in The Jester Challenge and I accept*
> *full duty of care for myself, my dependants and my fellow seafarers during*
> *my participation in the Jester Challenge.*

Skippers are unlikely to enlist onshore navigational and meteorological help and, in a parody of Blondie's views, we don't expect them to give a fig about level playing fields but we do expect them to behave like gentlemen as far as numbers on board and the use of an engine are concerned. They are simply content to reach their destination safely, taking their own finishing times to then compare routes, rigs, equipment, clothing, sleep patterns and diets. Jester Challenge skippers help each other as friends, not as adversaries. One skipper asked if he could take his cat - allowed! Another even asked, in all seriousness, if he could take his girlfriend on the understanding that she would do nothing other than look decorative - not allowed!

In the beginning some suggested I insisted on oil lamps, towed logs and sextants and while the Jester Challenge is for small vessels (many on very tight budgets) some of whom may well have been built in pre-GPS days, there's nothing Luddite about it. Satellite navigation predominates as well, unsurprisingly, as do wind vanes. With no nannying regulations Jester Challengers can carry - or not carry - what safety equipment they like based on personal experience. I rely on the maturity and experience of each skipper to make up his or her own mind on what suits their vessels and their own experience and mentality.

The Jester Challenge - a modern experiment in old-fashioned self-reliance, self-sufficiency and personal responsibility - replaces no existing race, is complimentary to the Royal Western Yacht Club's OSTAR and, so far after fourteen years, seems to be attracting the right type of entrant - both skipper and yacht. There is no vetting system other than my own gut feeling and no one knows how that works or how many obviously unsuitable applicants I have turned away!

That first Jester Challenge to Newport was marked by the first arrival being a Frenchman - the calm and amusing Eric Andlaur - which, considering that the French tend to dominate the OSTAR, would have been much to Hasler's pleasure and a rather satisfying conclusion. At Newport we were introduced to the more than hospitable and helpful Newport Yacht Club and the indomitable Norman Bailey who became our unofficial, one-man reception committee. Then and now nothing has ever been too much trouble for Norman.

The first arrival in the second Jester Challenge was the laughing Igor Zaretsky who, as a result, was to become Russia's Yachtsman of the Year.

However, before that, we decided to run a Jester Azores Challenge to give those who did not wish to go all the way to the Americas the chance to cut their teeth on a long-distance voyage but one with a destination close enough from which to return to the UK before the hurricane season.

Later still Tony Head - an enthusiastic Jester skipper and invaluable helper and mentor - suggested that even the Azores might be too far for those who really were beginners and so suggested we sent them, every odd year, to Baltimore in the Republic of Ireland. Another Jester Challenge skipper and the oldest so far - Roger Fitzgerald based at Pwllheli in north Wales - felt that two starts would make sense for this Challenge - one from Plymouth and one from Wales, to avoid the Welsh starters having to sail south to Plymouth before sailing north to Baltimore. So he devised a route that was the same distance from Pwllheli to Baltimore as Plymouth to Baltimore. These two routes (with the same starting times) were short enough for newcomers (and old hands who just wanted to keep in on the act) to sail there and back, well within a normal summer holiday period. The first Jester Baltimore Challenge coincided, by happy chance, with Baltimore's Pirate Week, so since then we have made sure that the JBC's dates continue to match Baltimore's amusing festivities. And there we have it. Skippers from eleven nations have taken part so far. Among this year's potential starters to the Azores we have four from France, two from Norway and one each from Australia, The Netherlands and Germany. Not bad for an event that has never been advertised but that relies purely on word of mouth and reputation. (The lack of a £1,800 entry fee and no regulations probably help!)

A good many Jester Challenge skippers have gone on to far greater things and while I accept that it is invidious to name a few names out of the many I have to praise Roger Taylor in *Mingming* who has ventured twice in to Arctic waters in his junk-rigged Corribee only 21 feet in length, while Igor Zaretsky, following his success in the 2010 Challenge, then entered the Golden Globe non-stop single-handed around the world race. Others too have enjoyed a new lease of life.

So what next? I am taking potential entries as far into the future as people are prepared to commit while we shall carry on much as we have done so far, with no half-witted regulations, no financial charges and no unrealistic time limits, but with the most amusing, adventurous, friendly and seamanlike skippers one could ever hope to meet.

Chapter 30

Excerpt from the novel *Death's Sting*

In 1994 I was serving with the Foreign and Commonwealth Office in Croatia where I witnessed or was involved with some horrific behaviour by a few individuals. I could not put much of this in my non-fiction book *Paid to Predict*, so decided to write a novel called *Death's Sting*. This, in part, centred around the murderous behaviour of a Croatian army colonel and yacht owner named Slavić and his French crewman, Sublette. Here, James (a retired Royal Navy officer and ex-European Community monitor) is being stalked by the colonel in his yacht *Helena* sometime after he, James, had returned to England with his Serb wife, Matea, and step son and daughter, Dino and Alicia.

Hoping they would now be safe, they are enjoying a sailing holiday on the south Cornish coast in their yacht *Sea Vixen*. Slavić, though, had never forgotten events in Serbia, and is intent on revenge and has caught up with them.

James settled *Sea Vixen* (a gaff cutter) on her course and looked around. *Helena* was lying at anchor outside Mevagissey's walled harbour, out of sight from the anchorage, *Sea Vixen* had just left…but ready to pounce. As James watched though his binoculars, he could make out Sublette - it would never have been Slavić - struggling with the cable's windlass and calculated that they probably had a forty-five-minute lead over the Croat. It wasn't much but as the time to cover the 13 miles to Looe Island in the strengthening breeze, would be under two hours, it might just be enough. The two yachts were roughly compatible in size, but Slavić's Bermudian-rigged ketch would be faster… and then what? If Slavić could catch them offshore, there was no doubt that he would use firearms. But close in, within sight and sound of people, James wasn't so sure.

The wind was rising, noticeably, with spindrift starting to blow off the increasing number of low white horses as they, too, began to chase *Sea Vixen*. Every so often a larger wave broke under the vessel's counter, lifting her stern, accelerating her down its leading edge. It was becoming exhilarating and, if had not been for their pursuer slowly gaining on them, it would have been thrilling. For all the physical delight of a 'cracking sail' James knew that the adrenaline flowing through his veins was not caused by the pleasure of the chase, the excitement of a race even – which it had become – but by the far greater fear of not reaching safety in time.

He assessed his decision: they could not have stayed at anchor for, during the following night, they would have been at Slavić's mercy, nor could they have sailed offshore for he would have followed them to his perfect killing ground: out of sight of land. Their only chance was to run downhill, in as fast a headlong rush as they dared in the rising wind, towards the nearest port, and only then inform the authorities that an armed vessel was in pursuit. James had considered Fowey as a suitable destination until a more subtle plan, a more deadly scheme, formed in his mind and for that to happen he needed an area with the necessary hydrographic features.

It might work. It might not work. Almost anything had to be worth the risk to be rid of Colonel Ante Slavić once and for ever; and if he took Jean-Claude Sublette with him then that would be a most welcome bonus.

James asked Matea to take the helm. She was calm and experienced and they would need those very strengths of hers if his plan was to succeed. Happy that, in the increasingly testing conditions, she had the vessel under control James ducked below to study the chart in minute detail through a magnifying glass. As his strategy had only an outside chance of succeeding, and wanting to involve Dino as much as made sense for someone of his young age, James tossed him the tide tables. 'You can be a real help Dino if you can tell me the time of high-water at Plymouth for today. The thirtieth of July.'

Dino eagerly turned the pages, 'Half past five this afternoon.'

'Good lad. It's going to get even more bumpy before it gets better so you look after Alicia down here.'

'Is it dangerous, *tata*?'

'Not a bit of it.' James reassured him.

'Will we still have fish and chips for supper?'

'I promise.'

In the cockpit, the lively tiller secure in her hands, Matea asked again, 'Why can't we just call the coastguard on the VHF radio. Then Slavić can be arrested and we will finally be rid of him.'

James had considered this most sensible of all the options open to him. He had considered it very carefully indeed, but he knew that that would entail years of painful cross-examinations, visits to the Hague and the perpetual reliving of that terrifying day at Drniš, all coupled to the possibility that one day Slavić might be free again or even be found not guilty. Against those odds he accepted that his solution was not ideal but he would never forgive himself for not trying. He knew, too, that his plan might not work and, worse still, he knew that it might backfire, spectacularly, in Slavić's favour. He kept the radio call as an option but as an option of last resort and one only to be activated when he was certain Slavić was close enough to civilisation to be apprehended.

He relayed none of this to Matea but said instead, 'It may come to that but he'll hear our radio call and then take even more desperate measures to destroy us or', James was thinking hard, evaluating all the possibilities, 'perhaps, even worse, back off for as long as he likes, playing on our fears. Possibly for months…'

As the nautical miles beneath *Sea Vixen*'s keel were reeled off, the weather deteriorated markedly as Dino's fair weather cumulus 'fluffies' gave way to lowering, hard-edged cumulonimbus, darkening all the time, laden with moisture.

'Look beyond the skylight, Dino,' James ordered through the main hatch, 'See how the clouds have changed?

'This is not the time for a meteorology lesson, *duša*,' Matea interjected angrily. 'Please!'

'Fraid so,' James called back, 'Rupert Brooke can sum such things up so perfectly.'

Rank upon rank, unbridled, unforgiving,
Thundered the black battalions of the gods.

'Now, thanks to those 'black battalions' I would like to put the third reef in the mains'l,' James shouted above the wind, 'to make her easier to handle but the bugger will certainly catch us then. As it is he has closed the gap to less than a mile. If he gets any closer we'll be within rifle range so we've got to make the harbour before he does. Once in sight and sound of people on the shore he won't dare.'

James bent beneath the boom to check the fast-closing coast, now three quarters of a mile to leeward, fringed with bursting spray. They had passed Fowey, they had passed Polperro, if they did not make it safely into Looe and were forced to run to Plymouth then Slavić would catch them before they were half-way across the nine-mile width of Whitsand Bay and James knew that that, most emphatically, was not an option.

His first plan, the only plan now remaining, simply had to work. It would be a close run thing but he was determined to see it through for he had no other choice. It was not only imperative that all four of them escaped Slavić's murderous intentions – which they could have done in the earlier ports – but, of far more importance for Matea's final peace, it was vital that the Croat was destroyed, utterly and finally…. Fowey and Polperro might have offered sensible, safe havens but, for his strategy to succeed, only Looe's underwater reef could bring about the ultimate, satisfying conclusion.

'Are we still aiming for Looe?' The tone in Matea's voice betrayed her fast-rising concerns.

James did not answer directly but said instead,

'They pass very quickly; these summer blows in the channel.' He tried to reassure her further, 'If, together, we can get it right…' then he stopped. He had no right to make promises he was unsure he could honour.

Matea's love for James was not always matched by her confidence, not in his decision–making but in her own ability to match up to his expectations. Now, though, was not the time to let him down. She said more calmly than she felt, 'Just tell me what to do and when to do it.'

'I love you,' was James's unhelpful reply. 'The next few minutes will be tricky as we meet the ground swell off the cliffs. Better double check that the children's lifejackets are tightly fastened. Not loose, how Dino likes his to be. Tell them to stay below, to hold on tight and do nothing unless I say so. I'll take the helm.'

While Matea did as he had asked James took another look beneath the boom. He knew well the passage between Looe Island and the mainland despite only ever attempting it at high water and on calm days when he could see the bottom. This time was different and, although expecting it, he did not like what he saw ahead. The half-mile passage between Hannafore Point and Looe Island was a continuous line of breaking seas that made it hard to gauge where the less shallow passage was… but he had sailed through often enough and, as luck had it, they were approaching the reef close to high water.

Checking astern James saw that, tenacious as expected, *Helena* was being guided directly down the track that *Sea Vixen* was carving through the foam and as the seas reached shallower water they were growing in height and increasing in gradient. With her long, heavy, lifting-keel *Sea Vixen* remained stable but the downwards rush on the face of each racing wave, with the rudder rock solid in his hands, was still unnerving. Any deviation from this mad, impetuous charge and they would be rolled sideways by a breaking sea and… James shuddered.

His plan also depended, crucially, on Matea having the strength to hoist the keel. If she failed then they would all fail.

Nearing the bar and with the crests of breaking seas stretching uninterrupted from shore to shore, James lined *Sea Vixen* up with a well-remembered transit on the far cliffs. It was not quite the deepest section of the reef which made it even more suitable for the task. With half a cable to go, he shouted down to Matea.

'Darling. Stand by. Get Dino and Alicia to help. It's got to happen first go… and fast!' He looked at the breakers piling up ahead then added, 'Shut the hatch but leave a small gap so you can hear my commands.'

If James had worried about any aspect of his plan it was this moment. With the keel lifted *Sea Vixen* would lose much of her directional stability. Controlling her for the crucial transit of the reef in the waves that were building steeper as the sea bed shoaled would require every ounce of his strength on the tiller and the quickest of reactions. His left shoulder simply had to cope.

'Mama and me are ready, *tata*.' Dino's little face was pressed to the gap in the hatch, his eyes wide with innocent excitement.

James shouted below, 'Bravo,' he encouraged. 'When I scream, 'now' hoist away for all you are worth.'

With the tiller gripped in both hands and the rudder humming and vibrating as each overtaking breaker accelerated the vessel to the point of instability, there was no turning back even had *Helena* not been astern. James knew that he would not be able to control the cutter with so much sail set if she lay across both wind and sea and he was relying on Slavić's belief that he, James, knew a passage to safety. So far, the Croat had behaved according to the 'rules'.

It was, literally, now or never. With a last-minute check that their adversary was still directly astern James judged the moment. As a heavy, breaking sea burst green and white across the cockpit James yelled, 'Now!' towards the companion hatch.

In the saloon, Matea and Dino hauled on the rope purchase that raised the keel. Dino's eyes bulged and his immature muscles strained but he knew he was playing a vital part in this unknown escapade. He didn't know why it was vital, he just knew that if James asked for something to be done at sea in a hurry, then he had to help. One day he would be told.

As the monstrous iron weight was raised *Sea Vixen* responded. Slewing to starboard, her round bilges lost all grip as another sea foamed across the deck. James tried to pull the rudder hard up to windward, his arm and back muscles working at the utmost limit of their strength, but it was solid in his hands. The cutter skidded sideways to port, broaching, close to being rolled…close to annihilation…but drawing one more foot less…one foot further from the deadly reef beneath.

Fifteen seconds was all it took to cross the bar with the cutter out of control in a mass of tumbling breaking surf, the rocks not four feet beneath her bilges. For those long, fifteen terrifying seconds she heeled to 45 degrees, the lathering seas reaching to her mast. Then, just as suddenly and just as violently, she rolled upright as the weight of water on her upper decks sluiced overboard to port. The bar was astern. They had made it.

"Lower the keel!" James shouted, and as stability returned and the rudder regained its grip *Sea Vixen* swung wildly back to her original course in the lee of the reef.

The transition to peace was one of the most pleasant physical sensations James would recall: though he would never admit that to his wife.

He looked astern. The picture of a beautiful yacht - or even an unattractive motor vessel - running at speed onto rocks is not a pleasant one. For a split-second James was appalled at the sight of *Helena* in her death throes… but sometimes a single bereavement is necessary for the many to survive.

In the very spot that *Sea Vixen*'s keel had been raised *Helena*'s varnished hull reared up as though lifted on the back of some vast oceanic leviathan. Then it stopped dead in the water, listing sharply and wallowing erratically as heavy seas swept, unimpeded across her now-stationary deck. The main mast snapped at the crosstrees and crashed forwards. A terrible crunching sound reached James's ears, audible even above the roar of the breakers. *Helena*'s keel, grinding itself on the rocks below, was ripping her garboard planks apart.

In calmer water now James ran forward to lower the mains'l while Matea furled the jib.

'We must go back and try to save their lives,' James shouted in her ear.

Appalled at this sudden and inexplicable reversal of James's strategy - from killing Slavić to saving the man who murdered her parents - Matea swung round shouting, 'Must we *duša*? Must we? What crazy thing are you now suggesting.'

'Yes! We must. It's a brotherhood of the sea thing. All seamen are obliged to help those in distress. We must check if he is all right.'

Matea looked more closely at James and saw that he was grinning broadly.

'Yes,' she smiled back, 'of course we must.'

With the engine running sweetly, James headed towards the bar where two yellow life jackets were bobbing among the flotsam. One of *Helena*'s crew, arms flailing and shouting loudly, was trying desperately to struggle free of the floating detritus, the other appeared lifeless. Ropes and torn sails grabbed at both bodies as they drifted clear of the reef and into deeper water.

James stopped *Sea Vixen* alongside the nearest head. Recognising the flabby, waterlogged features of Ante Slavić, his bulging lifejacket framing his obese face as it struggled to support his immense body, James was astonished that he could feel no compassion for a fellow seafarer. Matea climbed out of the cockpit to clutch his arm, both of them swaying together as the vessel rolled in the spent swell on the lee side of the reef. White faced, she stared down at the man who, for so long, had been her arch enemy, her nemesis, yet even at this defining moment she could feel no emotion as she watched, impassively, Slavić snatching and clawing in vain at the smooth sides of *Sea Vixen*'s gently rolling hull.

Without taking her eyes off the drowning man Matea made her confession and, in that moment, all fear left her. '*Duša*,' she said, surprisingly gently, "I don't want to see him live," James had lowered the boathook to within Slavić's reach but Matea pulled it aside adding, 'but I can't watch him die.' Fighting back what she would later call her 'tears of liberation' she swayed back to the cockpit and went below to comfort her children.

Wielding the boat hook James shouted at the Croat. 'Grab hold of this,' he ordered.

Slavić retched and spluttered, pausing for breath between each word. 'Thank - you,' he coughed hopefully, 'I - thought - you - said - your - boat - drew - nine - feet.'

"That's right, she does," James replied coolly,' but only four feet with the keel raised.'

The look on Slavić's face would remain another source of pleasure for the rest of James's life, but…there was one final task to perform. One final promise to be honoured.

As the Croat's fingernails scratched uselessly at the slippery–wet boat hook's varnished pole, James could not avoid a final taunt, 'Don't be afraid of dying, Slavić. You've caused and seen enough deaths for it to hold any fear for you.'

"*Pomoć*, James. *Pomoć*. Please."

'Too late Slavić. Far, far too late to ask for mercy,' and with these final words James thrust the metal hook hard into Slavić's inflated life jacket, giving it a violent twist as he did so to make quite sure. The sound of escaping air was another satisfying memory that, too, would last him well into old age.

Realising that James had no intention of 'helping those in distress at sea' Slavić screamed, his face puce, his eyes wide with panic, his mouth opening and shutting, 'You – bastard! You...' but his words turned to bubbles as his head sank through the foam until all that remained were blood and vomit rising slowly to the surface in one last, obscene image.

Calmly James stowed the boathook before manoeuvring *Sea Vixen* away from the immediate area of debris, then he grabbed the radio microphone, 'Mayday relay. Mayday relay. Mayday relay. This is yacht *Sea Vixen*. *Sea Vixen* reporting the foundering of an unidentified sailing vessel off Looe harbour. Two men in the water. Am attempting a rescue. *Sea Vixen*, out!'

The coastguard answered immediately, asking James to stand by until Looe's inshore lifeboat, was 'on scene'. They requested more details. James was circumspect with his answers.

The arrival of the RNLI's rigid-inflatable allowed *Sea Vixen* to continue her voyage until, with Dino, Alicia and Matea on the upper deck handling warps and fenders, they brought the cutter alongside Looe Harbour's western quay.

Safely secured, Dino took James's hand. "*Tata*," he asked, looking trustingly up into his stepfather's eyes, 'where's the boat that was following us?'

'Very sadly it hit the rocks.'

'Why did it do that?'

'It's what happens when you get your sums wrong.'

'You didn't get your sums wrong, did you *tata*?'

'Thanks to you and mama, Dino, we all got everything right. Especially your sums.'

'Was anybody hurt?' Dino's anxious face was still looking up at James.

'We tried to save them but unfortunately we were too late.'

Dino thought for a long time. 'Are we still going to have fish and chips?' he eventually asked.

'Of course, a double helping. Tell mama and Alicia that we are waiting.'

The following morning a police officer and the lifeboat secretary stood on the quay looking down at James. 'We would like to thank you for your help yesterday,' one of them shouted, 'Pity it ended in tragedy.'

'Tragedy?' James affected curiosity.

'We found two bodies on the rocks at first light. One had suffered a head wound, possibly caused when the mainmast collapsed and the other's life jacket was ripped open. Must have snagged in the rigging as the yacht foundered. Just so much dead weight. Helped to pull him down.'

'Poor buggers,' James said.

"We can't work out why they tried to cross the bar in such a strong onshore wind."

'Damned fools if you ask me.'

'Why, did you?'

'I knew the way,' James replied, a touch flippantly, knowing that from the shore it would have looked irresponsible.

'Oh well,' the constable replied, 'every skipper must answer for his own actions.' He pulled out a notebook. 'Interestingly,' he consulted the pages, 'among the effects washed ashore there was a plastic wallet containing the details of your own vessel. Plus a number of firearms in a waterproof container, including a sniper rifle with telescopic sights. The deceased was also wearing a pistol in a shoulder holster. Would you know why any of that would be?'

'Not a clue, officer. Not a clue.'

'Judging by other papers we have identified one of the crew as a wanted Croatian war criminal.'

'His death will save the lawyers a lot of work.'

'You don't seem too concerned?'

'War criminals deserve all they get.'

'They also deserve a fair trial.'

James thought for some time before replying, very deliberately. 'No, not always.'

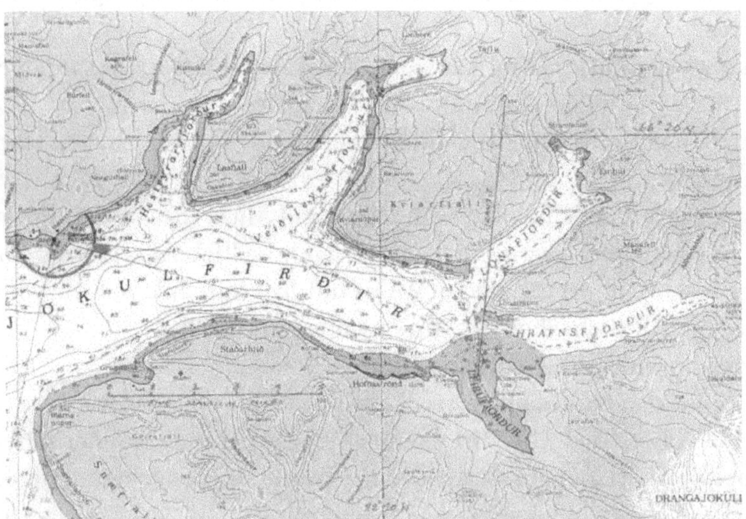

Iceland's four, last un-surveyed fjords showing *Black Velvet's* 'safe' tracks. (Danish Hydrographic Office).

Chapter 31

Excerpt from the novel *Skeletons For Sadness*

The following is a brief extract from the opening chapter of my novel covering the lead up to the Falklands campaign of 1982.

The black-browed albatrosses wheeled and soared between the deep valleys and charging crests of the South Atlantic's swells. A fold of skin above their eyes gave them an angry look that belied their peaceful purpose, but they were not the only life above that vast ocean. Skuas, heavy-bodied and evil, dived and screeched in their endless fight for food. Tiny, delicate Wilson's petrels flitted between the racing walls of white water, seldom gaining more than a few inches in height, their feet, paddling in air, occasionally broke the water's surface. The skua, follower of death, and the petrel, harbinger of bad weather: omens of doom to all but the most phlegmatic of seamen.

The seas north and east of Cape Horn have an unevenness about them not found further south. Off the Falklands they are seldom as mountainous, but their irregularity gives them a reputation nearly as ferocious as 'those great greybeards of Cape stiff'- the magnificent, breaking rollers that inhabit the Drake Passage and a terrifying place, as the seas and winds, following their uninterrupted circumnavigation, are squeezed through the 600-mile-wide gap between South America to the north and Graham Land to the South.

With saltwater dribbling down my face and oilskins I ducked below the main companion hatch, where the wind's howling was replaced by the more comforting clink of bottles in the locker above the starboard berth and the regular creaking of the yacht's frames as she laboured her way to windward. Somewhere a pencil rolled softly between the sides of a draw.

The saloon of a large wooden yacht at sea in bad weather has a womb-like security about it and *Nomad*'s in the South Atlantic was no exception. It smelt, and was warm and damp, the snugness emphasised by the compassionate glow from the single oil lamp swinging erratically beneath the main beam. Not yet dark beyond the large skylight, soft daylight shadows still swayed and circled across the polished wooden fittings, dancing in tune with those from the burning cotton wick. My affair with *Nomad* was profound and far closer than any I had known with a woman and, as her lover, I paid every compliment I could, not with bottles of scent or silk scarves but with jars of wood wax, tins of brass polish and pots of varnish.

Life was exactly as planned and with the muffled roar of approaching seas the only sound from the wilderness outside, it was close to perfection. Landfall after a lengthy passage is the second most exciting part of an ocean voyage, yet so often the saddest, for the end of a voyage means more than the safe arrival at a planned anchorage. It is the end of a world in miniature, the end of a naturally evolved routine – how I hated the word – the end of a micro civilization. It is also the end of an intimate interaction between people who, as so often in *Nomad*'s case, had seldom met for more than a few hours before departure. Making a landfall heralds an adjustment to the conventions of a larger society, with rules and regulations imposed by outsiders, bureaucrats, featureless, nameless and unknown. Conventions imposed by necessity but…

There is something very personal about a yacht's routine. It requires few guidelines, mostly common sense, and an understanding of three factors: the sea, the crew and the ship. I was often reminded that the very word 'sea-man-ship' summed it all up, and providing that I kept these vital ingredients in harmony, nothing should go wrong. But break that triangle at your peril. A good seaman should know how and when to give more or less emphasis to each factor without upsetting the delicate balance.

Ending a voyage implies the deliberate and unwelcome imposition of other people's rules. Ports have their uses but they are limited to the mundane. Perhaps Stanley would be different. Perhaps. Perhaps not. I almost didn't want to arrive. Didn't want my questions answered.

Chapter 32

A Selection of Letters

Some of the letters that follow are relevant to earlier articles and were sent to, or published by *The Daily Telegraph*, *The Oldie*, *The Field*, *Yachting Monthly*, the *Globe & Laurel* and the *Fleet Royal Marines Officer*.

The Daily Telegraph
23 July 1989

Sir,

Mr Ian Gillis and Mr Peter Lyons (Letters, July 18) need lament no more. Britain can, and should, preserve her 18th century wrecks on British soil. The wrecks of the Falkland Islands belong to the islanders (except in a very few cases) and should not be at the beck and call of any outside party no matter how worthy their cause.

The Falkland climate, devoid of acids in the air and trees with wood-destroying spores coupled with the near constant drying wind, is the most ideal place for these brave ships to remain.

The cost of removal, as we saw in the internationally deserving case of the SS *Great Britain*, is prohibitive. It would be far better to spend this money on stabilizing and preserving them in their present positions. The chances of the islanders agreeing to the removal of any wreck is slim for the *Fennia* experience still hurts. She was towed away in the mid-1970s shortly before her 'saviours' ran out of money and she was broken up for scrap in South America.

The islanders should now make some of their own funds available for preservation. Interested parties from abroad could, perhaps, sponsor vessels in which they have a national, historical or previous commercial interest.

The islanders can then build up a matchless collection of ships which will be preserved closer to their natural element than would be the case in any northern museum.

There are, too, other reasons for them to be kept where they lie. They are as much part of the Falkland scenery as the tussock-grass or diddle-dee. Many had second careers with the wool industry as storage sheds and some were repaired only to return after another encounter with an iceberg or a 'grey beard' of Cape Horn.

These ships are as firmly embedded in the folklore of the islands as the digging of peat or the ranching of sheep. They are part of the Falklands heritage and must remain so.

ES-T
Chairman the World Ship Trust

The Daily Telegraph
1 July 1992

Sir,

Following on from Lord Lewin's formation of the urgently needed National Ships Preservation Committee (report May 18) and the subsequent correspondence (May 28), there are a few more deserving cases 'on the books' of the World Ship Trust at the moment than the *Queen Mary*.

The Queen Mary Foundation in California has just told me that with the impending loss of the Walt Disney company as her present manager the future of this greatest of all ocean liners is about to rest in the none-too-sure hands of the port of Long Beach.

While the city of Long Beach says it intends to find a successor to the Disney company it has never been an active supporter of the *Queen Mary* and is now of the opinion that a more likely alternative is to scrap the ship.

By September it may be too late to save a ship that, were he still alive, would have been very much in John Masefield's mind when he ended his poem 'Ships' with the words:

> *They mark our passage as a race of men,*
> *Earth will not see such ships as those again.*

Tragically, quotes from Rupert Brooke's poem 'The Soldier' are likely to be more relevant.

ES-T
Chairman, the World Ship Trust

The Daily Telegraph
3 February 2000

Following complaints from the animal rights lobby about the then Countess of Wessex's fur hat.

Sir,

I support the Countess's decision to wear a fox fur hat. What a pity I was unable to counter her critics with a reply I was once forced to make when giving a lecture on sailing through an Arctic winter. As I donned my favourite Arctic-wolf fur hat to demonstrate its thermal properties, a strident voice harangued me about animal rights.

When she had stopped, I replied quietly 'Madam, it was him or me!' and I was able to finish the talk unheckled.

I shall be wearing it again this summer when at sea north of the Arctic circle.

ES-T

The Daily Telegraph
November 2006

Sir,

I received recently a letter about my book HMS *Fearless* in which the author complained of the smell of the pages. Perhaps all books should have the aroma of their subject matter in which case I shall arrange for the reprint to smell of burnt aviation fuel and frying chips!

ES-T

The Daily Telegraph
Circa 2018

The Prime Minister expressed concerns that we should beware of leaving the EU for then the UK would be entering 'uncharted waters'.

Sir,

We are at a loss to understand why Mrs May in particular, and Remainers in general, should be using the fear of 'uncharted waters' as one of the excuses for finding it difficult to leave the EU. It was the very taming of such regions, then most of the globe, that made this country the greatest trading and military nation in history. Across four centuries, the way ahead was paved by farsighted politicians and diplomats sponsoring gallant ships' companies and courageous explorers on foot, mule and camel. The Northwest passage, an uncharted area (and largely still is) held the key to shorter trading routes to the Far East, but no one baulked at attempting it.

Further afield, India and the East Indies produced spices; the West Indies supplied sugar; South America gave us guano and gold; South Africa offered diamonds; North America taught us to smoke while the inhospitable southern oceans brought us fish oils and whale bones. Wool from Australia, lamb from New Zealand and tea from China arrived despite crossing the most dangerous seas to be found anywhere on earth. Then we 'invented' the industrial revolution and won the prosperity that came with it.

None of these markets existed before intrepid explorers on land and sea, backed by politicians, risk-taking merchant traders, heroic military commanders and the most imaginative of inventors, forged their way across, and into, 'uncharted territories'. Now new forms of 'uncharted territories' - political, commercial and financial - should, once more, be seen as exciting challenges. Challenges that are waiting to be grasped with open eyes and widespread arms and not treated as black holes by those who can see no future outside the waning EU.

Our predecessors took huge financial risks but those audacious actions, performed by a far bolder, more enlightened establishment, made us what we are (or, rather, what we were). Now the lessons learned from four centuries of enterprise are to be forfeited because a timid, morally bankrupt collection of short-sighted politicians are frightened of taking the smallest risk: terrified of failing because they believe that successful endeavor can only be regulated into existence by the dead hand of the EU.

Of course there will be setbacks but the final prize, as our current 'leaders' should have learned by now, will be worth every one of the risks. Facing the challenges of 'uncharted territory' is what we have always done best and is, after all, what most of us voted for.

As we used to say in our adventurous youth, 'bugger the begrudgers, we'll do it our way'.

ES-T

The Daily Telegraph
27 July 2015

Sir,

Glorious, exciting and full of hope as it is there is something strangely bizarre about the British entry for the America's Cup.

In Saturday's pictures the starboard side of the mains'l has the Union Flag upside down, the accepted sign of a disaster at sea…and yet the port side of the sail has it the right way up: assuming, as with the other nations and their mains'ls, the wind blows from forrard to aft!

After all the money and attention to detail this rather public display of uncertainty will not, I trust, be a pointer to the final result.

ES-T

The Daily Telegraph
22 July 2016

Sir,

On the assumption that the wind blows from forrard to aft on Sir Ben Ainslie's catamaran it is unfortunate that the prominent union flag at the head of the mainsail is flying upside down The photograph of the British America's Cup entry shows quite clearly that the Union Flag at the head of the mains'l's starboard side is either upside down or back to front on the fair assumption that the wind blows from bow to stern. Bizarrely it is correct on the port side of the vessel.

I hope this signal of nautical distress is not a taster for things to come.

ES-T

The Daily Telegraph
4 November 2016

Following comments about Enid Blyton's writing, using this book as an example on whose cover was a painting of a dinghy being rowed with only one oar.

Sir,

Did the artist for the cover of the book *Five on a Treasure Island* (Letters, November 2) really mean the dinghy to go round in circles to starboard?

ES-T

The Daily Telegraph
23 November 2016

Sir,

Why do the As, Bs and Cs get all the best gales. Could the Meteorological Office please begin next year's storms with Zebedee and then work backwards through the alphabet?

ES-T

The Daily Telegraph
28 December 2018

In answer to the suggestion that civilian craft be used to combat illegal immigration.

Sir,

The idea of second-hand patrol boats, in conjunction with light spotter aeroplanes, (Letters, December 28) could indeed be a solution that might help stem the flood of illegal immigrants. It would, too, free up both the Royal Navy and the Border Force to confront drugs and arms smugglers, unlawful fishermen, real criminals and the Queen's enemies in general.

However, in both the RN and RAF there is a manpower problem and as the crews of the proposed small vessels and light aircraft need not be trained to service standards may I suggest the reintroduction of the Second World War's remarkably successful Royal Naval Volunteer (Supplementary) Reserve, along with an RAF equivalent.

Prior to 1939 the ranks of the RNV(S)R were mainly drawn from experienced yachtsmen, trawler men and general seaman and were available on an 'as required' basis. These experienced 'amateurs' conducted their own training and received no pay and thus were not a drain on sparse resources yet were irreplaceable once employed (and paid) in manning, for instance, the country's coastal forces. *Plus ça change?*

Sadly for me, so successful was the scheme that the age limit had to be reduced from 39 to 25 and, if implemented now, I do not see it being increased to 78!

ES-T

The Daily Telegraph
13 November 2020

Following a trail of letters about using out of date material.

Sir,

A few years ago, Peter Cameron, a Royal Marines helicopter pilot, suffered serious injuries on my boat.

Among others, the haemorrhaging leg wound required a tourniquet so, in the dark, we applied a government-issued 'first field dressing'.

Once he had been lifted ashore by the coastguard we inspected the packaging on the dressing. It was dated 1944. I am glad to report that Peter survived.

ES-T
PS. Conversation between the yacht and the 999 operator:

Yacht: We have the haemorrhage under control.
999 operator: Are you medically trained?
Yacht: No but between the four of us we have about 100 years of experience with gunshot wounds.
999 operator: GUNSHOT WOUNDS! GUNSHOT WOUNDS! You'll need the police!

The Daily Telegraph
22 February 2010

Sir,

Steven Broomfield's suggestion (Letters, February 22) of sharing the proceeds of oil with Argentina was precisely what was in mind in 1975. To refresh my memory of events I have dusted off the thesis that I wrote for the Royal Naval Staff College, Greenwich, on my return from commanding the Falkland Islands' Royal Marines' Naval Party 8901 in 1979.

Following a seismic survey in the mid-1970s it was estimated that twenty billion barrels of oil could be recoverable: apparently six times the then known

North Sea reserves. The tentative plans were for United Kingdom companies to drill the oil then simply pipe it ashore to Comodoro Rivadavia, an 'oil town' on the adjacent Argentine coast. There it would be refined and sold to the world's market to everyone's financial advantage, including that of the Falkland Islanders.

On 2 April 1982, Argentina forfeited any such collaboration, yet foresight might have saved the day – and lives – all round.

ES-T

The Daily Telegraph
6 February 2015

Sir,

Croatia has been found not guilty of 'genocide' in Krajina (Comment, February 4) but it should remain guilty of 'ethnic cleansing'. There is no other word for the forcible removal of the Serbs of Krajina during Operation Storm in 1995. Perhaps the reluctance to indict Croatia stems from the fact that both Germany and America rearmed Croatia with tanks and aircraft throughout 1994 without which the Serbs could not have been 'removed'.

When we learnt that the German government was, against the terms of the UN Embargo 713, importing Leopard tanks and aircraft in containers into Croatia, I was ordered by a French diplomat to cease monitoring the port of Ploĉe, in my area.

When I argued that that was precisely why we were employed as European Community Mission Monitors, I was ordered by a Greek (Greece held the presidency at the time) to continue monitoring but to falsify (his word) my daily reports to Brussels, to indicate that I had not been in the area and thus had seen nothing: but I was to continue to watch Ploĉe and report, privately, to the Greeks. I resigned from the Mission.

ES-T

The Daily Telegraph
2 April 2016

Sir,

Your report (Croatia's anger as Serbian cleared of war crimes. *The Daily Telegraph*, April 1) that Croatia condemns as 'shameful' the acquittal of the Serb Vojislav Seselj on charges of war crimes perpetuates the well-established Croatian 'holier-than thou' attitude towards its neighbours.

Remembering that only last week ex-Serbian President Radovan Karadžić was sentenced to forty years imprisonment is it not more shameful that the then Croatian President, Franjo Tuđman, was never indicted for similar crimes against humanity. After all, one of the aims of Croatia's Operation Storm on 4 August 1995 was the ethnic cleansing of over 200,000 Serbs from the Krajina region, with an estimated 20,000 of them murdered.

This equally shameful episode in the whole sorry mess of the Balkans in the 1990s was only possible with the tacit agreement and practical support (through the breaking of UN Arms Embargo 713) by Washington and Bonn.

ES-T

The Daily Telegraph
23 November 2016

Following a photograph of military training in a wood.

Sir,

I am glad the soldier in the Duke of Lancaster's Regiment, featured in your photograph (October 29), had a wood to fight in for his training.

I have, over the years, been obliged to take part in JEWTs – jungle exercises without trees – and even DEWDS – desert exercises without dunes. Others included, memorably, a NEWD – night exercise without darkness – during which, as second lieutenants under training, we were required to transit Woodbury Common's numerous obstacles wearing blindfolds.

The TEWT – tactical exercise without troops – is well-known to military officers while sadly our maritime forces seem to be heading for a series of NEWS or naval exercises without ships. I once conducted a SLEWP, appropriately named for the yacht club in which I was lecturing. When the projector broke during the second of fifty slides I was forced to continue with a slide show extravaganza without pictures.

ES-T

The Daily Telegraph
6 November 2018

Following a discussion of when and when not to wear a tie.

Sir,

When sunbathing – a rather vulgar Italian habit that I enjoy – I do not wear a tie. More seriously, a tie is necessary to add colour and individuality to an otherwise rather boring selection of men's formal suits. The ladies are luckier for they can change the combinations of colour and degrees of formality almost hourly: and what a joy that is!

The other occasion that a tie is less sartorially important but of vital practicality is when sailing in high latitudes. A tightly knotted Royal Cruising Club tie is the only method I have found to be all-but fool proof for preventing icy water creeping down ones back. A soggy towel freezes against the skin adding to the discomfort and, possibly, the danger of frostbite.

ES-T

Considered on Facebook to have been the most pointless letter of the month! I agree!

The Daily Telegraph
31 December 2018

Comment on a report about the French reaction to the channel migrants.

Sir,

What would Nelson do? Simple, welcome them all, men women and children, with open arms. The more the merrier to help man his fleet in the seemingly unceasing 'war' with France. It would also relieve the press gangs of their necessary but distasteful task. Positive results all round!

ES-T

The Daily Telegraph
18 November 2000

Sir,

In his characteristically robust letter (Nov 17), General Julian Thompson suggests that there are more questions than answers to whether or not there should be a 'Euro-army' and whether or not the United Kingdom should be part of it. Here are some more; small incidents maybe but still pointers to greater areas of international distrust.

Why, when as an FCO-employed European Community monitor in the Republic of Serbian Kyrenia, was I shown, in some secrecy by one Captain Dragan in his mountain camp overlooking Croatia, a section of regular Italian soldiers being trained by him 'against the day Italy decides to take back that part of northern Dalmatia lost to the Germans at the end of the Second World War'? Dragan knew well that his revelations to me would reach the outside world but not via the European monitoring system

Why, when sent to take over the team monitoring the Croatian coast in the Split area, was I ordered by my French superior (a senior diplomat) to relieve a regular Danish naval officer and underwater warfare specialist, who he had sacked for spying against the Croats – aka Germans? (He left, but conveniently 'forgot' to take his notes with him!)

Why, when discovered by another team in the north that the German government was, against the terms of the UN embargo, importing Leopard tanks (and aircraft in containers) into Croatia, was I ordered (by a different French diplomat) to cease monitoring the port of Ploĉe, then in my area?

Why, when I explained that that was precisely why we were employed, was I ordered by a Greek (they held the presidency at the time) to ignore the Frenchman and to carry out the legal monitoring but to falsify my daily reports to Brussels (and, particularly, to the French) to say that I had not been in the area and thus had seen nothing – but I was in fact to continue to watch Ploĉe and report, privately, only to the Greeks if I did see anything?

Which comes back to the most relevant of the General's unanswered questions: will British soldiers be sent on operations with which we disagree (and whose side might they take if the problem is internecine) and could we also find ourselves supporting a similar, morally disgraceful, illegal operation as that undertaken by the 1995 German and American-supported Croat army's cleansing of upwards of 20,000 Kryenian Serbs from land they had farmed for four hundred years?

European military unity? – don't even bother telling that to the marines for only a politician (who never has to suffer the physical consequences of his actions) could really believe in it.

ES-T

The Daily Telegraph
25 April 2021

Sir,

I am full of admiration for Mr Ian Rivers and his attempt to row west to east across the North Atlantic singlehanded and wish him God speed.

However, he should be grateful that your reporter, Dominic Nicholls, is not responsible for the passage planning. The route Mr Rivers plans, from New York to the Isles of Scilly, is not 'the wrong way'. The prevailing winds in that part of the North Atlantic also blow from west to east while the Gulf Stream could push Mr Rivers towards his destination at roughly 70 nautical miles per day. Furthermore, tropical storms in the North Atlantic, although not unknown, are most rare.

Finally, Mr Nicholls makes much of the fact that navigation will be by sextant as though this was a rare phenomenon. This fool-proof method of determining a vessel's position has been conducted by mariners for hundreds of years, so, bravo to Ian Rivers for choosing the most reliable navigational instrument available and the most sensible route.

ES-T

The Daily Telegraph
5 February 2022

Sir,

If I was offered penguin burgers in a Greenlandic brassiere (as James Pembroke posits) I would be extremely suspicious of the provenance of the birds on offer. Despite being a flightless bird they would have had to have 'flown' some 10,000 miles – or arrived in a 'freezer'.

For the record, I have eaten fresh penguin and not as a burger; in the Falkland Islands: fishy but palatable.

ES-T

The Daily Telegraph
27 April 2022

Sir,

Nikolai Tolstoy is right to raise the lack of surprise at Germany's tardiness in sending support to Ukraine. He might, though, care to comment on Germany's support of Croatia in the early 1990s when, along with the USA, Chancellor Merkel's government broke UN Arms Embargo 713. This helped to re-arm Croatia to such an extent that that country was, eventually, able to ethnically cleanse 200,000 Krajina Serbs from their 500-year-old homeland: generally regarded as the worst such crime since the holocaust. The interesting fact is Russia was supporting Serbia.

ES-T

The Daily Telegraph
2 September 2022
Sir,
Tomorrow (3 September) is Merchant Navy Day as proclaimed by His Majesty George V in recognition of the sacrifices made during the First World War, often unsung, usually unknown and that continue in conflicts to this day. That evening I shall greet supper with the grace that was said at the Nautical College, Pangbourne in the 1950s: *For what we are about to eat – thank God and the Merchant Fleet.*

ES-T

The Daily Telegraph
25 November 2022
Comments on a suggestion that sunset, or 'five bells', is the best time to start the evening's drinking.

Sir,
I admire Craig Heeley's drinking habits. Here, in South Devon, sunset tonight is at 1619 and 'five bells' will be struck rather earlier at 1430. Even for a Royal Marine that is a touch too soon for the first G&T. Ignoring the two dog watches 'five bells' at 1830 strikes me (and certainly my wife) as a more reasonable time to start the evening – regardless of when the sun sets.

ES-T

The Daily Telegraph
30 October 2023
Following lengthy discussions on Harold Wilson's mistress.

Sir,

In October 1968, Harold Wilson and Marcia Williams had near-adjoining cabins on board HMS *Fearless* at Gibraltar for the talks with Ian Smith over Rhodesia. One evening she and Gerald Kaufman were late back from a 'run ashore' and complaining that the naval staff car had not waited four hours for them outside a restaurant.

Arriving around midnight, Ms Williams was so angry that she stormed past the Royal Marines sentry guarding the Prime Ministers' sleeping quarters to protest.

Later, the Royal Marine was on a charge (later dismissed) for allowing Harold Wilson to be disturbed, but he had already had his revenge, for when Marcia Williams eventually returned to her own cabin and laid down on the bunk, it suddenly reverted to its daytime role as a sofa, squashing her horizontally against the bulkhead. The marine waited a very long time indeed before responding to her squeals.

This incident took mere seconds to be 'broadcast' throughout the ship, thus enhancing the long-rife rumours of 'an affair'!

ES-T

The Oldie
7 June 2021
Sir,

By sheer chance, as I was enjoying a corned beef salad in the sun this lunchtime, I turned the page of *The Oldie* to be met with the headline 'Where's the corned beef?'

Corned beef has formed the staple diet of every yacht I have had the pleasure of skippering in high latitudes especially when locally caught, shot or snared meat has been scarce. Indeed it formed the fundamental ingredient of so many meals in my youth while at sea. Yes, we called it 'bully beef' too but more often it was referred to as 'corned dog' or, when in arctic Norway, as 'dog in box'. I won't horrify you with my 'serving suggestions' but they include masses of red wine, garlic and vindaloo – perfect when the cabin temperature is well below freezing.

ES-T

The Field

21 March 1968
Three letters were received in reply, one each from East Africa, New Zealand and Saudi Arabia, all confirming that others had, too, witnessed such 'hypnosis'.

Sir,
Recently my company was posted to a remote corner of Oman where Major John Edward-Collins and I witnessed an unusual event. For some days our medical corporal, a Baluchi, had been teasing us by producing large scorpions and snakes from inside his shirt. He assured us that they were still poisonous but would not harm him as they were under a form of hypnosis. We, of course, were sceptical of his ability to hypnotise (or, as he would say, 'talk to') these creatures but he denied suggestions that they had been 'milked'.

Our chance to call his bluff came shortly after Christmas when we found a scorpion (later to be measured at just on five inches) in the open fireplace of the 'officers' mess' (beneath a date palm on the edge of a wadi).

As we knew it not been 'milked' or 'talked to' we immediately summoned the medical orderly who then turned down our invitation to pick it up. He would go nowhere near it, but instead called for an Arab private soldier, who, he said, would hypnotise it.

The scorpion, up to then, had been definitely hostile towards us and was kept at bay by a long stick. Because of this, we were amazed when it showed great fear on arrival of the soldier. It tried to back away but was thwarted by the fire.

The soldier sat on his haunches with his head in his hands and stared at the scorpion for two minutes. During this time we assumed he was plucking up the courage to pick it up. This was not the case and, after a total of three minutes, he suddenly stood up, turned to the medical orderly and declared that the scorpion was now safe.

The soldier had, as a child, read a certain part of the Koran to a holy man who had invested him with the powers of hypnosis. However, he would lose his power instantly, and permanently, if he were to kill any animal that he had made safe, although anybody else could do so. Indirectly therefore he did kill his victims as the scorpions were unable to catch their food. Although Major Edward Collins and I refused the invitation, it was apparently perfectly safe for us, or anyone else, to handle the scorpion. The amazing thing was the scorpion's complete change of attitude from belligerence to fear once the soldier arrived.

Since then I have spoken to others who spent many years in the Oman, and although they had heard of the ability to hypnotise poisonous animals, none had seen it done.

Perhaps some of your readers have witnessed this and can comment?

ES-T

The Field
Unrecorded date
For the Red Letter Days section.

Sir,
I do not hunt and I do not fish, instead I prefer to sail in places were other vessels are rarely encountered.

In doing so I have experienced a great many red letter days at sea but probably more 'red letter nights' for it is often between sunset and dawn that supreme happiness can engulf all other emotions. I have sublime memories of drifting along in the tropics under fair weather sails, beneath a full moon, with a tummy full of curry (and a tot or two) and a laughing crew. I compare those calm nights with others spent in an exhilarating crash to windward in a well-reefed, well-found yacht and, again, with a laughing crew. Other magnificent memories include swaying across the fore-tops'l yard, unfurling the sail of an outward-bound, square-rigger.

But the most crimson of all days - although it was, in practice, midnight - was at anchor in a flat calm among Iceland's north-western fjords in 1997. Earlier my son Hamish and I had tried to land three climbers into Depotfjord on Greenland's east coast from my twelve-ton gaff cutter that I had had especially built for high latitude exploring. Sadly, though, that year the *storis* - sea ice - was too thick for us to penetrate and so we returned the climbers to Reykjavik.

As four out of the five fjords of Iceland's north-western peninsula were tantalisingly uncharted we then set off through the Demark Strait. It was tough - below freezing and blowing half a gale - but we stood on to cross the Arctic Circle in order that King Neptune could board then, having assuaged 'His Majesty's' thirst, we turned for the entrance to Isafjôrdur and the unsurveyed fjords that lead off it.

Three weeks later, on 20 June – the summer solstice – and with our survey work complete – satisfyingly with a sextant, lead-line, compass and no GPS – we anchored in Leirufjôrður beneath the Drangajôrkull glacier, where it melts into the ocean. Following supper of roast puffin and freshly caught cod Hamish rowed ashore to explore the ice. Alone at last with my memories of the previous days, with the 'windy-up' gramophone playing operatic arias, with the liquid in my glass a fine malt, and with the sky a startling crimson as the sun set and rose almost simultaneously, I knew I would never feel more at peace at sea…and wrote so in the ship's log.

That evening remains the most intensely happy memory of all, even now after well over seventy years of cruising, for not only was our 3,500 mile voyage entering its final stage but it was also the culmination of our self-imposed surveying work that would, we hoped, find its way onto the charts. Even the unexpected 'impact hydrography' – the offending rock is now well tabulated in its correct position – had had its amusements! Here was contentment that no success in competitive sailing could ever match.

ES-T

The Field
26 April 2021
In support of Falkland Islands food!

Sir,
I am sorry to read in today's letters that Patrick Hickman-Robertson does not consider the Falkland Islands a destination for fine dining. I and my family lived in the Islands in the late 1970s when the food available might have been repetitive – not for nothing was the quite supreme roast hogget known as '365' – but since 'liberation' and my subsequent eight visits, I have enjoyed some of the finest and most exploratory food ever. Not only is everything local (rice might be an exception!) but the range and diversity impressive.

The tussock-fed beef is as fine (probably even finer) as anywhere; the lamb continues to impress; the locally caught mullet, trout, squid, Atlantic cod and the white-blooded ice fish are superb; vegetables are, now, locally grown; wild rhubarb and celery are delicious as are the jams (and wine) made from the tea and diddle dee-berries. For the more adventurous you haven't lived till you have enjoyed a fried penguin's egg; chewed on the root of the tussock grass or savoured a form of home-made potted shrimps from the krill. Mussels abound, totally untainted by pollution while the freshly shot geese and duck are more-than delicious. Need I go on?

ES-T

The Field
25 December 2020
Sir,
I am much saddened that Lieutenant Colonel Iain Saker (Letters December 24) had to wait for the RAF and, subsequently, the three-monthly supply ship to 'deliver Christmas' to him when in the Falkland Islands in 1989.

Christmas 1978 was one of the finest my family and I have ever experienced. Breakfast was fried gentoo penguin eggs; lunch was baked mussels from Yorke Bay followed by freshly smoked Warrah river trout. For the main course we enjoyed a superbly roasted upland goose (having first been marinated in a bucket of vinegar for twenty-four hours). Cheese was homemade cream cheese with wild garlic. We could have had (and did on New Year's Day) fabulous tussock-fed beef, or the unbeatable roast hogget which is more tender and with far more flavour than any northern hemisphere lamb. All this was accompanied by an Argentine Malbec and diddle-dee 'port'. Pudding was tea-berry tart, with lashings of real cream while tea, or 'smoko', after a dip in the sea at Gypsy Cove, was buttered krill pâté on toast and wild rhubarb tart. I don't remember what we had for dinner!

Fresh vegetables were a problem apart from the ubiquitous tussock grass bulbs far nicer than sprouts and rather cheaper than those other vegetables flown in by the RAF; although I am sure the Argentine Air Force, our rather tenuous link with the outside world, would have obliged. Everything was cooked in a peat-fired Aga.

What one can do with a dead leopard seal is, perhaps, best left to the survival handbooks rather than a Christmas Day menu.

With due respect to the colonel I cannot understand why he had to look beyond the Falkland Islands for 'Christmas'!

ES-T

The Field
28 April 2022
In yet further support of Falkland Islands food.
Sir,
I first travelled to the Falkland Islands, with my family, in 1978 for thirteen months, returned in 1982 and have visited no less than eight times since to commemorate but mostly to sail and explore. Thus I find it almost perverse that *The Field*, of all magazines, should only offer its readership, during the 40th anniversary year of the liberation of the Falkland Islands, an article written by a retired cavalry officer who does not know the islands; does not know the islanders; admits to being keen to leave the islands as soon as possible in 1982 following the barest of military involvement; who confesses to shooting wildlife with a machine gun; who used a helicopter to outwit his quarry and who complained that these last two facets were necessary as there was no food other than army rations.

Putting aside the fact that an imaginative cook can, with the bare minimum of extra ingredients and sauces, produce a delicious meal out of 'compo' there was, and still is, plenty of 'food' available without having to indulge in unsportsmanlike behaviour.

For a start there were – and still are – 600,000 sheep, easily bartered with a settlement manager; likewise with the beef cattle. All settlements keep chickens for meat and eggs. Fish, as your correspondent eventually discovered, are plentiful and the ubiquitous, almost-tame, upland goose can be snared using a bolas or, obviously a shotgun – but never with a machine gun. Krill, in season, can be scooped out of the ocean mashed and fried. The rock shags, also easily caught, make good eating as do, in extremis, the penguins and their eggs (the latter, again, when in season although perhaps this may not apply to a hungry soldier!). What a dead seal can be used for is best left for another time. 'Vegetables' are plentiful. Wild rhubarb grows around settlements and tussock roots make a good addition to the table, as does sea cabbage

In this 40th anniversary year of freedom it might have been more useful and instructive if *The Field* had concentrated on the amazing and hugely diverse wildlife that can be found across the Falkland Islands, instead of Roger Field's trite piece and questionable behaviour.

ES-T

Yachting Monthly
December 1995
Comments on the proliferation of divers.

Sir,
We seem to have a new concern in our midst, the proliferation of divers. Sailing in from the Western approaches late this summer, I plotted a course to take my gaff cutter between Nare Head and Gull Rock, a few cables offshore. As we neared the rock, we noticed three diving support craft flying Flag Alpha to the south of our track. As we did not want to bear away until well through the gap these were not considered an obstruction.

Once committed, and in the narrowest part, we saw that the passage was all but blocked by buoys, but by pinching we could just squeeze towards the main channel of which, although reasonably steep-to was going to be a tight fit. I aimed to give the buoys a berth of at least a cable, so again, no problem. However, at that precise moment the lead craft broke away and raced towards us. Alongside at 6 knots the diving supervisor bluntly shouted (and I repeat his words verbatim): "I order you to head north". He continued to scream instructions at us across four feet of water. Three of the six of us on board were qualified Ocean skippers and the remaining three were all very experienced. We replied (calmly and sensibly, I thought at the time) that his orders were impossible to obey and anyway, we were well clear. I, too, had to consider safety and as we were now too close for comfort to the mainland (and certainly too close for tacking to port) the only alternative was to bear away and towards, but still well clear of, the divers. Our escort remained oblivious to my own concerns and rites of safe passage.

The point is this. While acknowledging the vital adherence to the rules that govern Flag Alpha (I'm an ex-diver myself) there has to be a limit. The divers were, in this instance, blocking a legitimate passage and by ordering me to turn into water too shallow for our draught (and anyway, well away from their marked diving area) they behaved with an intolerable arrogance. As the diving supervisor continued to try to force us further north, we considered either he was oblivious to the danger his own craft was offering the divers ahead or, as must be the actual truth, there were no divers in our path anyway, and if they had been, they would have been well outside their own diving marks.

There are now so many divers in the Plymouth area demanding wide berths that yachtsman in these parts have often to sail many miles out of their way on what should be a simple and short passage from, say, Plymouth to the River Yealm.

The freedom of those who go afloat is one thing, but the assumption that, once you are flying Flag Alpha, you automatically have control of the sea lanes has to be something else. I regret to say that this problem is reaching near epidemic proportions and I puzzled over what should or could be done to ensure that we are not totally ruled by these people. We, too, have safety factors to consider, especially (as when we were off Nare Head) in an area where ability to manoeuvre is restricted by wind direction and the narrowness of the passage. There was plenty of room for both of us on that day, but that didn't seem to be enough for the diving superintendent.

The first question, therefore, is what can be done to ensure the divers don't assume that they can just hoist Flag Alpha anywhere they like and expect the rest of us to acquiesce meekly, regardless of inconvenience and danger. And the second question is: who would have had the right away if I had had time to hoist the 'restricted manoeuvrability' day signals?

ES-T

Yachting Monthly
March 1996
Following an article I wrote about the safety or otherwise of sailing the Dalmatian coast following Croatia's invasion of the Republic of Serbian Krajina and which was published in the March edition.

Sir,
I hesitated to write in defence of my article 'Is it Safe to go Back?' on the subject of Croatia as the reaction is exactly what I was expecting, but your correspondents protest too much.

At one point in the article, I say quite categorically: 'there is now no threat along the coast', but the lessons of the immediate past needed to be understood for fear of the future.

I believe, and so do others who have studied the coast and its problems as far as visiting yachtsmen are concerned, that the long-term future is not so assured as the Dayton Agreement would have us hope.

The Croatian ambassador's comment that Croatia has 'established sovereignty on its territory' and that of your Italian correspondent that 'military balance has been restored to the area' ignore the fact that this 'sovereignty' was realised solely with the military help of America and Germany. This underlines precisely why we should continue to worry for the Serbs have a long memory.

This 'restoration of sovereignty and military balance' was achieved by the near-total ethnic cleansing of 200,000 people who had populated the Serbian Krajinas for four centuries.

Secondly, the prices quoted were taken from the Adriatic Yacht Club of Croatia's own brochure and were correct at the time of submission to *Yachting World* (as were my comments about Foreign Office advice and insurance premiums). I'm delighted to hear that they have begun to fall from what, even then, were very competitive rates.

The small *Yachting World*-drawn map was, I agree, erroneous. In the text I explained that there were areas for where, I suggested, advice should be sought in advance as they might still be restricted: even the United Kingdom has such places. My advice now – as it was in Is it Safe to Go Back? Yes, but be prepared.

ES-T

Yachting Monthly
8 June 2012
This defence of a Jester Challenge skipper followed a coastguard statement.

Sir,
Peter Evans sailing *Federwolke*, a 22-feet Westerly Cirrus, was rescued by an RNAS helicopter from Culdrose when his boat was becoming overwhelmed in Force 9 winds. *Federwolke* was abandoned. After the rescue Terry Collins, Watch Manager, at Falmouth Coastguard said, 'The single-handed sailor, who had sailed from his home in Jersey to Plymouth before setting off to join the sailing challenge to the Azores, set off his Personal Locator Beacon as his yacht was being overcome by the incredibly rough seas. The conditions on scene were not suitable for a small craft such as this and we do advise anyone setting out on the water to take heed of weather forecasts and not to make journeys in conditions unsuitable for their vessel.'

Contrary to the Coastguard's statement, Peter Evans – a skipper in the 2012 Jester Azores Challenge that started from Plymouth on 27 May – sailed in fine weather with a fair forecast then, when bad weather hit him, he did everything right. Despite the coastguard's report, he had sailed as far as 120 nautical miles west of Ushant after six days of near calm conditions or light head winds but when a Force 9 was forecast (and, sensibly, before it hit him) he was already running back for shelter towards the Channel Islands or St Malo.

Size is not necessarily a factor in seaworthiness in gale force winds as many larger, fully-crewed vessel disasters prove. Much as I respect the coastguard service it does not help when they make uneducated, nannying comments without checking the truth. Sailing deliberately into a Force 10 is one thing but being caught out well offshore after many days at sea is another and thus should not be hinted at as being irresponsible.

I will defend my Jester skippers and what they do and how they do it to the end unless they seriously do not deserve it, but that has yet to be the case.

ES-T

To the Fleet Royal Marines Officer (FRMO) on the Commander-in-Chief Fleet's staff.

Late October 1978

The governor does not want us to be seen to be doing anything military as he thinks it will arouse suspicion among the islanders (and the Argentineans) so we are drastically curtailed although the locals do expect us to meet any contingency. They are always asking what we can do in an emergency and state that we would be useless because of our numbers, but when I ask the governor to allow us to practice I am told no for fear of giving rise to speculation…the overt Argentinean presence has begun to give me cause for worry….We are waiting to see if Argentina and Chile go to war on Thursday. It might affect us considerably.

ES-T

To the FRMO

Early 1979

I thought it time to let you know how things have been going since your visit as I am worried that we could be losing the momentum…You will be interested to know that His Excellency considered your visit to have been a waste of time. He pays only lip service to our presence and continues to demand that we keep a very low profile for fear that any move we make will panic the public – hence talk of a new barracks....would appear, to his eyes, to indicate an escalation of the threat (from Argentina)....I have fought and fought to be given regular briefings but am simply told that it is his job to decide when I should receive information. What a way to run a deterrent. The politicians and the FCO are the biggest threats to the defence of these islands...Why doesn't he come clean and tell the FCO, the MOD and the islanders that he doesn't want the military here except as cheap labour... Certainly our military position at the moment is verging on the farcical.

ES-T

To HMS *Endurance*

Early 1979
About this time HMS *Endurance* was preparing to sail from the UK for the southern hemisphere so I wrote to her first lieutenant:

Is there any chance that you can bring a pig (dead) for which I will pay you and a stilton or two plus a brace of pheasants (also dead) in your deep freeze for the New Year.

ES-T

Chapter 33

A Few (Very) Short Stories

by Tumblehome

For two years in the mid-1990s, I was asked to write a brief monthly column for *Yachting World* describing various 'awkward events' with which I had been involved. Many offer a 'lesson to be learned' while some contain a warning about the maintenance of morale! The magazine insisted that they were written under a *nom de plume* and chose 'Tumblehome'. (I preferred Sheepshank after the knot that shortens a rope.) Here are some of them, straight from *Yachting World*'s pages

The Gybe

I was delivering the elderly 50-square-metre yacht from Plymouth to Poole with a scratch crew of some, but not very much, experience. Nothing was in sight while we ran downwind on the port gybe, and so I felt safe enough to snatch a few minutes below, before the next watch needed guidance at 0400. While asleep on the saloon berth, I was woken by an enormous shout to get on deck. Ahead of us, and lit by our powerful lamp, was a 500-ton coaster on which there was no sign of life. The duty watch's mistake had been trying to steer the sloop out of the way by luffing up, the natural reaction for newcomers on whom I had earlier impressed the importance of not gybing without me.

I grabbed the tiller and, to the amazement of the crew, slammed the boat to starboard with the instant response I knew would occur. The boom swung across and caught the side of the steamer. However, if we had continued to turn lazily to port (there was no time to 'aft' the mainsheet to keep wind in the sail) we would have certainly been smashed in half by a sideways-on collision.

I had my ideas about ship-handling in an emergency confirmed and my crew now knew that the safe-looking ways are not always the preferred solution in such terrifying circumstances. What was a splintered boom compared with… we all shuddered at the thought of the alternative.

Bravado

It was the 1965 Fastnet Race and we were running in a wild night towards the Rock. Our boat was a Nicholson 36 with a skipper who was new to the sport (compared to his crew), and one very keen to make his mark.

'Bill,' we all queried at the change-over of night-time watches, 'don't you think we are a little over-canvassed?' But the skipper had once heard some aficionado ashore bragging that the only times he could ever guarantee to get the maximum out of the spinnaker was when he kept it flying until it blew out. Only then would be the time to change to a smaller one 'without an ounce of opportunity lost!'

Bill confidently announced that he would follow that advice. We did not believe him until about an hour later, the helmsman poked his head through the hatch and shouted, 'Bill, the spinnaker's gone. We were astonished to hear the order, 'Right set the next one down.'

We did too and were each rewarded with a bottle of beer in what was otherwise a dry ship. Later the skipper admitted that he had been 'hoist with his own petard'. When the moment came that he hoped would never come he didn't feel he could back down. Which actually is not the correct attitude towards seamanship: nor is it towards racing since we didn't even win our class.

Weathering the Start

I had rounded Portland Bill with a fair tide and a good weather forecast. Lyme Bay was its usual endless self for a yacht only 17 feet on the waterline and with no engine. Shortly after sunset the visibility reduced, bringing a vicious thunderstorm. The compass went haywire!

With the passing of the lightning, the wind freshened considerably and probably topped Force 6 at least. By sheer good fortune, I picked up Start Point light as three blurred smudges every ten seconds, so I was now able to head for it until hitting The Race that I knew would be running.

The visibility by then was too bad to attempt rounding Bolt Head before crossing Bigbury Bay, especially as my compass was now wholly unreliable… but I did have two other aids to position finding. With the tidal stream and wind conditions, I knew where I was if I stayed in the Start Race, which I did for the next exhausting, exhilarating, frightening four hours. During that time I tacked back and forth seaward 'til the Race lessened, and north until I could pick up that smudge of light at a dangerously high elevation. Providing that I did not sail out of the sides of the Race on the inbound legs, I was sure to pick up the light.

At dawn. the visibility was no better. but I was happy that I had, all along, remained in a patch of water I could identify. Eventually I crossed tacks with a steamer which was heading, I judged by her construction, for Fowey's china clay jetties. Managing to slip in behind her I checked our course against my compass and bore away safely for Plymouth.

The Very Foul Anchor

We had brought the heavy old Bristol Channel Pilot Cutter into Belle Île harbour, Brittany, which had been no mean feat, for only two of us had sailed before. It was though, at the last that things began to go wrong. The ship's head was brought to port until we were at right angles to the jetty, where the Admiralty pattern anchor and buoy rope were let go. Under power I began to reverse towards the wall to moor Mediterranean style. As the stern approached the shore the order to snub the cable was given - and it was followed by the question 'How does the cable grow?'

The fo'c'sle crewman looked, 'Short stay aft,' he shouted.

I didn't believe him. 'Look again,' I ordered. He did and this time barked 'Long stay aft.'

Of course it was, for the buoy rope had been wound in over the propeller shaft, successfully hauling the great hook up and under the rudder, where it was jammed with the bows firmly moored to the stern. The engine stalled and the tiller was immovable. At that moment the ferry appeared from around the sea wall 50 yards to port. Once it had passed close across our bows, we retrieved the immediate situation by anchoring with the kedge and running a warp ashore in the dinghy.

In the café that evening we were congratulated on a copy-book moor by the harbourmaster, who assumed we had aborted the first manoeuvre in mid-stream, to allow the ferry to pass unhindered. We accepted the offered *pastis* without blushes. It is always pleasant to have a cock-up taken for an accomplishment!

The Wrong Anchorage

The trainees were very impressed. After nearly running our distance, and not once having sighted land since leaving the Solent, I announced to them that the first landmark to appear ahead would be Nare Point, with the Lizard peninsula stretching away to the south.

As instructed, I was called when rocks appeared fine on the port bow and, identifying them as the Manacles, we came round to starboard. To start with I felt rather pleased with myself. This did not last however, for in the moderate visibility I could see no entrance to the Helford River

Eventually land did appear and, without losing any of my earlier self-assurance, we rounded it and sailed into what I hoped would be our anchorage. It wasn't - and we slid sedately on to St Austell Bay's sand. In the low cloud the Gwineas and the Dodman had replaced, to my extreme embarrassment, the Manacles and the 'other' Black Head.

Since rounding Start Point unseen, I had not only miscalculated our leeway but had also assumed that the log was under reading. It wasn't and we had not run our distance by about 15 miles.

I paid for much beer that night - and it wasn't in the Helford Passage Inn as promised.

Collision Regulations

I had been sailing single-handed, well north of the Arctic Circle. It was midwinter and I was moored to an ice floe while dangling a baited line to catch breakfast. I puzzled over what light signals to show for. I, or rather we, (I felt responsible for the ice flow once attached to it) had to abide by the International Regulations for the Prevention of Collision at Sea. This applied especially at high water when we floated free of the land to move slowly seaward in the offshore zephyr.

Originally deciding that I was at anchor (the Admiralty pattern anchor was firmly embedded in the floe which was then aground), I lit the mandatory riding light. In fact, I was probably moored even if the floe occasionally was not, and thus not required to show any lights.

However, on reflection we should perhaps have shown the lights of a fishing smack under sail for I had kept the stays'l set in the light offshore breeze to prevent the cutter from chafing against the low ice wall. But if so, we were 'not under command but under way' and sometimes 'not under command' and aground.

At other times we were restricted by our draught in our ability to manoeuvre, while all the time it could be argued that we were attached to a tow of over 200 yards in length. I made that at least eight conflicting signal requirements.

I could not solve the problem and certainly was not going to change the lights at every turn of the tide. In the end I blew out the anchor light on the assumption that no other fool would be afloat 200 miles north of the Arctic Circle in midwinter anyway.

The Ice Floe

My gaff cutter was moored to the low ice floe at the head of the fjord. It was January and we were 200 miles north of the Arctic Circle. It was also six in the evening and very cold.

I was sailing single-handed and enjoying the last 'night' (there was no true daylight) of an extended long weekend. The routine for a run ashore was to use cross-country skis to traverse the ice (men on skis can cross sea ice just one-and-a-half inches thick), then run along the coast road to the nearest village for a mug of hot chocolate. But not this time. Just fifteen yards short of the shore I found that around the semi-circumference of the fjord, the ice had broken away with the rise and fall of the tide, leaving a moat of mushy, broken ice – impassable, unless I had been prepared for a swim.

The unplanned run ashore that weekend was spent circumnavigating the two-mile-wide floe on skis. Some things can never be taken for granted and sea ice is one of them.

Beware the Know-All

I had anchored off Looe too many times to calculate but for some reason never at, or near, low water. On this occasion it was dusk and close to high water. Tim brought the chart into the cockpit and began studying it intently as he deduced my intentions.

'Don't you think we should drop the hook?' he asked tentatively.

'No, not yet,' I replied, full of confidence. 'I've been here many times. It's all right providing we don't go inside a line between the end of the breakwater and the rocks to the north.'

'Positive?'

'Positive!' I replied and gave the order when we were exactly on the transit.

Much later that night we returned from a run ashore to find the five-ton, long-keeled yacht about ten yards from the sea. To drive the point home, a rising easterly was about to push her further inland once the flood began. Tim went on to become commodore of our yacht club. I did not.

The Bicyclist

The elderly Bristol Channel Pilot Cutter was hove-to on the port tack, fore-reaching slowly in a westerly gale. Île de Ré lay to the south, with the coast of France eight miles to the north.

All was well and Roger had just taken over the middle watch. The skipper was asleep in his cabin aft and, as mate, I was on standby, fully clothed in the saloon.

Soon however, my dozing was interrupted when Roger's worried face appeared in the companion hatch. As he was not prone to panic, the quietness of his voice, coupled with an unaccustomed expression added considerable authority to his remarkable announcement.

'I have just seen a bicyclist peddling past the bowsprit.'

If Roger says he has just seen a bicyclist peddling past the bowsprit, then that was good enough for me. He does not exaggerate. I shot on deck.

Less than a cable away, the path at the back of the beach was visible though the spume. There was no time to call the watch below and so quite how the two of us managed to bring the 35-ton cutter through the wind and out to seaward on a reciprocal course, I have never understood.

Neither have I ever understood how we had managed to lose our ample sea room in one short watch in the first place. At dawn the skipper made no mention of the fact that we were on the wrong tack; he just smiled and we learnt something about seamanship - and leadership.

The Concrete Spinnaker

There was too much wind for the Twister's spinnaker, but a recently acquired brother-in-law was determined that we should have a go. He was new to the sport and, so far, it had not lived up to his perceptions of its exciting image. The vessel was chartered, and by the last day of our cruise, we had neither suffered any damage, or as far as I was aware, made any appreciable cock-up. I was keen to keep it that way.

The visibility inshore was hazy but allowed us, just, to make out the unmistakable sight of another yacht setting her spinnaker with no apparent fuss. My new brother-in-law didn't actually say that I was chicken, but merely pointed to the other boat and asked, very nicely, 'If it's good enough for him, why not for us?' I couldn't argue, and despite my better judgement we prepared the pole and bent on the clew, tack and halyard. With the sail half hoisted, the wind took charge. Inevitably with spinnakers, when things go wrong, they go wrong spectacularly. As we passed over the sail it caught the rudder and propeller, then released the shredded remains, to act as a most effective sea anchor with the mast head as the pivotal point. At that precise moment the visibility lifted to reveal that the 'spinnaker' inshore of us was a large, very solid observatory. Moral: seamanship not showmanship must always be the order of the day.

The Sardines

Halfway up the west Irish coast, on passage for Barra from Crosshaven in dirty weather and a five-ton sloop, my crew collapsed in tears and announced that he could go no further than our next destination. The reason for this breakdown wasn't actually the diet of sardines, or the fire in the galley (which had made cooking out of the question), or the complete failure of the heads (ensuring that the black bucket came into its own). Likewise, my crew had not bulked at finding the water tank full of draught Guinness (courtesy of Clare Francis!) that could only be drawn through the galley's sink hand-pump, or at the third full-blown gale in as many days 100 miles out in the Atlantic on a yacht only 17 feet on the waterline.

It was probably a combination of all these things that finally got through to him, added to the thought of another 1,200 miles to go after Barra. So, the conclusion was reached (perhaps understandably) that he hated sailing. We turned southwards to run before the wind and headed for Plymouth.

I realised, then, that sailing ability, beyond the basics, counts for little when choosing a successful crew for two-handed sailing. Compatibility in social habits, culinary tastes and drinking preferences count for far more.

Role Reversal

The local passage race from Plymouth to Fowey that year took place in a near flat calm. True to all our earlier experiences, it again seemed unlikely that we would make the party in the Royal Fowey Yacht Club, for my vessel of those halcyon days had no engine. However, a dusk-time zephyr carried us to the entrance of the river where its pull northward exactly cancelled out the ebb tide. Stationary over the seabed, we could see through our binoculars the party developing on the veranda, with our three wives intimately involved. But would they see us and at least acknowledge that we had reached closer to the finish line than on any other occasion during the previous eight years?

They did, and the club launch was despatched to bring in the one remaining straggler. To distant cheers, we were quickly taken in tow while the crew furled the sails and spruced themselves up.

These actions were a little premature for at that moment the launch's engine stopped – irrecoverably. So, to even heartier cheers, we quickly hoisted the mains'l and jib then changed places with the motorboat and her crew - the club's red-faced secretary. Out of the stronger tide in the river entrance we are able, under sail, to deliver our saviour and ourselves directly to the club's steps in safety. Which proves that yachts are not alone in having destinations and not times of arrival. We didn't buy a drink that evening.

The Unpaid Paid Hand

My crew for the 1974 two-handed Round Britain and Ireland race (RB&I) was an unknown quantity as he had stepped in at the last moment, after my original crew had been offered his own yacht to skipper.

Unexpectedly, once we had sailed, the new man turned out to be useless at sea, but promised to make up for his nautical failings by undertaking all the chores during each of the four compulsory stops. He insisted and I reluctantly agreed, for I knew I would be tired having been watch-on, stop-on during each of the four legs.

At Crosshaven all 'service-manned' yachts had to anchor in the river for 'security reasons' with no crews allowed ashore. (We believed that by singling us out in this way we were more of an obvious target for the IRA.) To make up for the lack of relaxation offered by the Royal Cork Yacht Club, a public-spirited local skipper invited us, plus a number of civilian crews to his motor yacht, that he too moored in mid-stream.

In accordance with our earlier agreement, my crew rowed me across for drinks while he returned to cook supper, after which he rowed me back again to the party then returned to wash up. At the end of the evening I blew a hunting horn and was collected. As I was rowed back to my own vessel, the voice of our host drifted across Crosshaven Harbour: 'Isn't it amazing how these military chaps manage to take their batmen with them - even on a two-handed race!'

The Mutiny

As we passed Leira Ness during the 1970 RB&I, both Roger and I were well aware that there was just half an hour before the Lerwick pubs shut. The rubber dinghy was pumped up and ready. I swung the yacht head to wind and shouted: 'Let go!' Roger just looked at me. 'Roger, let go the anchor!' Instead he flung the rubber dinghy over the side, jumped in and rowed ashore.

Puzzled, I anchored the 49-feet yawl myself. It was, by then, too late for a beer, but I rowed ashore anyway in the wooden praam in search of my crew and an explanation.

Roger greeted me in an illicitly open bar as though nothing had happened. We never once mentioned the incident until four years later, when he suddenly announced to my guests at a dinner party that it was time the reason for his well-known munity was clarified.

Apparently, I had cooked the eggs for breakfast that morning with too much garlic - and not for the first time either. Finally, his well-respected tolerance had stalled. We often sailed together after that, without a hitch but our eggs were always cooked separately.

The Visitor

With the impending visit of a senior member of the Royal Family to the fleet, of which we were part, the 49-feet wooden yawl was dressed overall. It was also pouring with rain and we were at the bottom of 30 feet of dripping, slimy seawall. Our visitor who, among other titles, was an Admiral of the Fleet, was rowed across the dock in a tiny praam dinghy in which he sat, imposing and self-conscious in the stern.

As he hauled his bulk over the yacht's side, the dressing line snapped at the main truck dropping forty or so sodden flags at his feet. Maritime dignity was restored by a tot in the saloon and a lively discussion of the race ahead. As he left, I asked our visitor if he would honour us with an entry in the visitors' book. 'Delighted,' he replied and bent to the task.

Halfway through his signature a huge drop of rainwater fell off the peak of his cap and splodged across the ink. 'Don't worry, Sir,' said Roger, my crew, as he leant across to the galley table, 'Have some elephant's bog roll!' I was aghast, but before I could remonstrate with Roger for destroying the recently salvaged decorum, our visitor said, 'Yes, thank you. That's what I always call it when the Queen is not listening!' They looked at each other and laughed at my pompous embarrassment.

Chapter 34

A Miscarriage of Justice:
The *Maria Asumpta* Case

On 30 May 1995, the 127-ton brig *Maria Asumpta* was lost on the north Cornish coast and three of her crew were drowned.

As a result, my good friend, her captain and owner, Mark Litchfield was imprisoned for eighteen months and appealed this sentence. The appeal failed. What was not generally known was that prior to the trial, the Marine Accident Investigation Bureaux had decided that there was no case to answer, yet the Crown Prosecution Service persisted. The trial judge, His Honour Sir Neil Butterfield, whom I knew, said after the trial that he, too, knew that Mark was innocent of manslaughter but that it was wise to let justice take its course in the certain knowledge that Mark would be found not guilty.

The trial, in Exeter Crown Court, was bizarre in parts. For instance at one stage the jury were sent to the jury room while a point of law was discussed. When they were called back in to the court the usher announced to the judge that the jurors were nowhere to be found. As there was no other entrance or exit to the jury room this was odd so the usher was told to try again. He found the twelve jurors hiding in the two (male and female) lavatories. Such was the standard of the jurors asked to deliberate on the case against an old Etonian, a former Royal Navy officer and the owner of one of the last privately owned square-rigged ships in the world. Mark did not have a chance against the young 'frippets' of Exeter - including the one elderly lady juror who was driven to court each morning by one of the prosecution witnesses, until stopped by the judge.

Following the failure of Mark Litchfield's appeal I wrote the following to the Appeal Court:

THE APPEAL COURT and the foundering of the *MARIA ASUMPTA*
An assessment of the sailing aspects by Ewen Southby-Tailyour.
Lord Justice Simon Brown:
'I can't understand - I don't see how we can be expected to.'
The three appeal judges in their summing-up:

'Even at the end of the appeal hearing, we confess to only an imperfect understanding of some of the technical detail.'

Introduction

1. The pamphlet produced by the Friends of the *Maria Asumpta* titled 'To Whom it May Concern' explains the trial and jury verdict.

2. A separate paper titled 'The Loss of the *Maria Asumpta* - Fuel Contamination Not the Cause' - by Captain John Lawson, Royal Navy - is a précis of the views of three experts in ship handling, diesel engines and naval architecture. That paper examines, in brief, the likely and unlikely causes of engine failure and should be read in conjunction with this paper. This paper is, too, a résumé of a longer paper by the same title that covers the most significant sailing aspects of the case as raised in the Court of Appeal by Lord Justice Simon Brown sitting with Mr Justice Rougier and Mr Justice Astill. All the original, detailed technical papers (sailing and mechanical) are available on request.

3. The Appeal Court judges introduced or emphasised a number of 'sailing' points that, in their view, helped to confirm Mark Litchfield's supposed guilt. In truth the appeal judges' astounding misapprehensions highlighted not only their absolute ignorance of the status of the *Maria Asumpta* as a motor vessel but of nautical affairs in general. It is clear to me that the judges snatched at these nautical straws in order to give their decision–making some apparent credence: yet nothing that I, nor any of the mariners who have followed this case closely, have seen and heard, indicates guilt to any degree either in the handling of the diesel fuel or the handling of the ship under sail.

4. The case hinged on whether or not contaminated fuel was, knowingly, put into the ship's tanks yet it was argued, quite erroneously (and disingenuously to confuse the jury at the trial) that as a sailing vessel she should not have been in the position in which she found herself shortly before she foundered. This is to ignore a most relevant fact: the *Maria Asumpta* was in every degree a full–powered motor vessel (in the correct, technical, naval architect's meaning of the expression) that went ashore due to an unexplained, sudden, unpredictable, catastrophic, double engine failure. Any references to her as a sailing vessel should have been, and should remain, an irrelevance but they have been used as smokescreens by the Appeal Court judges to back up their opinion that Mark Litchfield was guilty of hazarding his ship and thus guilty of manslaughter.

Court of Appeal findings

5. The following are points relevant to the sailing aspects of the case as presented by the Appeal Court judges and are taken from the Court of Appeal, Criminal Division Draft Judgement R v Litchfield (97/5973/W2).

6. It was the judges' submission – based in part, I believe, on the outrageous and wholly wrong assertions by a discredited sailing witness [name withheld] – that Mark Litchfield should not have planned the course he did because:
   a. It was along a dangerous shore.
   b. No engines are 'wholly reliable'.
   c. He could not sail out of trouble if his engines failed – the 'sail only criteria'.
   d. He allowed his ship to become embayed.
   e. His ship had 'just the one propeller'.
   f. His ship was 'single-skinned'.
   g. It was an area notorious for lobster pots and, apparently, loose fishing nets.
   h. The planned course itself was dangerous.

7. To which the reasoned responses based on experience and knowledge are:
   a. All shores are dangerous. The weather conditions on the day were perfectly acceptable for a motor vessel following the well-used and accepted inshore track.
   b. If in a court of law no engine is 'wholly reliable' why do merchant ships not carry back-up sails. Using this argument, though, no method of propulsion (including sails and oars) can be 'wholly reliable' – in which case the judges would have us never going to sea at all.
   c. The 'sail-only criteria' presented by the prosecution witness is an expression known to me solely in relation to sailing ships without engines. Its relevance began to cease at the turn of the century as the majority of sailing vessels were being fitted with auxiliaries. No motor-powered vessel can sail out of trouble if her engines fail but at least Mark Litchfield had that opportunity, although by then it was too late. If the engines had failed a few moments earlier he could have worn ship into Port Quin Bay and if they had failed a few moments later the *Maria Asumpta* would have safely weathered Rumps Point. Nowadays all sailing skippers expect to rely on their engines at some time to get their vessels past a headland, to avoid a lengthy tack offshore or to round a buoy against, say, a foul tide. Additionally, Mark Litchfield was going to have to rely totally on his engines off Padstow – a lee shore – for entering harbour, as do all ships whether motor or sail. The entrance to Padstow is surrounded by rocks

and islands: all vessels have to pass close to these regardless of the wind direction.

d   If a study is made of the planned course and the accepted wind direction of 315° T, then far from becoming embayed, the prosecution witness's (name withheld) mischievous contention through his phoney 'sail only' criteria, Mark Litchfield's course was safe for that wind direction, that coastal profile and his ship's tacking angle of 65° to the wind.

e. All merchant cargo ships have only one propeller and most only have one engine powering it yet the Maria Asumpta had two engines plus her sails.

f. To imply that, because the *Maria Asumpta* was 'single-skinned', Mark Litchfield had even more of a duty to keep off this 'dangerous' shore is a gross non-sequitur. Modern, steel motor vessels tend to be double bottomed with fuel often carried in the void space but except for those that carry dangerous cargoes, it is not, I think, a legal requirement. 'Single-skinned' is not a known expression – did they actually mean that the *Maria Asumpta* should have a double bottom – unheard of for wooden sailing vessels, motor vessels of a certain age and many small craft such as trawlers and coasters – or do they think that all ships should have, most unusually, a complete double hull. The ambiguity highlights a disturbing lack of knowledge and understanding particularly when produced as a judgement in court.

g. Lobster pots are found well offshore along almost all our coasts and can foul propellers even if they are not propelling the vessel. Perhaps no motor vessel should be allowed along this coast from now onwards. What fishing nets? I have never come across any unattended nets lying in wait to snag a sailing vessel's propeller. A loose net might, but a lobster pot would not stop a propeller of the size of *Maria Asumpta*'s: anyway, a permanent look-out was kept for these.

h. A number of fishermen, a lighthouse keeper and the lifeboat cox'n said that the course taken was close to the shore but these were opinions from people who did not, at the time, appreciate what was happening on board vis-a-vis the engines failing and the unexpected inshore tidal set. Nobody (except possibly the prosecution witness) has actually said that the *planned* course was dangerous. In fact the lighthouse keeper's evidence supported the defence case although the judges, because of their admitted lack of understanding, presented it as helping the prosecution's.

8. Importantly, (name removed) was a prosecution witness whose sole evidence as a 'sailing expert' was taken in preference to five others for the defence whose credit was, and remains, impeccable. Yet (the prosecution witness) as captain, once put a sail training ship on a well-marked reef in the West Indies through not using the correct charts. She was only saved by her stout, steel construction and he was dismissed from the post shortly afterwards; facts that were previously unknown to the prosecution (and, earlier, the MAIB) who called him. To my personal knowledge, the following was said of (the witness) by the commanding officer of a frigate: 'This officer should never be allowed to navigate a ship out of sight of land.'

9. Outside the Rules of the Road at Sea there are no regulations that dictate how a sailing vessel should be handled, yet the jury and the Appeal Court judges took only the discredited (the prosecution witness) word as law simply because he had written a book on sailing square-rigged ships.

10. The appeal judges did not accept the view that local prejudice was unhelpful to Mark Litchfield once the case had been moved from Cornwall to Exeter, but this is a nonsense. If it were necessary to move the case at all then the same criteria existed to move it totally outside the West Country's media influence. The same television stations (BBC and ITV – both of which showed dramatic film of the wreck each evening the trial was reported) and the same regional newspapers (the *Western Morning News*, the *Sunday Independent* and the *Evening Herald*) cover all of Devon and Cornwall, so moving the case to Exeter was nonsensical. If the excuse for not moving it further was as stated by the appeal judges ('To have moved it further would have caused problems with witnesses and a view') then nobody, and especially Mr Justice Rougier, considered the accused's position vis-a-vis a fair trial – yet the witnesses were not to be inconvenienced (most of whom came from upcountry anyway).

Summary

11. The *Maria Asumpta*:
    a. Was a fully powered motor vessel with sails.
    b. Had every right to be motoring along the track planned by her master in the prevailing weather conditions, setting sail when the opportunity allowed.
    c. Suffered an untabulated inshore tidal set contrary to that hinted at in the Admiralty Sailing Directions.

    d. Power was lost due to sudden, unexplainable, catastrophic, double engine failure.

12. Mark Litchfield:
    a. Was convicted of manslaughter due to the inability of the jury to grasp the technicalities of the evidence.
    b. Was condemned daily by adverse comment in the heavily biased, local (manipulated?) television and newspapers available to the jury each evening and morning of the trial.
    c. Had the support of the MAIB over the fuel issue.
    d. Was made a scapegoat after the lack of any 'Zeebrugge' prosecutions?

13. The Appeal Court judges:
    a. *On their own admission*, did not understand the complexities of the case.
    b. Presented spurious 'sailing' reasons why Mark Litchfield was at fault in order to justify their refusal to find a lurking doubt over the jury's decision.
    c. Supported (the prosecution witness) flawed evidence in preference to five experienced mariners.
    d. Were studiously unable to accept the overwhelming proof that clean fuel was in the ship's tanks and thus could not have been a cause of engine failure.
    e. Could not understand that the *Maria Asumpta* was a power-driven vessel.
    f. Described Mark Litchfield throughout the hearing as 'this arrogant man' – hardly the words of impartiality.

Conclusions

14. If acceptance of risk is justification for a manslaughter trial every time an unavoidable accident occurs then many professions would collapse. Significantly, in this case no risks were taken other than being at sea in the first place.

15. To avoid being charged after every accident are we now never to sail or motor (with engines that can 'never be wholly reliable') with 'just the one propeller', in a ship without double-bottoms (or double skins?), in coastal waters where we might encounter lobster pots and certainly never in proximity to land at any time in fine weather? As that appears to be the ruling, the maritime community needs to know the precise position.

16. The trial should never have taken place. The jury verdict was perverse and the Appeal Court judges, by their own admission, felt not competent to adjudicate.
17. Mark Litchfield is innocent of all charges and must be exonerated.

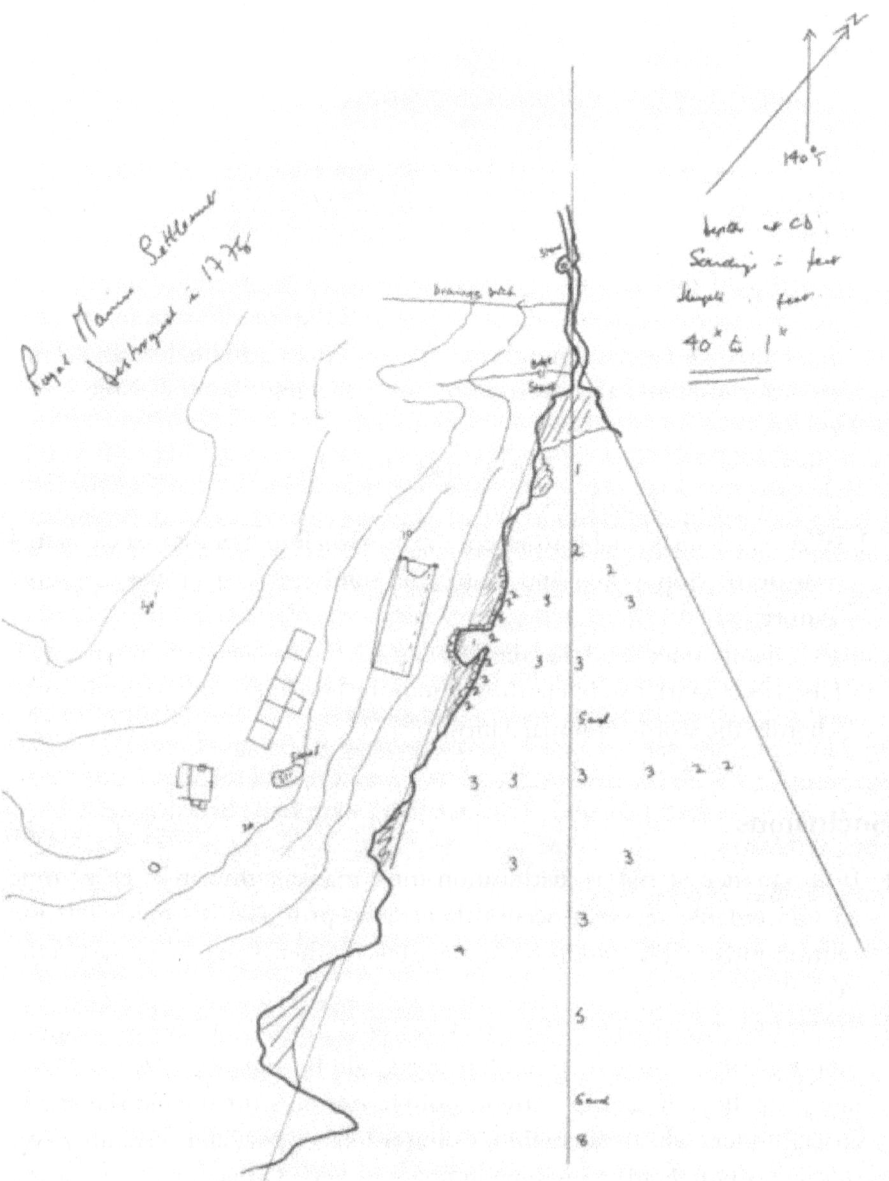

Brief survey of the Royal Marines camp on Saunders Island made in 1978.

Chapter 35

C Plath 26762 – The History of a Sextant

A version of the following written by Commander Phil Harper Royal Navy and myself was included in the publication *The Nautical Sextant* by W.J. Morris.

Few sextants carry their history with them, but my C Plath 26276 may be an exception. It was built in Germany late in the Second World War then 'liberated' in Wilhelmshaven from U–3008 in May 1945 by my father, Lieutenant Colonel Norman Tailyour. He was then commanding officer of 27 Battalion Royal Marines, a unit within 116 Infantry Brigade Royal Marines that was attached to the Canadian First Army and responsible for guarding about 200 German warships and submarines that had surrendered.

Norman Tailyour had owned various yachts before the war and, having been educated at the Nautical College Pangbourne, knew well how to use a sextant. In 1947, his friend and mentor, Lieutenant Colonel Patrick Phibbs, bought the 35-ton, 56-feet Bristol Channel Pilot Cutter *Olga*, and Norman was often invited to cruise along France's Biscay and Brittany coasts, using C Plath 26276 to navigate. From the age of five I, too, sailed in *Olga* and would occasionally take sun sights with this sextant but, to begin with, I left the figures for others to work out and plot.

Later, I also went to Pangbourne and was taught celestial navigation to 'O' Level standard so, during the summer holidays on board *Olga*, I could now produce my own intercepts and position lines. After joining the Royal Marines in 1960 I retrieved the sextant from *Olga* and used it in many Royal Ocean Racing Club races, including six Fastnet races during the 1960s and 1970s and, later, during six two-handed, round-Britain and Ireland races.

In 1963 I had been the Seamanship Training Officer for the Landing Craft branch at Poole, when C Plath 26276 was employed teaching celestial navigation. Then between 1963 and 1964 it travelled with me to HMS *Anzio*, an LST (landing ship, tank) in the Persian Gulf.

In the mid-1960s I was the sailing master of the Royal Marines' 'windfall' yacht *Sea Soldier* when I introduced young officers to the sextant.

When appointed officer commanding the amphibious detachment in HMS *Fearless* in 1973, C Plath 26276 was lent to the ship's navigating officer, who preferred to use it rather than the issued sextant, a much heavier Kelvin Hughes Admiralty Pattern 491. In 1978 I was sent to the Falkland Islands as officer commanding NP8901 and, naturally, C Plath 26276 went with me on the journey south. It was used extensively, mostly for horizontal sextant angles among the islands, while carrying out amateur surveys of the archipelago. These surveys formed the basis of more than one hundred pages of notes on the bays, inlets and landing beaches around the islands, notes which became useful to the commanders of the Amphibious Task Group during the Falklands campaign in 1982. Although C Plath 26276 joined me it saw little use. On my return, C Plath 26276 continued to be used during assignments at Poole and deployments to the Norwegian Arctic.

Having owned four yachts between 1973 and 2022, and after retiring from the Royal Marines I cruised between the Denmark Strait (the strait between Greenland and Iceland) and the Biscay coast, always with C Plath 26276. This sextant was particularly useful during three voyages surveying the last five uncharted fjords of north-west Iceland.

After eighty years of intensive use at sea, C Plath 26276 was in need of repair so on the recommendation of mutual friends, I took it to Commander Philip Harper, a serving Royal Navy navigator and commanding officer. By this time the aluminium screws used to secure the hinges and clasps of the original box had largely rotted away and the joints were coming apart. Many of the sextant's parts were corroded and both mirrors were in poor condition. The index mirror was almost completely destroyed, although I could still take a sight with it – just!

Phil cleaned, restored and renovated the instrument and its box. The horizon mirror was professionally re-silvered and a new index mirror was fitted. The sextant's original patina was preserved and the instrument made ready for another eight decades of hard use.

During the restoration, it became clear that there was something unusual about C Plath 26276. Even disregarding the extensive provenance, it was clearly a genuine wartime Kriegsmarine C Plath sextant, but the C Plath trademark (a stickman holding a sextant) was missing from both the arc and the handle. Fakes normally add the trademark to a non-original item, so this was more a cause for interest than concern. On removing the mirrors, the C Plath part markings were present confirming that the parts had been made in a C Plath factory. But why were the trademarks missing? Given the late serial number, it is surmised that this instrument was made up from parts in a machine shop in Germany after the C Plath factories in Ostrołęka and Sopot in Poland had been overrun by the Red Army in late 1944 or early 1945. It would then have been delivered to the Kriegsmarine and subjected to an examination. It seems by this stage of the war the Kriegsmarine merely stamped the certificates *Entspricht den Bestimmungen der Kriegsmarine* (Corresponds to the regulations of the Navy) and *Das Instrument is den fur Gebrauch aus fehlerfral zu bezeichnen* (The instrument is intended to be used without error). The sextant would then have been issued to a ship or submarine. In this case, it went to U-3008.

U-3008 was a new type of submarine – the Type XXI submarine Elektroboot, designed to operate at high speed underwater for extended periods. All Cold War diesel–electric submarines were based to a greater or lesser extent on this innovative German design. U-3008 was one of only two such submarines to complete a war patrol. She was launched on 14 September 1944 and commissioned on 19 October that year by Kapitänleutnant Fokko Schlömer.

Kapitänleutnant Helmut Manseck took command in March 1945. The boat sailed on one patrol from Kiel on 3 May 1945, returning on 21 May 1945. After the end of the war, U-3008 was secretly transferred to the United States Navy for trials and was then scuttled in a series of demolition tests in 1954. The hulk was raised and towed to the Navy dry dock at Roosevelt Roads where she was offered up for sale in 1955 for scrap.

What does the future hold for C Plath 26276? Liberating sextants from captured enemy ships is something of a habit in the family as my son, Hamish, is the owner of a Kelvin Hughes sextant which I 'liberated' from the Argentine logistic ship *Bahia Buen Suceso* in 1982. C Plath 26276 is therefore skipping a generation and has gone to my grandson, Jacob, who is starting a three-year degree course in Nautical Sciences at the Warsash Maritime School. As he aims to skipper super sailing yachts worldwide there is every chance that the instrument has much more travel and use ahead of it.

Chapter 36

A Final Summary

In 1946 my parents bought an ex-Royal Navy Fairmile B Class ML, *Naughty Princess*, in which we lived briefly but, as she came without propellers, ownership was short-lived.

Meanwhile, I had joined the Nautical College, Pangbourne where, in due course and as captain of sailing, I turned down the offer of an Olympic trial for, to me, sailing has never been about cut-throat competition. My only other claim to college fame was sacking a future Olympic double-gold medallist from my sailing team for winning a race by 'application of the 'rules' rather than through fair sailing. I disliked the manner in which many races were won or lost - in the protest room and not on the water.

Commissioned into the Royal Marines in 1960, I was introduced to the wooden, RNSA 14-feet dinghies, and I also bought my own Firefly dinghy which, in theory, I still own, as I gave it to Wellington College on permanent loan. Having completed initial training I specialised in the, then, dying art of the Landing Craft branch which included the complexities of amphibious operations, inshore pilotage, celestial navigation and, inevitably, Morse and semaphore.

Three tours in the Middle East acquainted me with the mysteries of the dhow and even a ridiculously dangerous, homemade sand yacht in the Oman desert. Two visits to Hong Kong offered chances to crew a junk - a fascinating experience, as was an outrigger off Kenya's coast. Later, reefing the foretops'l of the ill-fated brig *Maria Asumpta* in a rising channel gale was a sharp learning curve for a fifty-year-old.

During a year's appointment to a Plymouth-based commando I was asked to take over the duties, *inter alia*, as sailing master of the 50-square metre, 'windfall', *Sea Soldier*. I had skippered her often before and knew her as the highly-strung thoroughbred she was. Designed by Abeking and Rasmussen in 1936, she was a real delight to sail fully crewed or (much to the horror of the generals) single-handed. As well as being available for private hire from within the Corps she was also the Royal Marines' sail training vessel. Dozens of young marines and 'officers under training' grappled with her quirks, especially the temperamental Stewart Turner engine and the equally awkward Baby Blake heads. From first-hand experience, I know that countless south coast employees of young ladies would openly groan when they saw *Sea Soldier*'s duck-egg blue hull glide serenely into an anchorage in time for the six o'clock opening hour!

I never really liked ocean racing but in 1963 I was coerced into navigating a 'plastic', 30-feet sloop in the Fastnet. As the smallest entry and having been beset by a viscous gale while all others were safely back in Plymouth, we came last by well over a day. It had been a hideous week in a 'dry' vessel (alcoholically but most certainly not on deck or below) and with a humourless skipper. I swore 'never again' yet two years later, was tempted by the same skipper who, wisely now, owned a more suitable Nicholson 36. I was hooked but not by the 'racing' side of affairs – I left that to others – rather by the navigational challenges allied to those of a skipper's tactics and the eccentricities of the weather and tides. I went on to skipper or navigate four more Fastnets including, in 1969, as a fore-deck hand in the RORC's *Griffin III*. She had been so poorly maintained and stored by her bo'sun that when I debriefed the club's notoriously prickly secretary, I was invited never to renew my temporary membership. Among a number of other calamities, I had explained in straightforward language, there had been no charts of the course (until bought at the very last minute) the dinghy was stolen on the morning of the start, we ran out of water and food – 'oddly' there was plenty of tonic water and corn flakes – and had to jury rig the port, topmast shrouds and the steering gear. The Brookes and Gatehouse instruments failed as we rounded the Rock.

Which brings me neatly on to that next year's two-handed Round Britain and Ireland race when myself and Roger Dillon (before he joined the RCC and whose uncle had been the Secretary of the Royal Yacht Squadron) were generously lent, by Philip Tuckett, his beautiful, wooden 49-feet yawl, *Speedwell of Cremyll*, now, happily, owned by RYS and RCC member David Reynolds. During the work-up I was knocked out and overboard by the spinnaker boom, which only confirmed my view that it is not a gentleman's sail. As I came-to with the Hasler self-steering, servo blade slicing past my left ear at 6 knots, I watched Roger climbing over the stern pulpit and shouting 'Don't worry, Ewen, I'm coming in to help.' Just in time he remembered that we were two-handed! The lifebelt he threw was a genuine lifesaver for had I not been able to kick off my oversized sea boots I would never have reached its comparative security.

Moral: Train your crew to think quickly in a crisis – but not too quickly.

First lesson learned: Train yourself to be more sensible. I did and have never set a spinnaker since – a squares'l being a far more seamanlike downwind sail.

Second lesson learned: Confirmation that it is wise to wear sea-boots two sizes too big.

A few days later we were in Plymouth's Millbay Docks waiting for the three-man inspection team and, in true Royal Marines style, had laid everything out as for an admiral's inspection which, in effect, it was. To my horror I saw that the approaching inspectors were being led by the 'notoriously prickly' RORC secretary who, rather negatively and I thought ostentatiously, pointed out to his fellow inspectors the Royal Yacht Squadron's burgee at our masthead. I turned to Roger and said quietly. 'We may have a problem.' In the saloon, and in silence, Roger and I sat opposite the team while waiting for the inevitable inquisition - but it never came. After some anxious moments the secretary turned to his fellows and said, 'I know this young skipper and can safely state that this vessel and her crew are, in all respects, ready for sea. We need not carry out an inspection.' Then, turning to me he ordered, 'Now, Tailyour, I think you owe me a drink!' We, more than willingly, obliged and while I was, admittedly, flattered by this grossly undeserved accolade I knew, too, that he was taking a risk for, in truth, few if any sailing vessel can really be, 'in all respects', ready for sea. If the inspectors had so wished any number of reasons could have been found to prevent us sailing. On reflection I think it was his way of apologizing for kicking me out of the RORC.

Apart from the parties in Crosshaven, Barra, Lerwick (especially the Lerwick Boating Club) and Lowestoft (all accompanied by my windy-up gramophone and various '78s' including, famously, Jelly Roll Morton and his Red Hot Peppers playing the Kansa City Stomp!) the race highlight occurred when an off-course pigeon fluttered below into the saloon while we were becalmed somewhere south of Cork. Roger was fast asleep, naked and lying on his back in his bunk. Deep in its primeval brain the pigeon knew that it needed to find a twig, branch or bough…and it did!

I had entered the Royal Marines Sailing Club's new 36-feet wooden sloop in the first RB&I in 1966, but could not take part as I was then building the sand yacht in the Oman. In the end I entered for the first nine RB&I for much the same reasons that I enjoyed the Fastnets. I never had any aspiration to win but to remain firmly in the middle of the fleet where the best parties were. For the record, I eventually started in six, retired in three, was disqualified in one and finished two. The disqualification came in 1989 when, on entering the final compulsory stop of Lowestoft, my co-skipper, the late Colin de Mowbray, unilaterally and suddenly, decided that Brighton was a far better run ashore.

The 1993 RB&I race was another notable event for that was the year in which I had had built the third of my four *Black Velvets*, this one a gaff-rigged Tradewind 35. Notable too, as my son, Hamish was the youngest ever co-skipper, while becoming known for his bagpipe playing as we entered and left each of the four stops. We were the last to finish but it had all been so enjoyable.

Between 1978 and 1979 I served in the Falkland Islands and although I had under command a 150-ton motor vessel, it was much more fun to survey the coastlines under sail. So with good luck, a passing, cement-built, Colin Archer ketch, *Capricornus*, was briefly pressed into service. Then what a joy it was to explore a few of those unspoilt, unvisited waters under canvas.

On my retirement from the Royal Marines in 1992 the third *Black Velvet* was built specifically for high latitude exploring and certainly not for speed. She was strengthened around the waterline, was gaff rigged, filled with extra ballast to compensate, fitted with two robust heating systems and space for two and a half tons of 'cargo'. Unsurprisingly she could set no spinnaker but, instead, crossed a 27-feet squares'l yard.

For six seasons (and sometimes more than once a summer) *Black Velvet* (by then a commercially registered sailing vessel) was hired by the Devon Wildlife Trust to take four ornithologists at a time into the western approaches seeking the elusive Wilsons Petrel - known to the Trust as 'willy-watching patrols'.

This was hard work as the 'birders' refused to take any part in running the ship and such chores as cooking and washing up. I drew the line when vegans began appearing and it was only thanks to the Trust that *Black Velvet* was (most reluctantly) fitted with GPS following a complaint that my fixes with sextant, hand bearing compass and Walker Log were not accurate enough. Really!

Throughout most of my ownership of this third *Black Velvet* I held an annual 'Biscay booze cruise - and no marinas' with three like-minded friends from Stubbington, Pangbourne and the Royal Marines - Michael Shuttleworth (mate of the upper deck), Michael Groom (bunting tosser) and Peter Cameron (unpaid, paid hand). For many reasons that should not be elaborated here none of these 'adventures' made it in to print.

Then, in 1997, Hamish and I entered the RWYC's two-handed Iceland race but, unlike the other stripped-out competitors, we were laden with skis, sledges, climbing ropes, crampons, ice axes, fifteen pairs of climbing boots, three months of basic food and the same of sealed, bonded stores. We certainly used up the planned 'cargo' spaces - and more.

The fourth and final *Black Velvet*, a 30-feet Cornish Crabber, was by far my most favourite for she was ideal for the growing grandchildren and equally suitable for a single-handed, fading grandfather! Sadly the end came rather unexpectedly when, in 2021, I fell in from the dinghy and was trapped, upside down, over the side but, as before, I was able to kick off of my oversized boots and so struggle to the river's bank. Clearly the time had come so she was put on the market the next day and sold to a good home – but one on the North Sea coast and I do not envy her that.

Now as I prepare to lower the ensign for the last time it is with regret that there is no more opportunity to detail the day Claire Francis filled the first *Black Velvet*'s water tank with draught Guinness or of the satisfaction of tabulating the underwater profile of Friendship Bay's beach in Bequia. The sobering experience of rounding Land's End at 25 knots in the late Mike McMullen's radical trimaran *Three Cheers* during a December near-gale, must remain only in my memory, as does a transatlantic record attempt in Robin Knox-Johnston's huge catamaran *Sea Falcon*. Then there were the seventy-knot 'snake boat' chases across Hong Kong's darkened and debris-strewn waters and the winters in Arctic Norway developing small boat operations in support of the commando brigade, skills that became so valuable in 1982. There is no time either to describe the cat and mouse operations on the rivers and lakes of Northern Ireland or, sadly, all the hundreds of other amusing, frightening, instructive, adventurous incidents since that very 'nautical' christening in a snow-bound Nissen hut all those years ago. The torch passes. The final satisfaction being that my son, Hamish and now my grandson Jacob, have taken up the nautical baton with huge enthusiasm.

Chapter 37

The Glory of the Ride

Excerpts from a 'haul-down' report in 2022 I wrote for the Royal Yacht Squadron and the Royal Cruising Club to celebrate my final 'coming ashore'.

Edward Monkton was absolutely correct:

He knows not where he's going,
For the ocean will decide,
It's not the destination,
It's the glory of the ride.

Sailing and exploring by sea have been the two dominant factors in my life with both providing maximum, lifelong excitement, enjoyment and not a few frights.

Through service appointments and creative leave-planning I have been privileged, or lucky enough, to have sailed or motored in the Denmark Straight, Iceland's fjords and the Norwegian Arctic, to Patagonia, the Falkland Islands, South Georgia and to the southern Ocean; from Hong Kong to the West Indies via Bombay, to Oman, Malta, Cyprus, Crete, Sardinia, Corsica, Minorca and to the islands of the Dalmatian and Greek coasts; from the Gulf of Aqaba to the Baltic; from Florida to the Chesapeake river; from North Island, New Zealand and the east coast of Australia to the Maldives; from the Persian Gulf to the Outer Hebrides; from Italy's Lake Garda to the Canadian lakes; from Britain's rivers and canals to those of Germany and northern France....

And all in rowing and racing dinghies, day-boats, square-riggers, out-riggers, catamarans, trimarans, small gaff cutters, Bristol Channel pilot cutters, sailing trawlers, 'covert' Norwegian fishing trawlers, Bermudan sloops, ketches, yawls, schooners, naval whalers, admirals' gigs, kayaks and canoes, Arabian dhows, Chinese junks, a sand yacht and even (please excuse me) as a deck hand in a 'super yacht' while 'working my passage' from Nassau to Miami. To which list I must add inflatable and rigid raiding craft, assault and mechanised landing craft as well as small, medium and large hovercraft. Nor can I ignore a

North Sea oil rig, two transatlantic Cunard ocean liners, one troopship, a P&O cruise ship, an 'expedition' ship in South Georgia, a 150-ton motor vessel and a cement-built, Colin Archer ketch among the Falkland Islands; a 40-knot, water-skiing boat, a 5-knot narrowboat and an ex-Royal Navy 20-knot, 112-feet Fairmile B Class motor launch, a veteran of the Normandy beaches in 1944. Nor would I ever want to forget a variety of submarines, amphibious assault ships, frigates and aircraft carriers of various nationalities.

So there we are and it is now high time that I lowered the ensign, hoisted the riding light, poured the gin and raised a toast to what has been a truly 'glorious ride'!

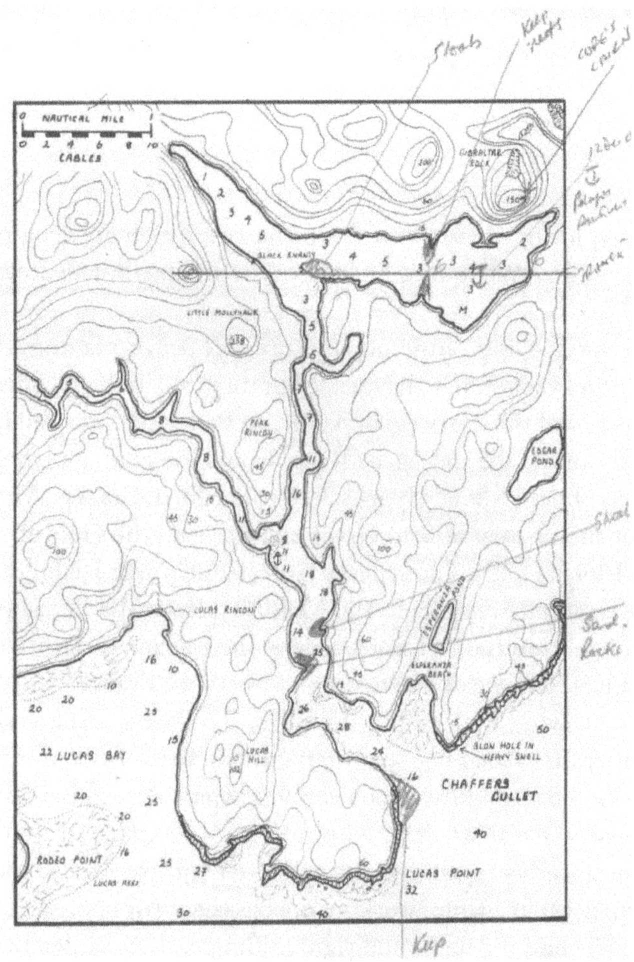

Corrections to my chart made during *Pelagic Australis's* visit.

Epilogue: The Sailor's Grave

Adapted by the author from the German original.

There are no roses on the sailor's grave,
No lilies on the ocean wave.
His tributes come with the seabirds' sweeping,
And the tears that flow when a young maid's weeping.

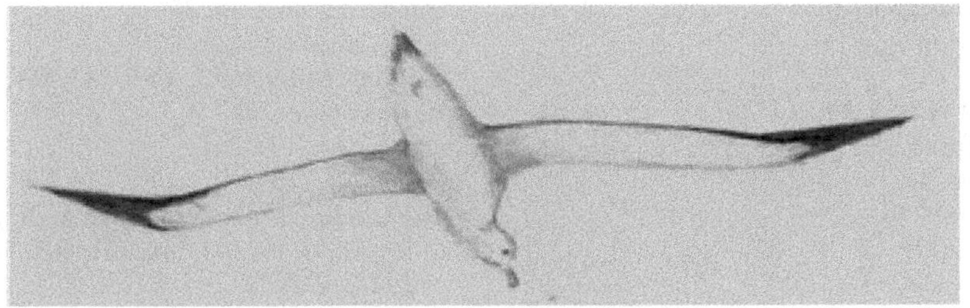